آئیے اردو پڑھیں

Let's Study Urdu

آ ئے اردو پڑھیں

Let's Study Urdu

An Introductory Course

Ali S. Asani

Harvard University

and

Syed Akbar Hyder

University of Texas, Austin

Yale University Press

New Haven and London

Publisher: Mary Jane Peluso

Development Editor: Brie Kluytenaar

Manuscript Editor: Noreen O'Connor-Abel

Production Editor: Ann-Marie Imbornoni

Production Controller: Karen Stickler

Marketing Manager: Timothy Shea

Cover Design: Mary Valencia

Cover Photograph: Michael Currier

Printed in the United States of America.

ISBN 978-0-300-11400-3 (pbk.: alk.paper)

Library of Congress Control Number: 2006939857

A catalogue record for this book is available from the British Library.

The paper in this book meets the guidelines for permanence and durability of the Committee on Production Guidelines for Book Longevity of the Council on Library Resources.

10 9 8 7 6 5 4 3 2 1

اپنے محبوب کی خاطر تھا خُدا کو منظور

ورنہ قران بھی اترتا بہ زبانِ اردو

اکبر الہ آبادی

In Memoriam

Annemarie Schimmel

(1922-2003)

who, during her lifetime, worked tirelessly to bring about a better appreciation

of Urdu literature and its culture

Contents

Chapter 9

Introduction

A member of the Indo-Aryan family of languages, Urdu is spoken by over 150 million people in many parts of the South Asian subcontinent. Designated the official language of Pakistan and one of the national languages of India, Urdu is also routinely spoken as a first or second language in South Asian diaspora communities in the Middle East, South and East Africa, Western Europe, North America, and Australia. In recent decades, Urdu has been glamorized by Bollywood, India's massive film industry, which routinely commissions prominent Urdu writers and poets to write scripts and compose song lyrics for the many movies it releases every year.

Urdu first emerged as a literary language in the fourteenth and fifteenth centuries when dialects of it (Gujri and Dakhani) were used in western and southern India for poetic compositions. In the late eighteenth century it received a special boost in northern India from the Mughal emperor Shah Alam II (r. 1759-1806), who had developed a special fondness for it. As the power base of the Mughal empire and the regional kingdoms that patronized Urdu eroded and finally gave way to British colonial rule over most of the subcontinent, Urdu writers adamantly sought new patrons. Whether in Hyderabad or in the Punjab, Urdu demonstrated marked resilience in the face of political upheavals.

Although Urdu has developed into a language with a great literary and cultural history, its spatial, temporal, and etymological origins are fraught with acute ambiguities, not to mention bitter controversies. The word *Urdu* itself is of Turkish origin and means "camp," most likely a reference to the surroundings of Delhi's Red Fort, at times referred to as *urdu-e mu'alla*, or "exalted camp." For many centuries, the area around the Red Fort was an important center of power for Turko-Persian dynasties originating in Central Asia, including the illustrious Mughals. It accomodated various linguistic and cultural traditions, some of which were Persianate and others Indic. Toward the end of the eighteenth century, the hybrid language of this area came to be referred to as *zaban-e urdu-e mu'alla,* or "the language of the exalted camp." This expression appears to have been truncated over time and simply became Urdu, which then came to signify the vernacular or local language spoken around the Red Fort.

Notwithstanding the use of the term Urdu to designate a specific language, it is important to remember that as late as the nineteenth century, what we today refer to as Urdu was also known as Hindi, Hindavi, Gujri, Dakhani, or Rekhta ("mixed language"). Historically, the linguistic spectrum encompassed by the Urdu/Hindi/Hindavi/Gujri/Dakhani/Rekhta framework has not been a rigid one and the boundaries and definitions of these dialects have been relatively fluid. This wide spectrum not only incorporated Persian vocabulary and a few Persian grammatical elements (Persian being the official language at many courts in pre-colonial South Asia) but also embraced elements from vernacular or local languages such as Dakhani (spoken in the Deccan), Gujarati, Avadhi, Khari Boli, and Braj.

The emergence of more rigid definitions of what constitutes Urdu is largely a consequence of British colonial policies and the growth of religiously based nationalisms in the late nineteenth and early twentieth centuries. As a result, many aspects of culture that were common to both Hindus and Muslims, including language, came to be perceived exclusively through religious lenses. Many came to believe that Urdu, because it was written in the Perso-Arabic script, reflected an Islamic orientation. Thus, a language that had to that point been spoken by Hindus and Muslims alike, and its script learned by all peoples regardless of their religious orientation, became inextricably linked to South Asian Muslim identity. Such a narrow association of the language with Islam alone overlooked two important facts: first, millions of South Asian Muslims did not speak Urdu, and second, many Hindus were counted among its greatest poets, writers, and devotees. In the eyes of the religious nationalists, Hindi, on the other hand, the language written in the Devanagari script and drawing vocabulary from Sanskrit, came to be identified with Hindus. Notwithstanding these narrow demarcations distinguishing Urdu from Hindi, Premchand, a renowned author who has been claimed by partisans on both sides of the Urdu/Hindi divide to be one of their own, declared: "In my view, Hindi and Urdu are one and the same language. When they have common verbs and subjects, there can be no doubt of their being one."

Many a writer in South Asia has continued to challenge the constraints that have been placed on these languages by freely mixing idioms. In response to the religious nuances that have come to surround both Hindi and Urdu, a handful of leaders (including Mahatma Gandhi) and writers (Sajjad Zaheer for instance), who were interested in fostering Hindu-Muslim unity, have promoted the use of the term "Hindustani" to refer to a mode of Urdu-Hindi defused of any religious charge. Unfortunately, the forces of communalism in contemporary South Asia have been so strong that this expression has failed to gain wide currency.

Although in many respects Urdu and Hindi are almost identical gramatically, in today's world Urdu is written in the Perso-Arabic script whereas Hindi is written in the Sanskrit-derived Devanagari script. Those persons and institutions who wish to focus on differences tend to identify Urdu more with the vocabulary of Persian and Arabic, and Hindi with vocabulary from

Sanskrit. We should remind ourselves that these distinctions between Urdu and Hindi are from certain perspectives quite arbitrary and the inexorable speculations as to what extent, if any, these languages differ from each other can continue endlessly to no avail.

This book attempts to steer a middle course in the Urdu-Hindi divide in that it uses, for the most part, words and expressions that are mutually intelligible to self-identified Urdu-Hindi speaking communities. In writing this book, we have become convinced more than ever that languages are open-ended networks. In a language such as Urdu, cultural and temporal variations pave the way for growth and development. Expressions that are commonplace in Hyderabad, India, might be seen as archaic and even quaint in Karachi, Pakistan. In an introductory book such as this, it is impossible to cover all the variations in the language. Nor is it possible to cover all the subtle lexical and grammatical nuances. Nevertheless, we hope that the course provides students with a strong enough foundation to pursue more advanced study. For those students who are interested in the highly Persianized form of Urdu that is commonly used in newspapers and journals, we have included sample reading passages at the end of the book.

Over the many years we have labored to produce this book, we have been deeply grateful to our wonderfully patient students for having tolerated earlier incarnations of the present work and for their invaluable suggestions. We also owe a special debt of gratitude to the following friends and colleagues who are responsible for many improvements in this book: Gaurav Shah, Ameek Ponda, Lata Parwani, Naseem Hines, Shafique Virani, Neelima Shukla-Bhatt, Amjad Alinani, Alex Keefe, Herman van Olphen, Shahnaz Hassan, Danielle Widmann, Sunil Sharma, Amy Bard, Azhar Abbas, Carla Petievich, Hussein Rashid, and Michael Currier. Special thanks to Bill

University of Texas, Austin, for carefully reading the entire manuscript and suggesting many corrections that have improved the book and to Bill Countie, Tony DiBartolo, and Margaret Keyes of Harvard's Media Production Center for their patience in recording the audio materials that accompany this course. This book would not have been possible without generous funding from the Consortium for Language Learning and Teaching and the enthusiastic support of the Consortium's executive director, Peter Patrikis.

In addition to dedicating this book to the late Annemarie Schimmel, we also wish to dedicate this work to our past, present, and future students with the hope that our efforts will inspire them to continue their study of Urdu and enable them to experience the trans-national and trans-temporal cultural traditions that Urdu embodies so well. We have given every consideration to first-time students of Urdu, that their experience of learning this language be both rewarding and enjoyable. We hope that those who use this book will come to appreciate a language that many consider the most romantic in the world.

How To Use This Book: A Note for Teachers and Students

The overall objective of *Let's Study Urdu* is to make students comfortable with reading, writing, and speaking Urdu in everyday contexts. Although the book may be used in a variety of instructional settings, it is specifically designed to fulfill the needs of a first-year (26 week) American college-level Urdu class that meets 4-5 times per week for fifty minutes per session. Depending on the speed with which students master the material, it is possible to extend the use of this book, particularly chapters 15 and 16, to the first semester of a second-year course. For each classroom session, we suggest that students spend at least an hour to an hour and a half outside of class reviewing the material and completing the relevant exercises. The book assumes that a teacher who is proficient in Urdu grammar and in reading, writing, and speaking the language is present in class to provide guidance for students. In our teaching experiences, we have noticed that the information from this book is communicated more effectively when students read assigned sections before coming to class. Keeping this in mind, the book is designed so that students can study much of the grammar explanations on their own as homework and devote the time they spend in the classroom to hearing and practicing the language. With this approach, the amount of time that the teacher needs to spend explaining grammar can be kept at a minimum, with classroom contact time being devoted to fostering interactive and learner-centered activities. The book is accompanied by an audio component that will help students develop their reading, speaking, and listening skills.

This book assumes that students have a working knowledge of the Urdu writing system and, as a result, it uses almost no transliteration. To attain mastery of the Urdu script, we recommend the companion volume to this book, *Let's Study Urdu: An Introduction to the Script* (New

Haven: Yale University Press, 2008).

Format

Each chapter is divided into several sections, with each section usually devoted to the

introduction of a particular point of grammar or idiomatic construction. After a series of

examples illustrating the relevant grammar, students are called upon to complete the relevant

exercises, labelled as **Reading and Translation Drills** and **Substitutions**. These exercises are

meant to reinforce the grammar that the student has learned in that section. While the **Reading**

and Translation Drills stress reading and comprehension skills, the **Substitutions** emphasize

writing skills as well as recall of vocabulary items. Some sections of the book include English to

Urdu translation exercises that help students develop their writing skills and reinforce grammar

and vocabulary. If the translation exercises are done orally, they can assist students in generating

Urdu within limited contexts so as to improve speaking proficiency. The first eight chapters of

the book also contain **Pronunciation Drills** that are designed to help students understand Urdu

syllabification and develop greater competency in pronouncing retroflexive, dental, palatal,

aspirated, and nasal sounds as well as those letters borrowed from Arabic and Persian languages.

The penultimate components of each chapter are the contextual dialogues, گفتگو (Conversation)

and **Conversation Practices,** which integrate vocabulary with the grammar units introduced in

the various sections of the chapter. These dialogues also help in the development of reading and

communication skills. As the book advances and students increase their command over grammar

and vocabulary, the dialogues flow more naturally. The گفتگو (Conversation) sections of each

chapter are connected to each other by a soap opera-like drama featuring two characters, Raj and

Nargis, and their families. As the Raj-Nargis romance unfolds from chapter to chapter, students are exposed to the language as it is spoken in a variety of everyday contexts. At the same time, the ongoing romance keeps them wondering and anticipating what will develop in the next chapter. These contextual dialogues are followed by popular **Songs,** taken for the most part from Bollywood, India's renowned film industry. Most of these songs, whether in excerpted form or in their entirety, are romantic in theme and their selection has been carefully keyed to the grammar sections. The rationale for this activity is fourfold: to develop aural comprehension skills, to appreciate certain flexibilities and nuances of Urdu grammar, to enhance pronunciation through singing, and to provide exposure to a very significant element of South Asian culture, whether in the Subcontinent or in the diaspora. We recommend that every class session devote at least 5 minutes to listening to and singing these songs. Students are not expected to totally comprehend the songs since they often require a knowledge of Urdu-Hindi prosody to which they have not been exposed. We recommend that after students have mastered a song, they watch a video clip of it from the Bollywood film in which it appears so as to be exposed to its visual context. To facilitate the identification of the films from which these songs are excerpted, we have included a list. We hope that the list will also be helpful for those who wish to locate the lyrics of the songs in their entirety from various websites on the Internet. Every chapter ends with a **Vocabulary** section that lists all new vocabulary items introduced in that unit. These vocabulary items are also found in the English-Urdu and Urdu-English glossaries that appear at the end of the book. After Chapter 16, the book contains several **Reading Passages** based on radio and television broadcasts, newspaper extracts, popular jokes, and recipes. The passages integrate major grammar points of the book and are designed to further strengthen reading and translation skills of culturally authentic language.

Suggested Teaching Strategies

Although the book provides plenty of mechanical and structured exercises and activities, teachers and students are encouraged to utilize the material in the book in an open-ended and creative manner. The **Reading and Translation Drills** are not only tailored to enhance reading and translation skills, but they may also be used effectively in dictation and aural comprehension exercises. They may also be creatively transformed into games. For example, the words composing one of the sentences included in the drills may be written individually on separate index cards to create a "jigsaw" puzzle that students need to solve by reproducing the original sentence with the various components in correct grammatical order. The **Substitutions**, a less controlled activity, may lead students to bring in new vocabulary words, an exercise that can be particularly effective when they are working in pairs. The **Translation** exercises may be written by students on the board in the classroom to assess grammar, idiomatic usage, spelling, and competency of the script. The گُفتگو (Conversation) and **Conversation Practice** sections present students with basic situations which they can reproduce through role-playing activities that bring in new vocabulary words and grammar structures from previous chapters. They can form the basis of skits which can be presented "live" in class or recorded on video. Students may also be creative in developing scenarios based on vocabulary from the songs.

Many of these strategies lend themselves to group activities or students working in pairs to elicit numerous creative responses. The class can be divided into groups, with each group creating situations or exercises that expand upon the material that the students have encountered in class. Groups may also compete with each other on the basis of vocabulary acquisition and degrees of comprehension. Activities based on students working in groups or pairs should aim at maximizing peer-facilitated learning that ensures in-depth mastery of the material.

Bibliography of Works Consulted

Barker, Muhammad Abd al-Rahman, et al. *Spoken Urdu: A Course in Urdu.* 3 vols. Ithaca: Spoken Language Services, 1990 [1987].

Barker, Muhammad Abd al-Rahman, et al. *An Urdu Newspaper Reader.* Ithaca: Spoken Language Services, 1986.

Bhatia, Tej. *A History of the Hindi-Hindustani Grammatical Tradition.* Leiden: E.J.Brill, 1987.

Bhatia, Tej, and Ashok Koul. *Colloquial Urdu.* London: Routledge, 2000.

Jain, Usha. *Introduction to Hindi Grammar.* Berkeley: Center for South and Southeast Asian Studies, University of California, 1995.

Kalsi, A. S., et al. *Modern Urdu Texts. Urdu Short Stories.* London: School of Oriental and African Studies, 1991.

Matthews, David J., and Mohammed Kasim. *Teach Yourself Urdu.* London: McGraw Hill/Contemporary Books, 2003.

Matthews, David J., and Christopher Shackle. *A Selection of Twentieth Century Urdu Verse.* London: School of Oriental and African Studies, 1991.

McGregor, R. S. *Outline of Hindi Grammar.* New Delhi: Oxford University Press, 1999.

Naim, C. M. *Introductory Urdu.* 2 vols. Chicago: South Asia Language and Area Center, University of Chicago, 1999.

Naim, C. M. *Readings in Urdu: Prose and Poetry.* Honolulu: East West Press, 1965.

Narang, Gopi Chand. *Readings in Urdu Literary Prose.* Madison: University of Wisconsin, South Asia Center, 1968.

Platts, J. *A Dictionary of Urdu, Classical Hindi, and English*. 1st Indian edition. Delhi:

    Munshiram Manoharlal Publishers, [1930] reprint 1977.

Schimdt, Ruth Laila. *Urdu: An Essential Grammar*. London: Routledge, 1999.

Shackle, Christopher, and Rupert Snell. *Hindi and Urdu since 1800: A Common Reader*.

    London: School of Oriental and African Studies, 1990.

Film Sources for Songs Cited in the Book

Chapter	Song	Film (Year)	Lyricist
1	چھلیا میرا نام	*Chaliya* (1960)	Qamar Jalalabadi
2	آوارہ ہوں	*Awara* (1951)	Shailendra
2	میرا جوتا ہے جاپانی	*Shree 420* (1955)	Shailendra
3	یہ دنیا گول ہے	*Chaudhvin ka Chand* (1960)	Shakil Badayuni
3	یہ دِل دیوانہ ہے	*Ishq par Zor Nahiiṅ* (1970)	Anand Bakshi
4	میں پل دو پل کا شاعر ہوں	*Kabhi Kabhi* (1976)	Sahir Ludhiyanvi
4	یہ نینا، یہ کاجل، یہ زلفیں	*Dil Se Mile Dil* (1978)	Amit Khanna
4	عمر تیری سولہ	*Beqabu* (1996)	Rahat Indori
5	دِل ہے کہ مانتا نہیں	*Dil hai ki mantaa nahiiṅ* (1991)	Faiz Anwar
5	یاد تیری جب آتی ہے	Private recording: Gaurav Shah	
6	زندگی امتحان لیتی ہے	*Naseeb* (1981)	Anand Bakshi
6	میرا دل بھی کتنا پاگل ہے	*Saajan* (1991)	Sameer
7	اچّھا تو ہم چلتے ہیں	*Aan milo sajna* (1970)	Anand Bakshi
7	یاد آ رہی ہے	*Love Story* (1981)	Anand Bakshi
7	شام ڈھل رہی ہے	Private recording: Gaurav Shah	
8	میری جان کچھ بھی کیجیئے	*Chhalia* (1960)	Qamar Jalalabadi
8	سانسوں کی ضرورت ہے جیسے	*Aashiqui* (1990)	Sameer
8	آنکھوں میں	Album recording Aryans	Jai Walia
9	تو چیز بڑی ہے مست مست	*Mohra* (1994)	Anand Bakshi

Chapter 1

1.1 Word Order in the Urdu Sentence

In Urdu the normal word order in the simplest sentence, reading from right to left, is as follows:

2	1
Verb	Subject
ہوں	میں

I am

Urdu sentences thus generally begin with the subject and end with the verb so that all other elements of the sentence fall between the subject and the verb.

3	2	1
Verb	Complement	Subject
ہوں	امریکن	میں

I am American.

The complement can be a noun or an adjective:

3	2	1
Verb	Complement	Subject
ہوں	خوبصورت	میں

I am beautiful.

When such a sentence is put in the negative, the verb can be replaced with the negative particle نہیں which can mean either "no" or "not."

3	2	1
Negative Particle	Complement	Subject
نہیں	امریکن	میں

I am not American.

For a more emphatic tone, نہیں can be followed by the verb:

4	3	2	1
Verb	Negative Particle	Complement	Subject
ہوں	نہیں	امریکن	میں

I am <u>not</u> American.

For an even more emphatic tone, the negative particle نہیں can come after the verb:

4	3	2	1
Negative Particle	Verb	Complement	Subject
نہیں	ہوں	امریکن	میں

I am (definitely/certainly) not American.

1.2 Conjugation of Verb ہونا and Pronouns

The first Urdu verb we will conjugate is the most common verb: ہونا (to be).

Singular Forms

Translation	Conjugational Form	Pronoun
I am	ہوں	میں
You (least formal) are	ہے	تُو
You (informal) are	ہو	تُم
You (formal) are	ہیں	آپ

2

| He/She/It is | ہے | وہ / یہ |

Plural Forms

We are	ہیں	ہم
You are	ہو	تُم
You are	ہیں	آپ
They are	ہیں	وہ / یہ

میں is the most common first person pronoun, although some people use the first person plural pronoun ہم in contexts that require a first person singular pronoun. The use of ہم in place of میں is generally considered a mark of humility, though in some instances, under the influence of English idiom, the substitution is used to connote the "royal we." In several regions of North India, people use ہم in the میں context quite commonly.

میں امریکن ہوں۔

I am American.

ہم امریکن ہیں۔

I am American.

We are American.

تُو is the least formal of the second person pronouns and should not be used unless one is on intimate terms with the addressee or unless an insult is intended. It is commonly used to address young children and sometimes servants as well. Interestingly, تُو is used when addressing God. In some regions, this pronoun is also used to address one's mother.

تُو اچّھا ہے۔

You are good.

تُم is the common second person pronoun. It can be used in addressing one person or several persons who are younger than you or a person or persons with whom you are on fairly familiar terms. It is also frequently employed to address individuals of a lower social status than the speaker, e.g., servants, taxi drivers.

تُم ہندوستانی ہو۔

You (singular) are Indian.

You (plural) are Indian.

آپ is the most polite and formal second person singular and plural form. When addressed to one person, آپ expresses respect. Thus, when you speak to a person for the first few times or when you address a person older than yourself, آپ should be used. In general آپ can be used for any person to whom you want to show respect. آپ is also used to express plurality, i.e. "you" (plural). On account of its use both for respect and plurality, the meaning of آپ is dependent on context. For example, the following sentence has two possible meanings:

آپ اسٹوڈنٹ (طالبِ علم) ہیں۔

You (respectful) are a student.

You are students.

Note: In highly formal speech آپ can sometimes be used as a third person pronoun of respect meaning "he or "she." This usage, which is even more formal and polite than the use of plural یہ / وہ (see below) , is only used for persons accorded the highest degree of respect, such as religious personalities. Example:

آپ ایک بہت مشہور پروفیسر ہیں۔

He (highly honorific) is a very famous professor.

وہ / یہ when used as pronouns can be either singular or plural, meaning "he," "she," "it," or "they." Again, when used in a plural context, these pronouns can connote respect for a single individual:

وہ پروفیسر ہے۔

He is a professor.

وہ پروفیسر ہیں۔

He (respectful) is a professor.

They are professors.

The latter example is ambiguous because ہیں can be used for a singular subject who is spoken of with respect or for a plural subject.

1.1 - 1.2 Reading and Translation Drill

ا۔ میں امریکن ہوں۔

تو امریکن ہے۔

تم امریکن ہو۔

آپ امریکن ہیں۔

۲۔ وہ ڈاکٹر ہے۔

ہم طالبِ علم ہیں۔

وہ پروفیسر ہیں۔

تو جاپانی ہے۔

۳۔ بابو ہندو ہے۔

شاد مسلمان ہے۔

مائیک عیسائی ہے۔

5

جین یہودی ہے۔

بلبیر سِکھ ہے۔

۴۔ ٹام کروز مشہور ہے۔

لتا مشہور نہیں۔

تو سُندر ہے۔

آپ خوبصورت ہیں۔

Translate into Urdu:

1.   He is Indian.

2.   She is Pakistani.

3.   They are Russian.

4.   You (least formal) are not a student.

5.   We are doctors.

6.   Brooke Shields is very famous.

7.   Anita is not famous.

8.   Sean Connery is very handsome.

9.   We are human.

10.   He is not Christian. He is Hindu.

Fill in the blanks with the appropriate form of ہونا

ا۔ میں عیسائی ـــــــــ اور راج ہندو ـــــــــ ۲۔ ہم ہندوستانی ـــــــــ ۳۔ وہ ڈاکٹر ـــــــــ ۴۔ کرن اور رام بھی ڈاکٹر ـــــــــ ۵۔ تو مشہور ـــــــــ ۶۔ تم سُندر ـــــــــ ۷۔ شیلا اور پوجا بھی خوبصورت ـــــــــ

1.3 Greetings and جی as Particle of Respect

Urdu does not have a uniform mode of greeting. The manner in which one person greets another is contingent upon a variety of factors: the age and gender of the two speakers, prior acquaintance or intimacy, their educational background, and the region in which they are located. At times, the perceived religious identity of the person who is being greeted may also play a part. As a result, the several forms of Urdu (and Hindi) greetings carry overtones of social status, regional identity, and religious affiliation. The following are a few commonly heard expressions:

1) آداب (literally, "respect") and آداب عرض (literally, "[my] respects are presented [to you])." These greetings, which are formal in tone, are religiously neutral in that they can be used between persons of different or identical religious affiliation. Depending on context, they may be said by a person of a younger age, or of an inferior social status, to an older person or one with a socially superior status. They are often accompanied by a gesture of respect in which the speaker moves his/her right hand to the forehead. Sometimes the gesture itself is used without any words and the act is called "آداب کرنا " or "سلام کرنا" ("presenting greetings"). If both greeters are of the same rank or not intimate with each other, the reply to these greetings is also آداب or آداب عرض. If there is a difference in rank or age, then the person with the superior rank or age may respond with a nod and the blessing "جیتے رہو" (literally, "may you live long"). For some people آداب and آداب عرض represent a formal and contrived set of greetings associated with the culture of nineteenth- and twentieth-century Urdu-speaking aristocracies of Delhi, Lucknow, and Hyderabad (India). Hence they choose not to use it as they feel it is outdated or old-fashioned. In contemporary Pakistan سلام علیکم ("salaam alaikum") and its

7

response سلام علیکم و)("*wa alaikum salaam*") have come to replace آداب and آداب عرض as

the standard formal greetings.

2) السّلام علیکم (pronounced "*as-salaam alaikum*") or سلام علیکم ("*salaam alaikum*") is an

Arabic greeting meaning "peace be upon [with] you." It is a common greeting between Muslims

in South Asia and, indeed, all over the Muslim world. The reply to this greeting is و علیکم السّلام

("*wa alaikum as-salaam*") or و علیکم سلام ("*wa alaikum salaam*") "may peace be upon you as

well." As mentioned above, this greeting has become prevalent in Pakistan, where in some

ultra-conservative circles it has become a marker of Muslim religious identity. It is important to

note, however, that notwithstanding the tendency in contemporary South Asia to politicize and

polarize greetings along religious lines, historically this is not a greeting that was exclusively

limited to Muslims. Hence, non-Muslims in some regions of South Asia and elsewhere still

continue to use it when greeting their Muslim acquaintances and friends.

3) نمستے is commonly used all over India as a form of greeting. Some consider it to be a

customary "Hindu" greeting, although a large number of non-Hindus in India use it as well when

greeting their Hindu friends and neighbours. نمسکار is a slightly more formal form of it. The reply

to this greeting is the same: نمستے or نمسکار. These greetings are all-purpose and cover a range of

usages such as "good morning," "good afternoon," "good evening," and also "goodbye." The

saying of نمستے is accompanied by a hand gesture: the greeter joins the palms of both hands in

front of himself or herself.

4) ہیلو and ہائی "hello" and "hi" are informal greetings common among the "English-medium"

educated and those who want a transreligious greeting which avoids any specific religious

identification. In modern-day India, it is quite common to hear, especially in urban areas, the greetings "hello" or "hi" at the beginning of a lengthy conversation that is entirely in Urdu/Hindi.

5) After the initial exchange of greetings, it is customary to inquire about health and well-being. This inquiry may take place in an informal or formal manner depending on context. In more informal contexts, and perhaps becoming increasingly widespread under the influence of English forms, the phrases "آپ کیسے ہیں؟" or "تُم کیسے/کیسی ہو؟" (literally, "how are you?") are frequently used. Equally informal is the ubiquitous "کیا حال ہے؟" literally, "what is [your] condition/state?" This has the same nuance as the American slang "what's up?" Usual responses are : "میں ٹھیک ہوں" or "ہم ٹھیک ہیں" (literally, "I am fine"). A slightly more colloquial response uses the echo compound "میں ٹھیک ٹھاک ہوں"

6) The etiquette of formal Urdu speech requires the use of polite and even ceremonious language. For this reason, the question "مِزاج شریف؟" (مِزاج = disposition, temperament; شریف = noble; literally, "[your] noble disposition?") is frequently employed. Again, etiquette of formal Urdu dictates that the reply should be modest, simple, and even humble so that one does not actually say how one is. Thus, the typical response to "مِزاج شریف؟" is "مہربانی" " thank you " (literally, "kindness, kind of you to ask"). One may also use "شُکریہ" which also means "thank you" as a reply. Sometimes variant expressions such as " بھگوان کی کرپا ہے " or " خُدا کی مہربانی ہے " (literally, "there is God's kindness/mercy (God = بھگوان (Hindu) or خُدا (Muslim); kindness = مہربانی/کرپا " i.e. thanks be to God) or آپ کی دُعا ہے (دُعا = prayers, "[I am fine thanks] to your prayers") may also be heard.

7) The asking of names can also be informal or formal. The informal "آپ کا نام کیا ہے؟" ("What is your name?") is most commonly heard. In formal contexts, polite and respectful phrases are employed: "آپ کا شُبھ نام کیا ہے؟" or " آپ کا اِسم شریف کیا ہے؟"

(literally, "What is your noble (شریف) name?" or "What is your auspicious (شُبه) name?").

Humility and modesty require the response to begin: "میرا نام ـــــــ ہے" (literally, "My name is ....).

8) Before taking leave of a person, one may formally or politely ask: " اِجازت دیجیۓ " (literally, "please give permission [to leave]"). Just as there is no uniform greeting when two Urdu speakers meet, there are no consistent words of parting, either. Traditionally " خُدا حافِظ " (literally, "God be your protector, God keep you") has been the standard form for saying "goodbye" among Urdu speakers, regardless of religious affiliation. With the unfortunate growth of religious nationalism, these words of parting have been associated by some to a Muslim identity. Consequently they will use either " پھر مِلینگے " ("we'll meet again") or " بائی " ("bye"). On the other hand, some Muslims feel that " خُدا حافِظ " is not a strong enough "Islamic" greeting, since they consider the word " خُدا " to refer to "god" with a small "g." Hence they prefer to use " اللّٰہ حافِظ " ("may Allah be your protector/ keep you"). As a result of right-wing religious influences, " اللّٰہ حافِظ " has become ubiquitous throughout Pakistan. In contrast, Muslim and non-Muslim Urdu speakers in India continue to use " خُدا حافِظ ".

9) The particle جی can be attached to ہاں (yes) or نہیں (no) to indicate respect for the person whom one is addressing. At times, the use of this particle by itself suggests affirmation of the validity of a statement or command:

یہ طالبِ علم ہے؟

Is he a student?

جی ہاں یہ اسٹوڈنٹ ہے۔

Yes, he is a student.

10

جی نہیں۔

No, he is not.

جی۔

Yes, he is.

جی can also be added as a suffix to nouns or proper names as a mark of respect, e.g., گاندھی جی "Gandhijii," or باپو۔جی "Baapuujii, father," or ماتا۔جی "Maataajii, mother."

1.4 Asking Questions

There are several ways of asking questions in Urdu:

1. *With a questioning intonation:*

آپ امریکن ہیں؟

Are you American?

With this option no interrogative word is used and the questioning intonation consists of a slight rise in tone when pronouncing the complement. In this example the complement is the noun "American"; hence the intonation will rise slightly when the speaker pronounces this word.

2. *With the interrogative word* کیا *at the beginning of the question:*

کیا، آپ امریکن ہیں؟

Are you American?

This is the simplest way of turning a statement into a question. Most questions that begin with کیا can be answered with either "yes" or "no"; hence this type of question is commonly called a yes-or-no question.

3. *With the interrogative word* کیا *at the end of the statement:*

آپ امریکن ہیں، کیا؟

11

You are American, aren't you?

There is an implication in this question that the questioner already knows the answer and is trying to confirm it.

4. *With the interrogative word or words immediately before the verb:*

آپ کیا ہیں؟

What are you?

Note that although the literal meaning of کیا is "what," it cannot always be translated into idiomatic English. Only the کیا in example no. 4 can be translated into English as "what." Sometimes کیا may also have an idiomatic meaning in Urdu that is not readily apparent in the literal English translation. Thus, the sentence in no. 4 above could, depending on the tone and intonation of voice with which it was said, be a rhetorical question "What are you?" or "Who are you?" implying that "you are nothing." Awareness of such nuances develops gradually through familiarity with the language and its cultural contexts.

5. *With the use of* کہاں

کہاں like کیا is another interrogative word. It means "where." Like کیا it usually comes right before the verb:

وہ کہاں ہے؟

Where is he?

1.3 - 1.4 Reading and Translation Drill

۱۔ آپ ہندوستانی ہیں؟

جی نہیں میں امریکن ہوں۔

کیا، وہ بھی امریکن ہیں؟

12

جی ہاں وہ بھی امریکین ہیں۔

۲۔ کیا وہ مشہُور ہیں؟

جی ہاں وہ مشہور ہیں۔

وہ ایلیزبیتھ ٹیلر ہیں۔

نہیں! وہ سندر نہیں!

۳۔ کیا آپ پروفیسر ہیں؟

جی ہاں میں پروفیسر ہوں۔

وہ طالبِ علم نہیں۔

کیا، ہندو اور مُسلم اِنسان نہیں؟

۴۔ وہ بہت مشہور ہے، کیا؟

نہیں نہیں ہم مشہور ہیں۔

تم کیا ہو؟

میں انسان ہوں۔

۵۔ پروفیسر جی کہاں ہیں؟

وائیٹ ہاؤس کہاں ہے؟

تاج محل کہاں ہے؟

ماتا جی کہاں ہیں؟

Translate into Urdu:

1. Are they students?

2. No, they are professors.

3. Where am I?

4. Is Nargis beautiful?

5.   Yes, she is beautiful.

6.   Yes, she is intelligent, too.

7.   Where is Amit?

1.5 Urdu Postpositions and Definite and Indefinite Articles

I am at Harvard.

The word "at" in the above sentence is a preposition. It is called a preposition because it comes before the locative noun, Harvard. Unlike English, Urdu does not have prepositions. It has instead postpositions. In other words, the equivalent of "in" or "at" in Urdu (میں) will follow the locative noun and not precede it:

verb	postposition	locative noun	subject
ہوں	میں	ہارورڈ	میں

میں گھر میں ہوں۔

I am in/at the house.

میں کالج میں ہوں۔

I am in/at college.

Note in the previous examples, the Urdu equivalents of the English articles "a," "an," and "the" are missing. This is because Urdu does not possess distinctive definite and indefinite articles. Thus گھر can be translated as "a house" or "the house." One way of emphasizing the indefinite nature of گھر is by placing the numerical adjective for one "ایک" before it:

ایک گھر a house or one house

میں ایک کالج میں ہوں۔ I am in a college.

1.6 Adjectives of Nationality

Many adjectives of nationality can formed by adding "ی" to the country's name:

جاپانی	=	ی	+	جاپان Japan
روسی	=	ی	+	روس Russia
ہندوستانی	=	ی	+	ہندوستان India
پاکستانی	=	ی	+	پاکستان Pakistan
بنگلہ دیشی	=	ی	+	بنگلہ دیش Bangladesh
چینی	=	ی	+	چین China
ایرانی	=	ی	+	ایران Iran

Two important adjectives do not follow this pattern:

امریکن   America   امریکہ

انگریز   England   انگلستان

Note: امریکی in place of امریکن is also acceptable. برطانیہ "Britain" can also be used to refer to United Kingdom. The adjectives انگلستانی and انگریزی refer to English as an attributive adjective rather than as an adjective of nationality. Thus:

یہ پتلون انگلستانی ہے۔ These pants are English

1.5 - 1.6 Reading and Translation Drill

۱۔   کیا، آپ ہارورڈ میں ہیں؟

جی نہیں۔ میں ایم۔ آئی۔ ٹی میں ہوں۔

ایم۔ آئی ۔ ٹی کہاں ہے؟

ایم۔ آئی ۔ ٹی کیمبرج میں ہے۔

۲۔   وہ لندن میں ہے۔

15

لندن بہت خوبصورت ہے۔

کیا، لندن فرانس میں ہے؟

جی نہیں۔ لندن برطانیہ میں ہے۔

۳۔   وہ بھی دفتر میں ہے۔

کیا، آپ بھی ایک دفتر میں ہیں؟

ہم دفتر میں نہیں ہیں۔

جناب! آپ کہاں ہیں؟

۴۔   وہ ایرانی ہے۔

نہیں، وہ ایرانی نہیں۔ ہندوستانی ہے۔

کیا، آپ بھی ہندوستانی ہیں؟

نہیں صاحب۔ میں روسی ہوں۔

Translate into Urdu:

1   Where is New York?

2.   New York is in America.

3.   Is America beautiful?

4.   No, America is not beautiful. Canada is beautiful.

5.   Where are you (informal)?

6.   I am in a (one) house.

7.   Where is Lisa? She is at the university.

8.   Are Raj and Nargis in the house?

9.   Yes, they are in the house.

10.   Where is Harlem? Is Harlem in New York?

1.7 Introduction to Possessive Adjectives

In this section, we will introduce only three possessive adjectives. A more detailed discussion and the grammatical construction of these adjectives will be included later. Possessive adjectives in Urdu, as in English, come before the nouns they modify.

Verb	Complement	Noun	Possessive Adjective
ہے	علی	نام	میرا

My name is Ali.

The three possessive adjectives introduced in this section are:

My = میرا

Your (formal) = آپ کا / آپکا

His/her (formal) or their = اُن کا / اُنکا

1.7 Reading and Translation Drill

۱۔ اُن کا نام ویلیم ہے۔

آپ کا نام کیا ہے؟

میرا نام علی ہے۔

آپ کا نام خوبصورت ہے۔

۲۔ میرا گھر نیو یارک میں ہے۔

آپ کا گھر کہاں ہے؟

میرا گھر بھی نیو یارک میں ہے۔

کیا، اُن کا گھر بھی نیو یارک میں ہے؟

17

۳۔ آپ کا کام کیا ہے؟

میں ڈاکٹر ہوں۔

اُن کا کام کیا ہے؟

وہ بھی ڈاکٹر ہیں۔

۴۔ آپ کا کام کہاں ہے؟

میرا کام بوسٹن میں ہے۔

بوسٹن کہاں ہے؟

بوسٹن امریکہ میں ہے۔

Translate into Urdu:

1. His name is Amit. He is American.

2. Her name is Devi. She is Indian.

3. Their house is in Pakistan.

4. Are they Pakistani? No, they are definitely not Pakistani.

5. What is their work?

6. They are all students. They are Iranian.

7. Your house is beautiful.

8. It's your house.

9. Where is Dacca? Dacca is in Bangladesh.

10. She too is Sikh. She is a professor at Panjab (پنجاب) University.

1.8 Pronunciation Drill: Short and Long Vowels

Column 2		Column 1	
میت	مِت	آب	اب
چیت	چِت	کاب	کب
ریت	رِت	کام	کم
میٹ	مِٹ	رام	رم
جھِم	رِم	ریم	رِم
سِمرن	سیما	روم	رُم
بو	سو	دام	دم
مونا	موٹا	تاب	تب
موسیٰ *	موسم	تان	تن
مسجد	مصالحہ	ران	رن
مالِک	مَلک	جام	جم
مالی	مَندِر	مات	مت
سالن	مالن	رات	رُت
صفا	دوا	ساجن	سجن
طاب	تاب	مُسافر	سفر
رابِط	ثابِت	صفائی	سفید
اَلم	عِلم	آم	عام

*The vertical line above the letter *"ye"* is a sign for a special letter, *"alif maqsura,"* which occurs occasionally in certain words of Arabic origin. It is pronounced as *"aa."* The *"ye"* functions simply as a carrier and is not pronounced. Hence the last syllable in this word would be

pronounced *"saa."* Other examples are: عیسیٰ *"iisaa,"* = Christ; ادنیٰ *"adnaa,"* = lowly; فتویٰ =
"fatwaa," = legal opinion based on Muslim jurisprudence.

1.9 گفتگو (Conversation)

نرگس:	آداب عرض جناب۔
راج:	نمستے، مزاج شریف؟
نرگس:	مہربانی، کیا حال ہے؟
راج:	سب ٹھیک ہے۔ آپ کا شُبھ نام؟
نرگس:	میرا نام نرگس ہے۔ آپ کا اسمِ شریف کیا ہے؟
راج:	میرا نام راج ہے۔ کیا، آپ امریکین ہیں؟
نرگس:	جی ہاں۔ میں امریکین ہوں۔ کیا، آپ بھی امریکین ہیں؟
راج:	نہیں۔ نہیں۔ میں ہندوستانی ہوں۔ آپ کا کام امریکہ میں کیا ہے؟
نرگس:	میں امریکہ میں ڈاکٹر ہوں۔ اور آپ؟
راج:	میں اِسٹوڈنٹ ہوں۔
نرگس:	اچّھا۔ آپ کہاں اِسٹوڈنٹ ہیں؟
راج:	میں ہارورڈ میں اِسٹوڈنٹ ہوں۔
نرگس:	ہارورڈ میں؟! کیا، آپ کا گھر کیمبرج* میں ہے؟
راج:	نہیں۔ میرا گھر سمرویل** میں ہے۔ آپ کا گھر کہاں ہے؟
نرگس:	میرا گھر کرکلنڈ اسٹریٹ*** پر ہے۔ اچّھا۔ اِجازت دیجِئے۔ پھر ملینگے۔
راج:	خُدا حافظ۔
نرگس:	خُدا حافظ۔

* Cambridge

20

** Somerville

*** Kirkland Street

1.10 Conversation Practice

Amit: Hello, Sheila, how are you?

Sheila: Fine, thanks. Are you Indian?

Amit: No. I am American. I am a student at Harvard. Are you American?

Sheila: No. I am Japanese. My house is in Tokyo.

Amit: Tokyo! Tokyo is very beautiful. Where is your house in Tokyo?

Sheila: My house is on Hito Street.

Amit: What is your job in Tokyo?

Sheila: I am a professor in Tokyo. I am at Tokyo University.

Amit: Good! We'll meet again. Goodbye.

Sheila: Goodbye.

1.11 Song

چھلیا میرا نام۔

چھلنا میرا کام۔

ہندو، مُسلم، سِکھ، عیسائی

سب کو میرا سلام۔

<u>Glossary for Song</u>

چھلنا = to cheat, to deceive

سب کو = to everyone, to all

سلام = greetings

21

1.12 Vocabulary

Note: The gender of nouns is indicated in parentheses: m - masculine; f - feminine

again, then	پھر
all	سب
also, too	بھی
America (m)	امریکہ
American	امریکن، امریکی
and	اور
Bangladesh (m)	بنگلہ دیش
beautiful	خُوبصورت / سُندر
Britain	برطانیہ
China (m)	چِین
Chinese	چِینی
Christian	عیسائی
condition, state (m)	حال
Dacca (m)	ڈھاکہ
disposition, health (m)	مِزاج
how are you? (formal)	مِزاج شریف؟
(lit. your noble	
disposition?)	
doctor (m/f)	ڈاکٹر
England (m)	انگلستان

English (nationality)	اَنگریز
English (adj)	انگلستانی، انگریزی
English (the language)	انگریزی
famous	مشہُور
fine	ٹھیک
gentleman, sir, mister	صاحب، جناب
give permission to leave (got to run)	اِجازت دیجِیئے
good; all right; o.k.	اچّھا
goodbye (lit. God be your protector)	خُدا حافِظ
greetings/hello/hi	آداب عرض، آداب، نمستے
to a Muslim (reply in parentheses)	سلام علیکُم (وعلیکُم سلام)
he/she	وہ، یہ
his/her (formal)	اُن کا/اُنکا
Hindu	ہِندُو
house (m)	گھر، مکان
human being (m)	اِنسان
I	میں
my; mine	میرا
in	میں

23

India (m)	ہندوستان / بھارت
Indian	ہِندُوستانی
intelligent, clever	ہوشیار
Iran (m)	اِیران
Iranian	اِیرانی
Japan (m)	جاپان
Japanese	جاپانی
Jew	یَہُودی
Muslim	مُسلِم، مُسلمان
name (m)	نام
auspicious name (m) (formal Hindi)	شُبھ نام
noble name (m) (formal Urdu)	اِسمِ شریف
no, not	جی نہیں، نہیں
noble, honorable	شریف
office (m)	دفتر
on	پَر
Pakistan (m)	پاکِستان
Pakistani	پاکِستانی
Russia (m)	رُوس
Russian	رُوسی

see you soon (lit. we will meet again)	پھر ملیں گے
Sikh	سِکھ
student (m/f)	طالبِ علم، اِسٹوڈنٹ، چھاتر (ہندی)
thanks (m)	شُکریہ
thanks (lit. kindness) (f)	مہربانی
they	وہ، یہ
their	اُن کا / اُنکا
university (f)	یُونیورسٹی
very; many	بہُت
we	ہم
what; also interrogative particle	کیا
where	کہاں
work/job (m)	کام
yes	جی ہاں، ہاں
you -- least formal	تُو
informal	تُم
formal	آپ
your (formal)	آپ کا / آپکا

Chapter 2

2.1 Demonstrative Pronouns and Adjectives

یہ and وہ function as both demonstrative pronouns and adjectives. As demonstrative pronouns

they signify, respectively, "this/these" or "that/those," their meaning depending on context. In

this chapter, they are used only in their singular form. Examples:

This is a boy.   یہ لڑکا ہے۔

That is a girl.   وہ لڑکی ہے۔

This is a house.   یہ گھر ہے۔

That is a shoe.   وہ جوتا ہے۔

As demonstrative adjectives, یہ and وہ modify both singular and plural nouns and also mean

"this/these" or "that/those." They are placed directly before the noun they modify. In this chapter,

they will be used only with singular nouns. Examples:

This boy.   یہ لڑکا۔

That girl.   وہ لڑکی۔

This house.   یہ گھر۔

That shoe.   وہ جوتا۔

2.2 Cardinal Numbers 0-10

Urdu numerals are written from left to right in their number form, just as the English ones are.

So 45 in Urdu is ۴۵. In this section we will begin with the first ten numbers.

صفر   •   0

ایک	۱	1
دو	۲	2
تین	۳	3
چار	۴	4
پانچ	۵	5
چھ	۶	6
سات	۷	7
آٹھ	۸	8
نو	۹	9
دس	۱۰	10

2.3 The Interrogative کون

کون is an interrogative meaning who/which. Like the other interrogative words that we have encountered so far (کہاں، کیا), the preferred position of کون is right before the verb.

راج کون ہے؟

Who is Raj?

وہ لڑکا کون ہے؟

Who is that boy?

If کون is the subject of the sentence, then it is placed at the beginning of a sentence.

کون ہے؟

Who is it?

2.4 The Postposition سے

سے in Urdu can be translated as "from" or "since." When appearing with an interrogative word,

سے appears after it. Like میں, سے is a postposition and occurs after the noun or interrogative it qualifies. An interrogative that frequently uses the postposition سے is کب or "when." کب سے is thus "since when."

وہ کہاں سے ہے؟

Where is he from?

وہ یہاں کب سے ہے؟

Since when has she been here?

وہ وہاں دو سال سے ہے۔

He has been there since (lit. for) two years.

سے may also be used after locatives such as "here" and "there."

here = یہاں

from here = یہاں سے

there = وہاں

from there = وہاں سے

میرا گھر یہاں سے دور ہے۔

My house is far from here.

اُن کا گھر یہاں سے نزدیک ہے۔

His/Their house is near [from] here.

Note also the following idiomatic usage:

far from x = x سے دور

close to x = x سے نزدیک

28

2.1 - 2.4 Reading and Translation Drill

۱۔ یہ گھر ہے۔

یہ گھوڑا ہے۔

وہ چیز ہے۔

وہ طالبِ علم ہے۔

۲۔ یہ گھر لال ہے۔

وہ طالبِ علم سکھ ہے۔

وہ چیز کہاں ہے؟

یہ ٹوپی بہت خوبصورت ہے۔

۳۔ کلنٹن کون ہے؟

پاکستانی صدر کون ہے؟

وہ کون ہے؟

وہ علی ہے۔

۴۔ جون کہاں سے ہے؟

جون ٹیکساس سے ہے۔

ٹیکساس کہاں ہے؟

ٹیکساس امریکہ میں ہے۔

۵۔ کیا، وہ بھی ٹیکساس سے ہے؟

جی ہاں، وہ بھی ٹیکساس سے ہے۔

وہ ٹیکساس میں کہاں سے ہے؟

وہ ٹیکساس میں ہیوسٹن سے ہے۔

۶۔ میرا گھر یہاں سے دور ہے۔

کیا، اُن کا گھر بھی یہاں سے دور ہے؟

جی نہیں، اُن کا گھر یہاں سے نزدیک ہے۔

آپ کا گھر وہاں سے دور ہے۔

۷۔ امریکہ پاکستان سے دور ہے۔

امریکہ کینیڈا سے دور نہیں۔

امریکہ کینیڈا سے نزدیک ہے۔

پاکستان بھی ہندوستان سے دور نہیں۔

2.1 - 2.4 Substitutions

Replace the phrases within brackets in the following sentences with the Urdu equivalents of the

English phrases listed below.

۱۔ میں (ٹیکساس سے) ہوں۔

from New York

from California

from Pakistan

from India

۲۔ میں (ٹیکساس میں)(ہیوسٹن سے) ہوں۔

from Mumbai, in India

from Tokyo, in Japan

from Montreal, in Canada

from Chicago, in Illinois

۳۔ میں لاہور میں (پانچ سال سے) ہوں۔

for two years

for one year

for three years

for four years

۴۔ راج (گھر میں)(دس سال سے) ہے۔

for nine years   here

for eight years   there

for seven years   in one office

for six years   at Harvard

۵۔ (آپ کا کام)(ہارورڈ سے)(دور) ہے۔

not very near from there their school

far   from the office   your house

near from New York   her work

not far from the university my job

2.1 - 2.4 Translations

1.   What is this?

2.   This is a horse. It is my horse.

3.   Where is Ali from?

4.   Ali is from France.

5.   Where in France is he from?

6.   He is from Paris.

7.   How long have you been here?

8.   We have been here for ten years.

9.   Is Boston far from New York?

10.   No. It is not very far.

11.   Who is Sheila? Sheila is a student. She is from Japan.

12.   Where is that shoe?

13.   This girl is very intelligent.

14.   Their house is near New York.

15.   His heart is not here!!

2.1 - 2.4 Questions

Answer the following questions in complete sentences.

۱۔   آپ کا نام کیا ہے؟

۲۔   آپ کہاں سے ہیں؟

۳۔   آپ یہاں کب سے ہیں؟

۴۔   آپ کا گھر کہاں ہے؟

۵۔   کیا، آپ کا گھر ہارورڈ سے نزدیک ہے؟

۶۔   ہارورڈ ایم۔آئی۔ٹی سے دور ہے؟

۷۔   آپ کا کام یہاں کیا ہے؟

۸۔   کیا، آپ کا جوتا جاپانی ہے؟

۹۔   کیا، آپ کا گھر لال ہے؟

۱۰۔   کیا، سلمان خان مشہور ہے؟

2.5 Pronunciation Drill - Aspirations

Column 2		Column 1	
گھل	گُل	پھر	پر
کھِل	کِل	بھار	بار
کھولنا	کولنا	پِھر	پر
گھر	گر	پھان	پان
گھوڑی	گوری	تھن	تن
گدھا	گدّا	تھان	تان
بھائی	بائی	تھالا	تالا
کھانا	کانا	ٹھائگر	ٹاکا
گھوڑا	گورا	جھولا	جُولا
سبھی	سبی	جھال	جال
تبھی	جبی	چھال	چال
کھال	کال	چھانا	چاہنا
ڈھول	ڈول	دھم	دم
پھل	پل	دھام	دام

٢.٦ گفتگو (Conversation)

نرگس:　　　　نمستے جی۔ کیا، آپ یہاں ٹورسٹ افسر ہیں؟

ٹورسٹ افسر:　جی ہاں۔ آپ کا شُبھ نام کیا ہے؟

نرگس:　　　　میرا نام نرگس ہے۔ میں بوسٹن سے ہوں۔

ٹورسٹ افسر:　اچّھا! بوسٹن کہاں ہے؟

نرگس: بوسٹن امریکہ میں ہے۔ وہ بہت خوبصورت ہے۔

ٹورسٹ افسر: آپ امریکہ میں کب سے ہیں؟

نرگس: میں وہاں آٹھ سال سے ہوں۔ میں وہاں ڈاکٹر ہوں۔

ٹورسٹ افسر: آپ کا کام کہاں ہے؟

نرگس: میں ایم۔آئی۔ ٹی میں ڈاکٹر ہوں۔

ٹورسٹ افسر: اچّھا! ایم۔ آئی۔ ٹی بہت مشہور یونیورسٹی ہے۔

نرگس: ہاں وہ بہت مشہور ہے۔اچّھا، کیا، تاج محل یہاں سے دور ہے؟

ٹورسٹ افسر: نہیں، نہیں۔ تاج محل یہاں سے دور نہیں، نزدیک ہے۔ وہ آگرہ میں ہے۔

وہ بہت سندر ہے۔

نرگس: شکریہ۔ اچّھا جی۔ نمستے۔

ٹورسٹ افسر: نمستے جی۔

2.7 Conversation Practice

Rob: Hello, who are you?

Stranger: Hello, hello. My name is Jay. I am a tourist officer here. Are you from

America?

Rob: What?! No. I am from Canada. Canada is close to America.

Stranger: Yes, yes. Canada is very famous. What do you do [lit. what is your work] in

Canada? Are you a doctor? Are you a computer software engineer?

Rob: No, I am a professor. How long have you been a tourist officer?

Stranger: I have been a tourist officer for nine years. I have been in Delhi for ten years.

How long have you been in Canada?

Rob: I have been in Canada for seven years. Is Jaipur far from here?

Stranger: Jaipur? Yes, yes. Sir, what is Jaipur?

Rob: Oh no! Are you really (واقعی) a tourist officer? Jaipur is very famous. It is in

              Rajasthan. You are not a tourist officer! You are a vagabond! Where are the

              police?

Stranger: Yes, I am a vagabond. Goodbye, sir!

Rob: Goodbye!

(Rob runs from the stranger)

2.8 Songs

۱) آوارہ ہوں
یا گردش میں ہوں
آسمان کا تارا ہوں
آوارہ ہوں

۲) میرا جوتا ہے جاپانی
یہ پتلون انگلستانی
سر پے لال ٹوپی روسی
پھر بھی دل ہے ہندوستانی

Glossary for Songs

گردِش = revolving, turning, wandering (f)   پے = on (alternate form of پر)

آسمان = sky, heaven (m)   پھر بھی = yet, still

تارا = star (m)

35

2.9 Vocabulary

boy (m)	لڑکا
eight	آٹھ
far	دُور
five	پانچ
four	چار
from	سے
from where	کہاں سے
girl (f)	لڑکی
hat (f)	ٹوپی
head (m)	سر
heart (m)	دِل
here	یہاں
horse (m)	گھوڑا
near	قریب / نزدیک
nine	نو
one	ایک
pants, trousers (f)	پتلون
president (m/f)	صدر
red	لال
seven	سات
shoe (m)	جوتا

since when	کب سے
six	چھ
sky (m)	آسمان
star (m)	تارا
ten	دس
that, those	وہ
there	وہاں
thing (f)	چیز
this, these	یہ
three	تین
vagabond, wanderer (m)	آوارہ
when	کب
who	کون
year (m)	سال / برس
yet, still	پھر بھی
zero	صِفر

Chapter 3

3.1 Nouns: Gender and Plural

All nouns in Urdu are either masculine or feminine. Within the category of each gender there are two more categories: marked masculine nouns - those ending in the letter "*alif*" ا - (e.g. لڑکا "boy") and unmarked masculine nouns - those ending in with any other sound - (e.g. گھر "house"); marked feminine nouns - those ending in "*choTii ye*" ی - (e.g. لڑکی "girl") and the unmarked feminine nouns - those ending with any other sound - (e.g. چیز "thing"). As a rough guideline you should remember that most nouns that end with ا are masculine and those that end with ی are feminine. There are important exceptions to these rules: پانی (water), بھائی (brother), دہی (yogurt) are masculine whereas ہوا (air, wind) and دُنیا (world) are feminine.

Common Marked Masculine Nouns

boy	لڑکا
shoe	جوتا
dog	کتّا
banana	کیلا

The word final long "*aa*" vowel that is normally indicated by the letter "*alif*" ا at the end of words is indicated in some words by the letter "*choTii he*" ہ. Therefore, nouns ending in this letter are usually considered as marked masculine nouns. For example:

rent	کرایہ

wonder, wink, charm	کرشمہ
precious stone	نگینہ
song, melody	نغمہ

Note: The noun جگہ (place) is one of the few exceptions to this rule. Even though it ends in a "*choTii he*" it is a feminine noun.

Forming Plurals of Marked Masculine Nouns

To form the plural of marked masculine nouns the final "*alif*" is changed to "*e*," i.e. "*baRii ye*" (ے).

boys	لڑکے
shoes	جوتے
dogs	کتّے
bananas	کیلے

Nouns that end in "*choTii he*" in the singular may retain this letter in the plural since this letter, in the word final position, may also be pronounced as "*e*." Alternatively, the "*choTii he*" may be replaced by a "*baRii ye*."

rents	کرایہ کرائے
wonders, winks, charms	کرشمہ کرشے
precious stones	نگینہ نگینے
songs, melodies	نغمہ نغے

Common Unmarked Masculine Nouns

office	دفتر
house	گھر
house, buildings	مکان
name	نام
year	سال

Forming Plurals of Unmarked Masculine Nouns

Unmarked masculine nouns in the plural are written and pronounced in the same manner as in their singular counterparts: i.e., they show no change. For example:

Singular		Plural	
office	دفتر	offices	دفتر
house	گھر	houses	گھر
name	نام	names	نام

Common Marked Feminine Nouns

girl	لڑکی
bread	روٹی
hat	ٹوپی
sari	ساڑی اساڑھی

Forming Plurals of Marked Feminine Nouns

Marked feminine nouns, that is those that end in "*choTii ye*," form their plurals by the addition of اں at the end of the singular noun:

girls	لڑکیاں
breads	روٹیاں
hats	ٹوپیاں
saris	ساڑی/ساڑھیاں

Common Unmarked Feminine Nouns

thing	چیز
night	رات
world	دُنیا
table	میز

Forming Plurals of Unmarked Feminine Nouns

Unmarked Feminine Plurals are formed with the addition of یں to the singular noun:

things	چیزیں
nights	راتیں
worlds	دُنیائیں
tables	میزیں

Summary of endings of singular and plural nouns

Type of noun	Ending in singular	Ending in plural
Marked masculine	"aa" ا or ہ	"e" ے
Unmarked masculine	any except "aa"	no change
Marked feminine	"ii" ي	"iaan" یاں
Unmarked feminine	any except "ii"	"en" یں

3.1 Translation

Translate the following words into Urdu and provide their Urdu plurals and gender:

1. house	7. boy	13. hat	19. night
2. human	8. girl	14. dog	20. orange
3. actor	9. horse	15. apple	21. room
4. office	10. shoe	16. bread	22. photograph
5. student	11. thing	17. carpet	23. store/shop
6. work	12. year	18. banana	24. table

3.2 Attributive and Predicate Adjectives

The attributive adjective in Urdu, as in English, comes immediately before the noun it modifies.

2   1

لڑکا   اچّھا

noun   attributive adjective

a good boy

On the other hand, when the adjective follows the noun or pronoun it modifies it is a predicate adjective. In Urdu, a predicate adjective occurs in a sentence whose main verb is هونا . It comes after the noun/pronoun it modifies but before the verb.

2   1

اچّھا   لڑکا

predicative adjective   noun

Attributive

وہ اچّھا لڑکا ہے۔

42

That is a good boy.

Predicative

وہ لڑکا اچّھا ہے۔

That boy is good.

وہ اچّھا ہے۔

He is good/fine.

میں اچّھا ہوں۔

I am good/fine.

3.3 Marked and Unmarked Adjectives

Urdu has two kinds of adjectives: the marked adjective and the unmarked adjective.

Marked adjectives

Marked adjectives agree in number and gender with the nouns they modify. When modifying a masculine singular noun, they end in "*alif*" ا ; in "*baRii ye*" ے when modifying a masculine plural noun; and in "*choTii ye*" ی when modifying a feminine singular or plural noun.

Masculine singular:

Good boy   اچّھا لڑکا

Good office   اچّھا دفتر

Masculine plural:

Good boys   اچّھے لڑکے

Good offices   اچّھے دفتر

Feminine singular:

Good girl   اچّھی لڑکی

43

Good things اچّھی چیز

Feminine plural:

Good girls اچّھی لڑکیاں

Good things اچّھی چیزیں

The marked predicate adjective, like its attributive counterpart, agrees in number and gender with the noun/pronoun that precedes it.

This boy is good	یہ لڑکا اچّھا ہے۔
These boys are good	یہ لڑکے اچّھے ہیں۔
This girl is good	یہ لڑکی اچّھی ہے۔
These girls are good	یہ لڑکیاں اچّھی ہیں۔

Unmarked Adjectives

Unmarked adjectives are those that do not end in one of the marked endings: "*alif*" ا, "*baRii ye*" ے, or "*choTii ye*" ی. Regardless of the gender or the number of the noun they modify, they do not change their form.

Masculine singular:

Handsome boy	خوبصورت لڑکا
Clever shopkeeper	ہوشیار دکان والا
Red apple	لال سیب

Masculine plural:

Handsome boys	خوبصورت لڑکے
Clever shopkeepers	ہوشیار دکان والے
Red apples	لال سیب

Feminine singular:

Beautiful girl	خوبصورت لڑکی
Clever wife	ہوشیار بیوی
Red book	لال کتاب

Feminine plural:

Beautiful girls	خوبصورت لڑکیاں
Clever wives	ہوشیار بیویاں
Red books	لال کتابیں

3.4 Cardinal Numbers 11-20

گیارہ	۱۱	
بارہ	۱۲	
تیرہ	۱۳	
چودہ	۱۴	
پندرہ	۱۵	
سولہ	۱۶	
سترہ	۱۷	
اٹھارہ	۱۸	
انیّس	۱۹	
بیس	۲۰	

Note: The spellings of numbers from 11-18 end in "*choTii he*" ہ. These numbers are pronounced the same way as they would have been if they ended in "*alif*" ا. They do not inflect to agree with number and gender of nouns they modify as they function as unmarked adjectives.

Ordinal numbers 1-10

Ordinal numbers usually act as marked adjectives and decline in number and gender according to the noun they modify.

Masculine singular	Masculine plural	Feminine	Number
		singular and plural	
پہلا	پہلے	پہلی	first
دوسرا	دوسرے	دوسری	second
تیسرا	تیسرے	تیسری	third
چوتھا	چوتھے	چوتھی	fourth
پانچواں	پانچویں	پانچویں	fifth
چھٹّا	چھٹّے	چھٹّی	sixth
ساتواں	ساتویں	ساتویں	seventh
آٹھواں	آٹھویں	آٹھویں	eighth
نواں	نویں	نویں	ninth
دسواں	دسویں	دسویں	tenth

From number 7 onward you can see a pattern of attaching the suffixes ("vaaṅ," "veṅ," "viiṅ") واں، ویں، ویں to the number in order to get its ordinal form. With a few exceptions, this remains true with all numbers higher than seven. When these suffices are added to the numbers 11-18 which end in a "choTii he" one has the choice of retaining or dropping the "choTii he." For example:

eleven گیارہ   eleventh گیارہواں   or   گیارواں

46

۱۔ یہ بڑا لڑکا ہے۔

یہ بڑی لڑکی ہے۔

یہ بڑے لڑکے ہیں۔

یہ بڑی لڑکیاں ہیں۔

۲۔ وہ چھوٹا دفتر ہے۔

کیا، وہ چھوٹا مکان ہے۔

وہ خوبصورت نام ہے۔

وہ بہت خوبصورت گھر ہے۔

۳۔ ایک روٹی اچّھی ہے۔

پندرہ روٹیاں اچّھی ہیں۔

یہ روٹی سستی ہے۔

وہ روٹی بہت مہنگی ہے۔

۴۔ کیا، یہ چیز صاف ہے؟

جی نہیں، جناب۔ یہ چیزیں صاف نہیں۔

وہ چیز کالی ہے؟

نہیں صاحب۔ وہ چیز لال ہے۔

۵۔ پہلا دفتر بہت صاف ہے۔

دوسرا دفتر بہت بڑا ہے۔

کیا، تیسرا دفتر بھی بڑا ہے؟

چوتھا دفتر چھوٹا ہے، کیا؟

۶۔ پانچواں پھل مزیدار ہے۔

یہ اچھّی میزیں ہیں۔

وہ لال جوتے کہاں ہیں؟

بڑا کمرہ وہاں ہے۔

۷۔ علی ہوشیار لڑکا ہے۔

جینا ہوشیار لڑکی ہے۔

کیا، بولیوود میں سب اداکار ہوشیار ہیں۔

ہارورڈ میں سب لڑکیاں ہوشیار ہیں۔

۸۔ یہ لال سیب بہت مزیدار ہے۔

وہ پیلا سنترہ بھی بہت مزیدار ہے۔

یہ بارہ سیب مزیدار نہیں۔

وہ سولہ سیب مزیدار ہیں۔

3.1-3.4 Substitutions

Substitute the adjectives and/or nouns in brackets with the Urdu equivalents of the English

words indicated below:

۱۔ علی بہت (اچّھا) لڑکا ہے۔

handsome

intelligent

tall

famous

۲۔ رادھا بہت (خوبصورت) لڑکی ہے۔

good

48

intelligent

tall

young (small)

۳۔ وہ چیزیں بہت (مزیدار) ہیں۔

good

yellow

expensive

cheap

۴۔ یہ جوتا (لال) ہے۔

yellow

good

expensive

cheap

۵۔ یہ قالین (سفید) ہے۔

black

round

expensive

beautiful

۶۔ (شیلا) (پہلی لڑکی) ہے۔

second boy   He

third doctor   Ali

fourth student   I

49

sixth student   Michelle

۷۔   وہ کتاب (نیلی) ہے۔

inside

above

fifth

small

round

3.5 Pronunciation Drill: Perso-Arabic Sounds I

Column 3	Column 2	Column 1
مقبرہ	عادت	ثابت
مُرغی	عِبرت	اکثر
غضب	عینک	اخبار
بغداد	عدالت	خراب
بغل	عام	خزانہ
شغل	عرب	خاموش
سُراغ	غم	خبر
ژولیدہ	غازی	خالی
مِژگاں	غُصّہ	خرگوش
اژدھا	غنیمت	خربوزہ
اژدر	غوری	خِدمت
طرح	غزل	خُدا
طریقہ	فارِغ	بُخار

50

نرگس:	آداب عرض جناب۔ کیا حال ہے؟
دکان والا:	آداب عرض۔ سب ٹھیک ہے۔ یہ پھل بہت اچّھے ہیں۔
نرگس:	ہاں۔ یہ لال سیب اور پیلے سنترے اچھّے ہیں۔ کیا یہ سستے ہیں؟
دوکان والا:	جی ہاں۔ بہت سستے ہیں۔ یہ کون ہیں؟
نرگس:	یہ سُلوچنا ہے۔ سُلوچنا لندن سے ہے۔
دوکان والا:	اچّھا! ویلکم! لندن میں آپ کب سے ہیں؟
سُلوچنا:	میں لندن میں سترہ سال سے ہوں۔ میں وہاں طالبِ علم ہوں۔ یہ دکان بہت صاف ہے۔ یہ کیلے بھی بہت مزیدار ہیں۔
دکان والا:	شکریہ۔ یہ نیلی قالین بھی سندر ہے۔
سُلوچنا:	ہاں، بہت سندر ہے۔ کیا، یہ مہنگی ہے؟
نرگس:	ہاں، ہاں۔ بہت مہنگی ہے۔ وہاں دوسری دکان ہے۔ قالینیں وہاں سستی ہیں۔
سُلوچنا:	وہ دکان صاف نہیں!
نرگس:	نہیں، نہیں۔ وہ بہت بڑی اور صاف دکان ہے۔ اچّھا پھر ملینگے۔
دوکان والا:	اچّھا۔ خُدا حافظ۔

3.7 Conversation Practice

Tourist:	This store is very good.
Guide:	Yes, but (مگر) this is an expensive store. The fifth store over there is cheap.
Tourist:	Is it clean?
Guide:	Yes, it is clean and very big.
Tourist:	What are those big yellow things?

51

Guide:	These are delicious oranges and those are delicious red apples.
Tourist:	Are the oranges expensive?
Guide:	No, they are very cheap. The apples are also cheap. This bread is also delicious.
Tourist:	Who is that beautiful girl in the picture?
Guide:	That is Madhuri Dixit. She is an actress. She is very famous.
Tourist:	Is she Punjabi?
Guide:	No, she is from Maharashtra.
Tourist:	Maharashtra is in India. Mumbai and Bollywood are in Maharashtra. There are many beautiful actresses and handsome actors in Bollywood.
Guide:	Yes. The actor in that picture over there is Shahrukh Khan. He too is very famous.

3.8 Songs

۱) یہ دُنیا گول ہے
اُوپر سے خول ہے
اندر تو دیکھو پیارے
بالکل پولم پول ہے

۲) یہ دِل دیوانہ ہے
دِل تو دیوانہ ہے
دیوانہ دِل ہے یہ
آہ ہا ہا۔۔۔۔دِل دیوانہ

Glossary for Songs

گول = round, circular; a circle (m)

خول = cover; case; sheath (m)

دیکھو = see (informal imperative)

پیارے = dear one (term of address)

پولم پول = hollow

3.9 Vocabulary

above	اوپر
absolutely, completely	بالکل
actor	اداکار
actress	اداکارہ
apple (m)	سیب
banana (m)	کیلا
big	بڑا
black	کالا
blue	نیلا
book (f)	کِتاب
bread (f)	روٹی
carpet (f)	قالین
cheap; inexpensive	ستا
clean	صاف
cow (f)	گائے
delicious	مزیدار
dog (m)	کتّا

53

eighteen	اٹّھارہ
eighth	آٹھواں
eleven	گیارہ
expensive	مہنگا
fifteen	پندرہ
fifth	پانچواں
first	پہلا
fourteen	چودہ
fourth	چوتھا
fruit (m)	پھل
hospital (m)	ہسپتال
inside	اندر
job/work (m)	نوکری
mad, ecstatic; crazy	دیوانہ
Maharashtra (m)	مہاراشٹرہ
night (f)	رات
nineteen	انّیس
ninth	نواں
orange (m)	سنترا (سنگترہ)
picture/photograph (f)	تصویر
room (m)	کمرہ
round, circular; a circle (m)	گول

second; another	دوسرا
seventeen	سترہ
seventh	ساتواں
shop/store	دُکان/دوکان
shopkeeper/store owner	دُکان والا/دوکان والا
sixteen	سولہ
sixth	چھٹّا
small	چھوٹا
table (f)	میز
tall	لمبا
tea (f)	چائے
tenth	دسواں
third	تیسرا
thirteen	تیرہ
twelve	بارہ
twenty	بیس
white	سفید
wife (f)	بیوی
world (f)	دُنیا
yellow	پیلا

Chapter 4

4.1 Possessive Adjectives

The postposition کا (and its forms کی and کے) are used to form possessive adjectives in Urdu. کا in Urdu functions roughly like "of" or "apostrophe s, 's" in English. Like a postposition, it follows a noun or a pronoun. When it follows a noun or a pronoun, the کا and its preceding noun/pronoun is transformed into a possessive adjective or an adjectival phrase:

گھر   کا   +   آپ

[noun] [possessive postposition] [pronoun]

(your house)

In the above sentence آپ کا is a possessive adjective. In Urdu, possessive adjectives are marked adjectives that reflect the gender and number of the item(s) possessed. The gender and number of the possessor has no impact upon the possessive adjectives. Possessive adjectives, like their attributive counterparts, precede the nouns they modify. Thus, if the possessed object is *masculine singular*, the relevant noun/pronoun is followed by the possessive particle کا :

Your shoe	آپ کا جوتا
Ali's shoe	علی کا جوتا
Radha's shoe	رادھا کا جوتا

In the above examples, because جوتا the possessed object is *masculine singular*, it is preceded by the masculine singular form of the possessive particle کا. If the possessed object is *masculine plural*, then it is preceded by the masculine plural form of the possessive particle کے :

Your shoes	آپ کے جوتے
Ali's shoes	علی کے جوتے
Radha's shoes	رادھا کے جوتے

If the possessed object is *feminine singular or plural*, then the possessive particle کی precedes it:

Your thing	آپ کی چیز
Ali's thing	علی کی چیز
Radha's thing	رادھا کی چیز

Your things	آپ کی چیزیں
Ali's things	علی کی چیزیں
Radha's things	رادھا کی چیزیں

When کی ، کے ، کا follow pronouns, they have special forms. Below is a list of these special forms. Only the pronoun آپ does not change its form with the possessive particle.

میرا	=	کا	+	میں
میری	=	کی	+	میں
میرے	=	کے	+	میں
تیرا	=	کا	+	تو
تیری	=	کی	+	تو
تیرے	=	کے	+	تو

57

تمہارا	=	کا	+	تم
تمہاری	=	کی	+	تم
تمہارے	=	کے	+	تم
آپ کا	=	کا	+	آپ
آپ کی	=	کی	+	آپ
آپ کے	=	کے	+	آپ
اُس کا	=	کا	+	وہ (singular)
اُس کی	=	کی	+	وہ (singular)
اُس کے	=	کے	+	وہ (singular)
اُن کا	=	کا	+	وہ (plural)
اُن کی	=	کی	+	وہ (plural)
اُن کے	=	کے	+	وہ (plural)
اِس کا	=	کا	+	یہ (singular)
اِس کی	=	کی	+	یہ (singular)
اِس کے	=	کے	+	یہ (singular)
اِن کا	=	کا	+	یہ (plural)
اِن کی	=	کی	+	یہ (plural)
اِن کے	=	کے	+	یہ (plural)
ہمارا	=	کا	+	ہم
ہماری	=	کی	+	ہم
ہمارے	=	کے	+	ہم

4.1 Substitutions

Replace the words in brackets with the Urdu equivalents of the English listed below:

ا۔   یہ (میرا) دوست ہے۔

his

her

our

your (formal)

their

۲۔   وہ (ہماری) چیز ہے۔

my

your (informal)

its

his

her

۳۔   (اُس کا) مکان بڑا ہے۔

my

our

your (least formal)

their

her

۴۔   یہاں (شیلا کے) جوتے ہیں۔

my

his

Ravi's

Stephanie and Lisa's

your

۵۔ وہاں (بل گیٹس کی) گاڑیاں ہیں۔

Amitabh Bacchan's

Madhuri Dixit's

our

their

her

4.1 Reading and Translation Drill

۱۔ وہ ہماری گاڑی ہے۔

وہ ہمارا گھر ہے۔

وہ ہمارے قلم ہیں۔

وہ ہمارے گھر ہیں۔

وہ ہماری چیز ہے۔

۲۔ کیا، یہ بہت مہنگی چیز ہے؟

یہ مہنگا گھر ہے۔

یہ مہنگی کتابیں ہیں۔

یہ مہنگے قلم ہیں۔

۳۔ یہ سستی ٹوپیاں ہیں۔

یہ بہت سستی دکان ہے۔

یہ سستے گھر ہیں۔

یہ سستی گاڑیاں ہیں۔

یہ بہت ستا کاجل ہے۔

۴۔ تیرا گھر مہنگا ہے۔

ہمارا جوتا ستا ہے۔

تمہاری بیٹیاں جوان ہیں؟

آپ کی زندگی ایک خوبصورت غزل ہے۔

Fill in the blanks with appropriate possessive adjectives and then translate into English.

(my)	۱۔ _____ گھر یہاں سے دور ہے۔	
(our)	۲۔ _____ چیزیں بہت خوبصورت ہیں۔	
(his)	۳۔ _____ جوتا جاپانی ہے۔	
(their)	۴۔ _____ ٹوپیاں ہندوستانی ہیں۔	
(our)	۵۔ _____ مکان یہاں سے دور نہیں۔	
(her)	۶۔ _____ کتابیں بہت مہنگی ہیں۔	
(your, least formal)	۷۔ کیا، _____ دِل ہندوستانی ہے؟	
(my)	۸۔ جی نہیں۔ _____ دِل امریکی ہے۔	
(your, most formal)	۹۔ _____ دفتر یہاں سے بہت نزدیک ہے۔	
(your, informal)	۱۰۔ _____ دوست دس سال سے بوسٹن میں ہیں۔	

61

4.2 Asking and Telling Age

<u>Note</u>: Many people in South Asia, as in many Western nations, do not consider direct questions about their age to be polite or in good taste. Although it is crucial to learn how to make such inquiries, students should be aware that this kind of question should not be undertaken casually. Generally speaking, asking the age of young children or people younger than one's self is considered acceptable. For older persons or people whom one does not know well this may become a sensitive issue.

Asking Age

The sentence pattern used to ask a person's age is as follows:

4	3	2	1
ہے؟	کیا	عُمر	Possessive adjective declined to modify a feminine noun.

The possessive adjective is declined in the feminine form because عُمر the noun for "age" is feminine.

آپ کی عمر کیا ہے؟

What is your age?

اُس کی عمر کیا ہے؟

What is his/her age?

Alternatively, one may ask age by using a variation of the expression کتنے سال "how many years." In this case, the word سال is followed by appropriate form of کا، کے، کی agreeing with the subject. For example:

62

آپ کتنے سال کے ہیں؟

How old are you? [lit. how many years are you?]

وہ کتنے سال کا/ کی ہے؟

How old is he/she? [lit. how many years is he/she?]

Telling Age

The usual pattern for telling one's age is as follows:

4	3	2	1
verb agreeing with subject	کا، کے، کی agreeing with subject	# of years and سال	subject

میں بیس سال کا ہوں۔

I (masculine singular) am 20 years old.

شیلا دس سال کی ہے۔

Sheila is 10 years old.

ہم پندرہ سال کے ہیں۔

We (masculine plural) are 15 years old.

One may also tell age by using the noun عُمر with the appropriate possessive adjective, but this is less common.

میری عُمر بیس سال ہے۔

I am 20 years old [lit. my age is 20]

شیلا کی عُمر دس سال ہے ۔

Sheila is 10 years old [lit. Sheila's age is 10]

4.3 Cardinal Numbers 21-30

۲۱	اکّیس
۲۲	بائیس
۲۳	تئیس
۲۴	چوبیس
۲۵	پچّیس
۲۶	چھبّیس
۲۷	ستّائیس
۲۸	اٹھائیس
۲۹	اُنتیس
۳۰	تیس

4.2 - 4.3 Reading and Translation Drill

۱۔ میرا دوست اکّیس سال کا ہے۔

آپ کی عمر کیا ہے؟

میں بائیس سال کا ہوں۔

اُس کی عمر کیا ہے؟

۲۔ راج تئیس سال کا ہے۔

کیا، نرگس چوبیس سال کی ہے؟

میرے دوست پچّیس سال کے ہیں۔

اِس کی عمر کیا ہے؟

۳۔ تمہاری لڑکی کی عمر کیا ہے؟

وہ چھبّیس سال کی ہے۔

64

ہماری کلاس کی لڑکیاں ستائیس سال کی ہیں۔

سب لڑکے اٹھائیس سال کے ہیں۔

۴۔ اُن کا بڑا بھائی اُنتیس سال کا ہے۔

مگر اُن کی بڑی بہن تیس سال کی ہے۔

کیا، تو بھی سولہ سال کی ہے؟

نہیں، نہیں۔ میں اٹھارہ سال کی ہوں۔

Translate into Urdu:

1. Is his older sister twenty-one years old?

2. My sister and I are twenty-five years old.

3. How old are you?

4. These are twenty-eight delicious oranges.

5. Are these thirty red apples?

4.4 Order in a Noun Phrase

Thus far we have learned that nouns may be preceded by various elements including possessive adjectives (میرا، آپ کا، راج کا), attributive adjectives (اچّھا، ہوشیار), demonstratives (وہ، یہ), and numbers. They may sometimes be preceded by interrogatives as well. Examples of some interrogatives that frequently precede a noun include کون (who, which), کونسا (which one), کِتنا (how much, how many), and کیسا (what kind or sort of, how). (Note: کونسا، کتنا، کیسا are marked interrogatives; the "aa" ending, as in the case of marked adjectives, may change to "ii" or "e" depending on the gender and number of the noun that follows.) When a noun is preceded by two or more of these elements, the following order should be observed:

65

Noun	Attributive Adjective	Demonstrative,	Possessive Adjective
		Interrogative,	
		Number	

Examples:

میرا وہ ہوشیار لڑکا یہاں ہے۔

That clever son of mine (lit. my that clever son) is here.

نرگس کی دو چھوٹی بہنیں سُندر ہیں۔

Nargis' two younger sisters are pretty.

(Note: سُندر is used here as a predicate adjective and hence follows the noun.)

4.4 Translation Drill

Translate the following sentences into idiomatic Urdu:

1. Which beautiful daughter of his is an actress? (use کونسی for which)

2. Nilufer's second blue carpet is from Iran.

3. Those two big black dogs of yours are no good!

4. These seven-year-old yellow photographs, on the table, are mine.

5. All of Reshma's elder sisters are very tall.

6. How many of Raj's crazy friends are in America?

4.5 Pronunciation Drills - Nasals

Column 4	Column 3	Column 2	Column 1
بھنگڑا	زنگ	لاؤں	سنگ
سنگھاڑا	اُمنگ	جہاں	رنگ
گھنگرو	انگ	وہاں	بھنگ

مہنگا	انگریز	یہاں	ترنگ
ٹھنڈک	فرنگ	ہوں	ڈھنگ
منگنی	نارنگی	جوں	تنگ
سانس	تانگہ	سوں	پلنگ
جنگ	جھانسہ	دوں	گاؤں
شنکر	پھانس	چھاؤں	پاؤں

Perso-Arabic Sounds II

Column 3	Column 2	Column 1
طشت	فاخِر	خمیر
طِفلی	فخر	اختر
اطفال	قاضی	صاحب
غالِب	قلم	صدمہ
اِقبال	قبیلہ	صدر
ذوق	قافِلہ	ضمیر
قمر	قِسمت	مضمون
فِراق	قالین	وُضو
خُمار	قانون	طالِب
تقی	قِیامت	طالبان
مقصد	مقام	ظُلم
مقتل	قتل	ظالِم
طوطا	ضمانت	ظفر

67

راج: آداب عرض نرگس جی۔ کیا حال ہے؟

نرگس: سب ٹھیک ہے۔ یہ میرے بھائی شاد اور فراز ہیں اور یہ میری بہنیں نغمہ اور نیلوفر ہیں۔

راج: یہ میرا کتّا ٹائیگر ہے اور یہ میری بلّی چیتا ہے۔

نرگس: تمہارا کتّا اور تمہاری بلّی بہت سُندر ہیں۔

راج: ہاں، یہ جرمن ہیں۔ آپ کے بھائی اور آپ کی بہنیں یہاں کب سے ہیں؟

نرگس: میرے بھائی اور میری بہنیں یہاں بائیس سال سے ہیں۔

راج: اچّھا۔ اُن کی عمریں کیا ہیں؟

نرگس: شاد چوبیس سال کا ہے، فراز ستائیس سال کا ہے۔ نیلوفر بائیس سال کی ہے اور نغمہ تیس سال کی ہے۔

نغمہ: نہیں۔ نہیں۔ میں تیس سال کی نہیں ہوں! میں صرف انتیس سال کی ہوں۔

راج: یہ کتّا بھی انتیس سال کا ہے۔

نرگس: کیا! یہ کتّا اِتنا بوڑھا ہے؟

راج: بوڑھا؟! کیا، نغمہ بوڑھی ہے؟

نغمہ: نہیں۔ میں بوڑھی نہیں ہوں اور راج کا کتّا بھی بوڑھا نہیں۔ ہم جوان ہیں۔ ہمارے دِل جوان ہیں۔

4.7 Conversation Practice

Steve: Hello. I am Steve. I am from New York. Where is Sheila?

Seema: Sheila is not at home. I am her sister Seema and this is our little brother Babu.

Who is he?

Steve:	This is my friend Amar. This is his cat Dimple.
Seema:	Hello, Amar. Dimple is very beautiful. How old is she?
Amar:	She is five years old and she is very smart.
Babu:	I also am five years old and I am very smart!
Seema:	Where is Dimple from? She is not an Indian cat!
Steve:	She is from Afghanistan. She is an Afghani cat!
Seema:	Amar, are you from Afghanistan?
Amar:	No, no, I am from Bangladesh.
Babu:	Is Bangladesh far from India?
Amar:	Bangladesh is very close to India. It is a very beautiful country.
Babu:	My sisters and I are from India. There are no good cats in India.
Steve:	Well! We've got to run. We'll meet again. Goodbye!
Seema:	Yes, we will meet again. Goodbye!
Babu:	Goodbye, little Dimple!

4.8 Songs

۱) میں پل دو پل کا شاعِر ہوں
پل دو پل میری کہانی ہے
پل دو پل میری ہستی ہے
پل دو پل میری جوانی ہے

۲) یہ نینا، یہ کاجل، یہ زلفیں، یہ آنچل
خوبصورت سی ہو تم غزل

کبھی دل ہو، کبھی دھڑکن

کبھی شعلہ، کبھی شبنم

تم ہی ہو تم میری ہمدم

زندگی تم میری، میری تم زندگی

۳) عُمر تیری سولہ

نخرے تیرے سترہ!۔۔۔ خطرہ! خطرہ! خطرہ!۔۔۔۔

سترہ نخروں والی تیرا ہر نخرہ ہے ۔۔۔ خطرہ!

Glossary for Songs

ہستی	= existence (f)	دھڑکن	= heartbeat (f)
نینا	= eye (m)	شُعلہ	= flame, spark (m)
کاجل	= kohl, collyrium (m)	شبنم	= dew, dew drop (f)
زُلف	= curl, tress (f)	ہمدم	= companion, bosom friend (m/f)
آنچل	= hem of sari, veil, or shawl (m)	نخرہ	= coquetry, flirting (m)

4.9 Vocabulary

age (f)	عُمر
all	سب
brother (m)	بھائی
but/however	مگر، لیکن
car (f)	گاڑی
cat (f)	بلّی
country (m)	مُلک

70

danger (m)	خطرہ
daughter (f)	بیٹی
elderly (adj.); elderly person	بوڑھا
friend (m/f)	دوست
ghazal (love poem) (f)	غزل
how much, how many?	کِتنا، کِتنی، کِتنے
life (f)	زِندگی
moment (m)	پل
more, additional (adj.)	اور
old (thing)	پُرانا
only	صِرف
pen (m/f)	قلم
poet (m)	شاعِر
sister (f)	بہن
sometimes	کبھی
story (f)	کہانی
thirty	تِیس
this much	اِتنا
twenty-one	اکِیّس
twenty-two	بائِیس
twenty-three	تِئِیس
twenty-four	چوبِیس

twenty-five	پچّیس
twenty-six	چھبّیس
twenty-seven	ستّائیس
twenty-eight	اٹّھائیس
twenty-nine	اُنتیس
what sort of, what kind of, how	کیسا، کیسی، کیسے
young (adj.), youth (m/f)	جوان
youth, youthfulness (f)	جوانی

Chapter 5

5.1 The Present Habitual Tense

Verb Infinitives

All verb infinitives in Urdu end in ﺎﻧ. For example:

to read/study	پڑھنا
to go	جانا
to do	کرنا

Urdu Verbal Stems

In order to derive the stem (sometimes also called the root) from the infinitive, the ending ﺎﻧ is dropped. The stem of پڑھنا is thus پڑھ, that for جانا is جا, and that for کرنا is کر.

The Present Habitual Tense

To conjugate verbs that indicate actions that occur in the present or are habitual or frequent, the suffixes تا، تے، تی, are added to the verbal stem to create the present participle. The choice of suffix is determined by the number and gender of the subject of the sentence. Thus تا is the suffix for the verbal stem if the subject is masculine singular, تے if it is masculine plural, and تی for both feminine singular and plural subjects. To complete the tense the appropriate present tense of the ہونا verb also needs to be added. For example, the stem of the Urdu verb "to read or study" is پڑھ. In order to say "he is reading or studying" we add the suffix تا to the verb stem (since the subject is masculine singular) to get پڑھتا which grammatically is the masculine present participle. To this is added ہے the present tense of the verb ہونا corresponding to the subject "he." The result is the sentence وہ پڑھتا ہے which means "He reads/studies." Note: The present habitual tense does not denote that the subject is currently engaged in a particular act or process (e.g. he/she is reading). For this situation there is a separate tense, the present continuous, which will be introduced in Chapter 7. The following table illustrates the conjugational forms of the verb پڑھنا in the present habitual:

Verbal Infinitive: پڑھنا

Stem: پڑھ

Urdu Feminine	English	Urdu Masculine
	Singular	
میں پڑھتی ہوں۔	I study.	میں پڑھتا ہوں۔
تو پڑھتی ہے۔	You (least formal) study.	تو پڑھتا ہے۔
تم پڑھتی ہو۔	You (informal) study.	تم پڑھتے ہو۔
آپ پڑھتی ہیں۔	You (formal) study.	آپ پڑھتے ہیں۔
وہ پڑھتی ہے۔	He/she studies.	وہ پڑھتا ہے۔
	Plural	
ہم پڑھتی ہیں۔	We study.	ہم پڑھتے ہیں۔
تم پڑھتی ہو۔	You (informal) study.	تم پڑھتے ہو۔
آپ پڑھتی ہیں۔	You (formal) study.	آپ پڑھتے ہیں۔
وہ پڑھتی ہیں۔	They study.	وہ پڑھتے ہیں۔

Note: In Urdu, the verb جانا, "to go" does not need a postposition "to."

ہم کالج جاتے ہیں۔

We go to college.

کیا، تم سنیما جاتے ہو؟

Do you go to the movies?

5.2 The Present Habitual Negative

In negative sentences, the negative particle نہیں is placed right before the conjugated present

habitual verb and the auxiliary (the form of ہونا) is dropped unless the tone is emphatic:

میں نہیں پڑھتا۔

I don't study.

میں نہیں پڑھتا ہوں۔

I don't study (emphatic).

For still more emphasis, the negative particle may also be placed after the verb.

میں پڑھتا نہیں۔

I do not study at all.

In case the subject is feminine plural, and the negative particle نہیں precedes the verb, then the

feminine present participle is nasalized:

وہ نہیں پڑھتی۔

She does not study.

میں نہیں پڑھتی۔

I do not study.

وہ نہیں پڑھتیں۔

They (feminine) do not study.

ہم نہیں پڑھتیں۔

75

We (feminine) do not study.

The feminine plural present participle loses this nasalization when the negative particle نہیں

follows it, e.g., ـ ہم پڑھتی نہیں

Here is a list of common Urdu verbs that you should memorize:

to eat	کھانا
to drink	پینا
to stay or to live	رہنا
to go	جانا
to come	آنا
to do	کرنا
to work	کام کرنا
to write	لِکھنا
to sing	گانا
to dance	ناچنا
to play	کھیلنا
to understand	سمجھنا
to give	دینا
to bring	لانا
to take	لینا
to see	دیکھنا

5.1-5.2 Conjugation Drill

Conjugate the following verbs in the present habitual tense (assume that the subject is masculine):

کھیلنا	رہنا	کھانا	پینا	
				میں
				تو
				تم
				آپ
				وہ (singular)
				وہ (plural)
				ہم

Conjugate the following verbs in the present habitual tense (assume that the subject is feminine).

لکھنا	کام کرنا	آنا	جانا	
				میں
				تو
				تم
				آپ
				وہ (singular)
				وہ (plural)
				ہم

Conjugate the following verbs in the negative present habitual tense (assume that the subject is feminine).

گانا   ناچنا   کھیلنا   سمجھنا

میں

تو

تم

آپ

وہ (singular)

وہ (plural)

ہم

5.1-5.2 Reading and Translation Drill

۱۔   میں سیب کھاتا ہوں۔

تو آم کھاتا ہے۔

تم پھل کھاتے ہو۔

آپ سنترے کھاتے ہیں۔

۲۔   وہ پانی پیتا ہے۔

وہ شراب پیتی ہے، کیا؟

ہم لسّی پیتے ہیں۔

وہ کوک پیتے ہیں۔

۳۔   علی دلّی میں نہیں رہتا ہے۔

ہم امریکہ میں رہتے ہیں۔

وہ گھر میں رہتی نہیں۔

78

تم بھارت میں کب سے رہتے ہو؟

۴۔ شیلا وہاں اسکول نہیں جاتی ۔

کیا، تم بھی اسکول جاتے ہو؟

نہیں، میں اسکول نہیں جاتا۔

وہ لڑکیاں کہاں جاتی ہیں؟

۵۔ کیا، تو یہاں آتی ہے؟

نہیں، یہاں خطرہ ہے۔ میں یہاں نہیں آتی۔

مگر نرگس یہاں آتی ہے۔

راج اور نرگس وہاں جاتے ہیں۔

۶۔ میں دفتر میں کام کرتا ہوں۔

وہ شاعر صاحب بھی دفتر میں کام کرتے ہیں۔

ہم دفتر میں کام نہیں کرتے ہیں۔

تم گھر میں کام کرتے ہو؟

۷۔ وہ لڑکیاں دلّی میں نہیں رہتیں۔

کیا، آپ وہاں نہیں پڑھتیں؟

ہم نوکری نہیں کرتے۔

شیلا اور رینو فٹبال نہیں کھیلتیں۔

۸۔ فِل کالِنز کہاں گاتا ہے؟

کیا، پالا عبدل کبھی ناچتی ہے؟

مائیکل جیکسن بھی ناچتا ہے۔

شاہ رُخ خان اچّھا ناچتا ہے۔

۹۔ وہ اُردو سمجھتی ہے۔

79

وہ اُردو سمجھتی ہے مگر لکھتی نہیں۔

کیا، آپ عربی سمجھتے ہیں؟

ہاں۔ میں عربی کم سمجھتی ہوں۔

۱۰۔ میں ایک سیب لیتا ہوں۔

میں دس سنترے لیتی ہوں۔

کیا، آپ پانچ پھل لیتی ہیں؟

نہیں۔ وہ آٹھ پھل نہیں لیتیں۔

۱۱۔ راج بہت کام کرتا ہے۔

سیما کہانیاں لِکھتی ہے کیا؟

ہم وہاں بہت جاتے ہیں۔

کیا، تم کلب میں بہت ناچتے ہو؟

5.3 Times of the Day, Days of the Week, and Other Time Phrases

Times of the Day

morning (f)	صُبح
afternoon (f)	دوپہر
evening (f)	شام
night (f)	رات
day, daytime (m)	دِن

Days of the Week

Sunday (m)	اِتوار
Monday (m)	پیر
Tuesday (m)	منگل

Wednesday (m)	بُدھ
Thursday (f)	جُمعرات
Friday (m)	جُمعہ
Saturday (m)	ہفتہ

Other Expressions of Time

today (m)	آج
tomorrow (m)	کل
yesterday (m)	کل
day after tomorrow (m)	پرسوں
day before yesterday (m)	پرسوں
every	ہر
every day (m)	ہر روز، ہر دِن
every week (m)	ہر ہفتہ
every month (m)	ہر مہینہ
every year (m)	ہر سال
sometimes	کبھی کبھی
nowadays	آج کل

5.4 The Particle کو with Temporal Words and Phrases

The particle کو has many uses in Urdu. We will discuss these uses in great detail later. Suffice to

say here that certain time expressions are marked by (or followed by) کو. All times of the day,

with the exception of صُبح (morning), are marked by کو. Similarly all the days of the week are

also marked by کو. کو after these expressions may be variously translated as "on," "in," or

81

"during." However, none of the other expressions of time introduced above (such as آج، کل،

سال) use کو.

میں دِن کو اسکول جاتا ہوں اور شام کو کام کرتا ہوں۔

I go to school in the day and work in the evening.

وہ صُبح گالف کھیلتا ہے مگر رات کو پڑھتا ہے۔

He plays golf in the morning but studies at night.

لڑکیاں اِتوار کو اِسکول نہیں جاتیں ۔

The girls do not go to school on Sunday.

میں آج کل بہت مصروف ہوں۔

I am very busy these days.

میرا خاندان ہر سال پاکستان جاتا ہے۔

My family goes to Pakistan every year.

Note: The short "a" vowel at the end of the words for Friday and Saturday, جمعہ and ہفتہ, changes to "e" when marked by کو. For explanation, refer to the discussion on the oblique case of nouns in Chapter 6.

5.5 Review of Urdu Sentence Structure

The normal word order in an Urdu sentence is:

4	3	2	1
Verb	Locative Phrase	Temporal Phrase	Subject
پڑھتا ہوں	گھر میں	ہر روز	میں

Any change in this order usually implies that the element placed out of normal sequence in the sentence is meant to be emphasized:

ہر روز میں گھر میں پڑھتا ہوں۔

The temporal phrase ہر روز, "every day," is emphasized in this sentence by being positioned at the beginning of the sentence before the subject.

5.3 - 5.5 Substitution and Response Drill

Substitute the phrases in brackets with the Urdu equivalents of the English words indicated below:

۱۔   میں (اِتوار کو) کام نہیں کرتا۔

                on Monday

                on Saturday

                in the morning

                in the evening

۲۔   ہم (کبھی کبھی) سنیما جاتے ہیں۔

                every night

                on Friday

                on Thursday

                every year

۳۔   میں (آج) پڑھتا ہوں۔

                on Tuesday

                every week

                on Wednesday

                in the afternoon

۴۔ کیا، تم لوگ (پیر کو) مصروف ہو؟

on Thursday

every month

tomorrow

today in the evening

Fill in the blanks with the appropriate form of the present habitual tense:

۱۔ میں ہر روز دفتر _____ (go)

۲۔ ہمارے دوست بہت _____(work)

۳۔ وہ لڑکی لائبریری میں _____ (studies)

۴۔ میں اور اُس کا بھائی شام کو_____ (come)

۵۔ میرے بھائی لندن میں _____ (live)

۶۔ ہر روز شام کو وہ لڑکیاں _____ (dance)

۷۔ کیا، تم اُردو _____ (understand)؟

۸۔ جی نہیں۔ میں اُردو _____ اور_____ (read and write)

۹۔ ہم لوگ سب فٹبال_____(play)

۱۰۔ کیا، آپ ہر صُبح پھل _____ (eat)؟

۱۱۔ مڈونا بہت اچّھا _____ (sing)

۱۲۔ لڑکیاں جُمعرات کو نہیں_____(come)

۱۳۔ کویتا اور نیلو مٹھائی نہیں _____ (give)

میرا دوست روی _____ (is)۔ روی ایم۔ آئی۔ ٹی میں _____ (studies)۔ روی بہت اچّھا اسٹوڈنٹ _____ (is)۔ روی کے دو بھائی رمیش اور راج _____

84

ریمیش اور راج اُردو _____ (understand)۔ مگر اُردو (are)۔

وہ لوگ کیمبرج میں _____ (live) اور ہر روز صُبح کالج _____ (don't read)۔

_____ (go)۔ وہ دوپہر کو دفتر میں _____ (do work)۔ وہ ہر اِتوار کو نائیٹ کلب میں

_____ اور _____ (sing and dance)۔ کبھی کبھی شام کو وہ کافی

_____ (drink) اور مٹھائی _____ (eat)۔

Answer the following questions both orally and in writing:

١۔   آپ ہر روز دوپہر کو کیا کرتے ہیں؟

٢۔   آپ گھر کب جاتے ہیں؟

٣۔   کیا، امریکن لوگ اِتوار کو کام کرتے ہیں؟

٤۔   آپ کا دوست کہاں پڑھتا ہے؟

٥۔   کیا، وہ کبھی کبھی سنیما جاتا ہے؟

٦۔   آپ لوگ منگل کو کیا کرتے ہیں؟

٧۔   کیا، آپ جمعرات کو مصروف ہیں؟

٨۔   آپ کے پروفیسر کب کام کرتے ہیں؟

٩۔   آپ کے دوست ہر صبح کیا کرتے ہیں؟

١٠۔   کیا، آپ شام کو کافی پیتے ہیں؟

5.6 The Verb چاہنا with Nouns and Verbs

In this section we will be discussing two uses of the verb چاہنا, to want, to desire.

1. چاہنا with a noun:

The noun becomes the object of چاہنا, that is the object which is desired:

چاہتی ہوں۔	پھل	میں
verb	inanimate object of verb	subject

I want fruit.

2. چاہنا with a verbal infinitive:

The verbal infinitive in this construction becomes the object of چاہنا:

میں	کھانا	چاہتا ہوں
subject	verbal infinitive	verb

I want to eat.

Note that in such a construction only the verb چاہنا is conjugated. The verbal infinitive remains unchanged. To form the negative, the particle نہیں may be inserted before the verbal infinitive with the auxiliary of ہونا being optionally retained or not for emphasis:

میں	نہیں	کھانا	چاہتا (ہوں)
subject	negative	verbal infinitive	verb

For additional emphasis, the negative may be placed between the verbal infinitive and verb:

میں	کھانا	نہیں	چاہتا (ہوں)
subject	verbal infinitive	negative	verb

For even more emphasis, the negative can be moved to the end of the sentence:

میں	کھانا	چاہتا	نہیں!
subject	verbal infinitive	verb	negative

5.6 Substitutions and Translations

Replace the phrases within brackets in the following sentences with the Urdu equivalents of the English phrases listed below.

۱۔   میں (بیس آم) چاہتا ہوں۔

21 fruits

86

22 apples

23 houses

24 things

۲۔ کیا، (تم) (ایک گاڑی) (چاہتے ہو؟)

    want   25 pens   they

    want 26 oranges   you (formal)

      wants 27 hats   she

    want 28 mangoes   Raj and Nargis

۳۔ (ہم)(ناچنا چاہتے ہیں۔)

    want to sing   I

    want to play   you (least formal)

    want to drink   you (informal)

    wants to understand Rob

۴۔ علی(کتاب) (لکھنا) چاہتا ہے۔

    read   newspaper

    give   that thing

    drink   water

    take   30 books

۵۔ (وہ)(تاج محل)(دیکھنا چاہتی ہے)۔

    wants to go   New York   Steve

do not want to go   cinema   Steve and Amber

    want to stay at home   people

Translate into Urdu:

1.   We want to sing every evening.

2.   My friend and Rishi want to eat Indian food in an Indian restaurant.

3.   He wants to come to America; he does not want to live in India!

4.   She wants to understand Chinese not Russian.

5.   All of them want to read the newspaper in the morning.

6.   I want to go to the movies but Sheila wants to stay in the house.

7.   Do you (formal) want to work in the White House? No, I don't want to work in

the White House. I want to eat dinner and dance in the White House.

5.7 Pronunciation Drill: Retroflexes

Column 3	Column 2	Column 1
دوڑنا	چھوڑنا	برا بڑا
پھوڑنا	توڑنا	کرا کڑا
جھاڑ	پہاڑ	گرا گڑا
داڑ	باڑ	جرا جڑا
واڑا	باڑھ	گھورا گھوڑا
کاڑا	جاڑھ	مورا موڑا
جھگڑا	تگڑا	گِری گھڑی
تنگڑی	پگڑی	سِری سیڑھی
کھوڑی	نگوڑی	مورنا موڑنا

Repeat the following sentences to practice retroflexive sounds:

۱۔ بڑا گھوڑا دوڑتا ہے۔

۲۔ بڑا پہاڑ اچّھا ہے۔

۳۔ نگوڑی گھوڑی بوڑھی ہے۔

۴۔ گھوڑا گھڑی گاڑتا ہے۔

5.8 گفتگو (Conversation)

نرگس: کیا، یہ لکھنؤ اِسٹیشن کا ٹکٹ گھر ہے؟

کلرک: جی ہاں۔ آپ کہاں جانا چاہتی ہیں؟

نرگس: میں بنارس جانا چاہتی ہوں۔ فرسٹ کلاس کا کرایہ کیا ہے؟

کلرک: فرسٹ کلاس کا کرایہ دو سو روپے ہے۔ آپ کہاں رہتی ہیں؟

نرگس: میں امریکہ میں رہتی ہوں مگر ہر سال ہندوستان آتی ہوں۔ یہاں میرا خاندان رہتا ہے۔ اچّھا، فرسٹ کلاس کا کرایہ بہت زیادہ ہے۔ سیکنڈ کلاس کا کرایہ کیا ہے؟

کلرک: میڈم یہ بہت مُشکل ہے۔ سیکنڈ کلاس میں جگہ نہیں ہے۔

(راج آتا ہے۔)

راج: نرگس! تم یہاں؟ تم کیا کرنا چاہتی ہو؟

نرگس: راج، میں بنارس جانا چاہتی ہوں۔ وہاں کے مندر دیکھنا چاہتی ہوں اور ساڑیاں خریدنا چاہتی ہوں۔

راج: میں بھی بنارس دیکھنا چاہتا ہوں اور میں بنارس میں پان بھی کھانا چاہتا ہوں۔ یہ ٹرین کے دو ٹکٹ ہیں۔

نرگس: راج! تم بہت اچّھے ہو! میں کتنی خوش ہوں!

89

كلرک: ‏(راج سے) آپ کیوں ٹکٹ دیتے ہیں؟ کیا، آپ یہاں کام کرتے ہیں؟

راج: ‏نہیں نہیں۔ میں آسمان کا تارا ہوں۔ میں کام نہیں کرتا، صرف پیار کرتا ہوں۔

نرگس: ‏راج! تم تو بالکل پاگل ہو! یہ ٹرین کب جاتی ہے؟

راج: ‏یہ شام کو جاتی ہے۔ اچّھا تمہارے شوق کیا ہیں؟

نرگس: ‏میں بہت کتابیں پڑھتی ہوں۔ ٹینیس اور شطرنج بھی کھیلتی ہوں۔

راج: ‏کیا تم اب شطرنج کھیلنا چاہتی ہو؟

نرگس: ‏نہیں۔ میں مصروف ہوں!

5.9 Conversation Practice

Have a conversation with your partner about his/her activities in the morning, afternoon,

evening, and night. You should have at least 6-8 questions for your partner and vice versa. All

answers should be in complete sentences. Your conversations should incorporate as many of the

following vocabulary words as possible:

صبح، دوپہر، شام، رات، کھانا، پینا، دیکھنا، رہنا، ناچنا، گانا، چاہنا، خاندان، سمجھنا، آج کل، ہفتہ، اتوار، کبھی کبھی، کام کرنا، آنا، جانا۔

Be creative and feel free to bring in other vocabulary that we have encountered so far.

5.10 Songs

۱) دِل ہے کہ مانتا نہیں
مشکل بڑی ہے رسمِ محبّت
یہ جانتا ہی نہیں۔۔۔۔

90

۲) یاد تیری جب آتی ہے

دل میں طوفان لاتی ہے

آنسو ہیں میری آنکھوں میں

ہر سانس میں تیرا نام ہے۔

یاد تیری۔۔۔۔۔

<u>Glossary for Songs</u>

آنسو = tears (m)

سانس = breath (f)

رسمِ محبّت = rites, customs of love

یاد = memory, rememberance (f)

طوفان = storm (m)

5.11 Vocabulary

afternoon (f)	دوپہر
Arabic (f)	عربی
to bring	لانا
busy	مصرُوف
to buy	خریدنا
chess (f)	شطرنج
to come	آنا
to be convinced, to listen, to obey	ماننا

crazy, mad, insane	پاگل
to dance	ناچنا
day (m)	دِن
day before yesterday; day after tomorrow	پرسوں
definitely, sure	ضرُور
difficult	مُشکِل
to do	کرنا
to drink	پینا
to eat	کھانا
evening (f)	شام
every	ہر
every day (m)	ہر دِن، ہر روز
every month (m)	ہر مہینہ
every week (m)	ہر ہفتہ
every year (m)	ہر سال
eye (f)	آنکھ
family (m)	پرِوار، خاندان
fare, rent (m)	کِرایہ
food (m)	کھانا
Friday (m)	جُمعہ
to give	دینا

to go	جانا
happy	خُوش
hobby/hobbies (m)	شوق
hundred	سو
to know	جاننا
less	کم
to live or to stay	رہنا
a lot, very much	زِیادہ
love	پیار (m)/ مُحبّت (f)/ عِشق (m)
to love	پیار کرنا، مُحبّت کرنا
mango (m)	آم
memory, remembrance (f)	یاد
Monday (m)	پیر
morning (f)	صُبح
newspaper (m)	اخبار
now	اب
occasionally, now and then	کبھی کبھی
people, folk (m)	لوگ
place/vacancy (f)	جگہ
to play	کھیلنا
rupee (Indian/Pakistani currency) (m)	روپیہ

Saturday (m); week (m)	ہفتہ
to see	دیکھنا
to sing	گانا
to study/ to read	پڑھنا
Sunday (m)	اِتوار
sweets (f)	مِٹھائی
to take	لینا
temple (m)	مندِر
that, which, who (relative pronoun and conjunction)	کہ
these days / nowadays	آج کل
Thursday (f)	جُمعرات
today (m)	آج
tomorrow/yesterday (m)	کل
Tuesday (m)	منگل
to understand	سمجھنا
water (m)	پانی
Wednesday (m)	بُدھ
when (relative pronoun)	جب
why?	کیوں
wine/alcohol (f)	شراب
to work	کام کرنا

to write	لِکھنا
yogurt drink (f)	لسّی

Chapter 6

6.1 Postpositions

Unlike English, Urdu does not have prepositions. Instead it has postpositions: that is, the prepositional counterpart in Urdu comes after the noun or pronoun it modifies. Some postpositions consist of only one word and are called simple postpositions while others consist of more than one word, hence they are called compound postpositions.

Common simple postpositions include:

at, in	میں
on	پر
from, by, with, since	سے
to	کو
until, up to	تک

Compound postpositions are usually formed with the particle کے or occasionally with سے.

Some important examples include:

near	کے پاس
concerning, regarding, about	کے بارے میں
far from	سے دور
with	کے ساتھ
before	سے پہلے، کے پہلے
after	کے بعد

on top of	کے اوپر
under	کے نیچے
across, in front of	کے سامنے
behind	کے پیچھے
near, close to	کے نزدیک / کے قریب
beyond, in front of, ahead of	کے آگے
inside	کے اندر
because of	کی وجہ سے

Note: Pronouns that precede compound postpositions beginning with کے assume their possessive forms as discussed in Chapter 4. Thus, the pronoun میں before کے ساتھ becomes میرے, hence میرے ساتھ. Similarly, the pronoun میں before کی وجہ سے becomes میری وجہ سے.

6.2 The Oblique Case -- Oblique Forms of Nouns

Whenever a noun or a pronoun is followed by a postposition, the noun/pronoun (and its modifying adjective) goes into the oblique case. Without the postposition, the noun/pronoun and adjectives modifying them are said to be in the nominative case. Some nouns/pronouns reflect the oblique case by slight changes in their forms while others remain unchanged.

Exception: Some pronouns followed by a compound postposition use their possessive forms and not oblique forms. See section 6.6 below.

Oblique Forms of Nouns

Masculine Singular Nouns

When a postposition is used after a marked masculine singular noun which ends in final *"alif"*

ا , the *"alif"* is changed to *"baRii ye"* ے . If the noun ends in a *"choTii he,"* the *"choTii he"* is either changed to *"baRii ye"* or retained and pronounced as "e." For example:

Nominative: the boy   لڑکا

Oblique: on the boy   لڑکے پر

Nominative: child   بچّہ

Oblique: on the child   بچّے پر / بچّہ پر

Unmarked masculine singular nouns (i.e., those that do not end with final *"alif"*) do not change their form in the oblique. Example:

Nominative: office   دفتر

Oblique: in the office   دفتر میں

Masculine Plural Nouns

When masculine plural nouns go into the oblique, the suffix *"oñ"* وں is attached to them.

Marked masculine nouns which end with *"baRii ye"* ے in the nominative plural, drop this ending before taking the *"oñ"* وں suffix. Examples:

a) <u>Marked</u>

Nominative: boys   لڑکے

Oblique: with the boys   لڑکوں کے ساتھ

b) <u>Unmarked</u>

Nominative: offices   دفتر

Oblique: in the offices دفتروں میں

Feminine Singular Nouns

When feminine singular nouns are followed by a postposition, their form remains unchanged regardless of whether they are marked or unmarked. Examples:

a) <u>Marked</u>

Nominative: girl   لڑکی

Oblique: from the girl   لڑکی سے

b) <u>Unmarked</u>

Nominative: table   میز

Oblique: on the table   میز پر

Feminine Plural Nouns

All feminine plural nouns take the *"oṅ"* وں ending in their oblique forms. Note: The *"oṅ"* وں

suffix is added to the singular form of feminine nouns.

a) <u>Marked</u>

Nominative: girls   لڑکیاں

Oblique: from the girls   لڑکیوں سے

b) <u>Unmarked</u>

Nominative: tables   میزیں

Oblique: on the tables   میزوں پر

Summary of Oblique Form Endings for Nouns

Type of noun	Singular Oblique Ending	Plural Oblique Ending
Marked masculine	*"e"* ے	*"oṅ"* وں
Unmarked masculine	same as nominative	*"oṅ"* وں
Marked feminine	same as nominative	*"oṅ"* وں
Unmarked feminine	same as nominative	*"oṅ"* وں

99

6.2 Drill Exercise

Give the nominative plural, singular oblique, and plural oblique forms of the following nouns:

۱۰ـ ملک	۷ـ میز	۴ـ ٹوپی	۱ـ کیلا
۱۱ـ دوست	۸ـ قالین	۵ـ کام	۲ـ سیب
۱۲ـ پھل	۹ـ گاڑی	۶ـ بھائی	۳ـ مہینہ
۱۹ـ تصویر	۱۷ـ کتاب	۱۵ـ جوتا	۱۳ـ مکان
۲۰ـ دکان	۱۸ـ کہانی	۱۶ـ بوڑھا	۱۴ـ روٹی

6.3 Oblique Forms of Demonstratives

When یہ (this) is followed by a postposition, its oblique singular form is اِس. When وہ (that) is followed by a postposition, its oblique singular form is اُس. The oblique plural form of یہ is اِن and that of وہ is اُن. Examples:

Nominative Singular	Oblique Singular
this boy	on this boy
یہ لڑکا	اِس لڑکے پر
that boy	on that boy
وہ لڑکا	اُس لڑکے پر

Nominative Plural	Oblique Plural
these girls	with these girls
یہ لڑکیاں	اِن لڑکیوں کے ساتھ
those girls	with those girls
وہ لڑکیاں	اُن لڑکیوں کے ساتھ

6.4 Oblique Forms of Adjectives

Marked Adjectives

a) <u>Singular Masculine</u>: These adjectives change the word final *"alif"* ا ending to *"baRii ye"* ے in the oblique.

Nominative	Oblique
this good boy	with this good boy
یہ اچّھا لڑکا	اِس اچّھے لڑکے کے ساتھ
that big house	in that big house
وہ بڑا گھر	اُس بڑے گھر میں

b) <u>Plural Masculine, Singular Feminine, Plural Feminine</u>:

These adjectives do not change their form in the oblique.

Plural Masculine:	اچّھے لڑکوں کے ساتھ	with the good boys
Singular Feminine:	اچّھی لڑکی کے ساتھ	with the good girl
Plural Feminine:	اچّھی لڑکیوں کے ساتھ	with the good girls

Unmarked Adjectives

These adjectives do not change their form in the oblique, regardless of number or gender. Study the following examples with the adjective ہوشیار (intelligent).

Masculine Singular Nominative	ہوشیار لڑکا
Masculine Singular Oblique	ہوشیار لڑکے سے
Masculine Plural Nominative	ہوشیار لڑکے
Masculine Plural Oblique	ہوشیار لڑکوں سے
Feminine Singular Nominative	ہوشیار لڑکی

Feminine Singular Oblique   ہوشیار لڑکی سے

Feminine Plural Nominative   ہوشیار لڑکیاں

Feminine Plural Oblique   ہوشیار لڑکیوں سے

6.5 Oblique Forms of Pronouns

When certain pronouns are followed by postpositions, they assume a special form. Here is a list

of the pronouns in their nominative and oblique forms.

Singular

Nominative	*Oblique*
میں	مُجھ
تو	تُجھ
تم	تم
آپ	آپ
وہ	اُس
یہ	اِس

Plural

Nominative	*Oblique*
ہم	ہم
تم	تم
آپ	آپ
وہ	اُن
یہ	اِن

6.6 Note on کا، کے، کی

As we have learned previously, کی، کے، کا are particles indicating possession. The gender and number of the object being possessed determines which form is used: کا for masculine singular, کے for masculine plural, and کی for feminine singular and plural. They function just as postpositions after nouns, as they put nouns into the oblique case.

the boy's name	لڑکے کا نام
the boys' names	لڑکوں کے نام
the girl's thing	لڑکی کی چیز
the girls' things	لڑکیوں کی چیزیں

When preceding کی، کے، کا, certain pronouns, however, take the possessive form instead of the oblique:

میرا	=	کا	+	میں
تیرا	=	کا	+	تو
تمہارا	=	کا	+	تم
ہمارا	=	کا	+	ہم
میری	=	کی	+	میں
تیری	=	کی	+	تو
تمہاری	=	کی	+	تم
ہماری	=	کی	+	ہم

6.4-6.6 Reading and Translation Drill

١۔ مجھ میں کیا خرابی ہے؟

مجھ میں بہت خرابیاں ہیں۔

اِن چیزوں میں بہت خرابیاں ہیں۔

تم میں ایک بھی خرابی نہیں۔

۲۔ اِس پلنگ پر کیا ہے؟

اِس پلنگ پر ایک کتاب ہے۔

اِس بڑی دکان پر کون آتا ہے؟*

اِس بڑی دکان پر بہت لوگ آتے ہیں۔*

۳۔ وہ مجھ سے ڈالر لیتا ہے۔

کیا، وہ تجھ سے کتابیں لیتا ہے؟

نہیں، وہ مجھ سے نہیں، اُن سے کتابیں لیتا ہے۔

وہ لڑکیاں ہم سے کھانا نہیں لیتیں۔

* دکان پر, literally meaning "on the store," idiomatically implies "at the store."

Fill in the blanks with the appropriate form of the noun, pronoun, or adjective.

۱۔ _____ بہت اچّھا ہے۔ (the fruitseller)

۲۔ _____ کام اچّھا ہے۔ (the fruitseller's)

۳۔ _____ دفتر بڑا ہے۔ (my)

۴۔ _____ دفتر میں پندرہ لڑکیاں کام کرتی ہیں۔ (my)

۵۔ _____ کہاں ہے؟ (that book)

۶۔ _____ نام کیا ہے؟ (that book's)

۷۔ _____ اچّھی ہیں۔ (these books)

۸۔ _____ میں کیا ہے؟ (these books)

۹۔ میں _____ کے ساتھ کھیلتا ہوں۔ (good boys)

10. _____ لڑکوں کے نام کیا ہیں؟ (your [informal])

11. یہ _____ ہے۔ (good thing)

12. _____ کے اوپر کیا ہے؟ (these good things)

13. کیا، _____ میں خرابی ہے؟ (me)

14. نہیں، _____ میں خرابی نہیں۔ (you [least formal])

15. _____ میں بارہ کمرے ہیں۔ (that big house)

16. _____ میں بیس کمرے ہیں۔ (our office)

17. _____ پر کون ہے؟ (at these stores)

18. نہیں۔ وہ _____ سے کتابیں نہیں لیتا۔ (me)

6.7 The Interrogative کون and Its Oblique Forms

کون in its nominative form means "who" or "which."

وہ لڑکا کون ہے؟

Who is that boy?

یہ صاحب کون ہیں؟

Who is this gentleman?

کون صاحب ہیں؟

Which gentleman is it?

When کون goes into the oblique, its singular form is کِس while its oblique plural form is کِن.

In the oblique form, it may mean "whose," "whom," "which," or "what."

یہ کِس کی کتاب ہے؟

Whose book is this?

وہ کِس کا گھر ہے؟

Whose house is that?

یہ کن کے اخبار ہیں؟

Whose (plural) newspapers are these?

آپ کن کے ساتھ گاتے ہیں؟

With whom (plural) do you sing?

یہ چیز کس کتاب میں ہے؟

In which book is this thing?

کلاس کس وقت ہے؟

At what time is the class?

In the last example we see that the oblique case can exist even when a postposition is not explicitly present. (The Urdu sentence does not have a postposition for "at" after the noun وقت).

Since the postposition is implied, this form is known as the implied oblique. In idiomatic Urdu, postpositions are often left out after temporal and locative nouns but their existence is nevertheless assumed. This assumption is evident in the fact that the noun and adjective related to time and location of an action go into the oblique case without an explicit postposition.

وہ کس وقت گھر جاتا ہے؟

At what time does he go home?

It is assumed that وقت is followed by a postposition, پر, but the rules of idiomatic Urdu do not recommend that the postposition be explicitly stated. But as the use of the oblique form of the interrogative adjective کس illustrates, the noun وقت that it modifies is in the oblique case.

In many locative expressions, the same rule is applied.

وہ دفتر جاتا ہے۔

He goes to the office.

دفتر is in the oblique case with the postposition میں or پر implied after it.

$$وہ ڈاکخانے جاتا ہے۔$$

He goes to the post office.

ڈاکخانہ has been changed into ڈاکخانے because of the implied postposition which puts it in the oblique.

Note that کِس can be followed by کی ،کے ،کا (depending upon the object it is modifying) when inquiring about the possessor of a thing:

$$وہ کس کا گھر ہے؟$$

Whose house is that?

$$وہ کس کے پھل ہیں؟$$

Whose fruits are those?

$$وہ کس کی چیز ہے؟$$

Whose thing is that?

6.8 Note on کے لئے

The compound کے لئے can mean "for," "for the sake of," or "in order to." Nouns and adjectives preceding it will be in the oblique case:

$$وہ علی کے لئے آتا ہے۔$$

He comes for Ali.

$$وہ اِس لڑکی کے لئے آتا ہے۔$$

He comes for this girl.

$$وہ اچّھے کیلوں کے لئے آتا ہے۔$$

He comes for good bananas.

In addition to nouns and adjectives, verbal infinitives can also occur before کے لئے. In such instances, the infinitives will take the oblique case. For example, کھانا will become کھانے , کرنا will become کرنے , etc.

وہ کھانے کے لئے آتا ہے۔

He comes [in order] to eat.

وہ ناچنے کے لئے آتی ہے۔

She comes [in order] to dance.

Exception: Several pronouns followed by کے لئے do not go into the oblique case. Instead, they assume the possessive form.

for me	میرے لئے	=	کے لئے	+	میں
for you	تیرے لئے	=	کے لئے	+	تو
for you	تمہارے لئے	=	کے لئے	+	تم
for us	ہمارے لئے	=	کے لئے	+	ہم

See also section 6.6.

The لئے construction also has two common idiomatic usages:

| therefore | اس لئے |
| why | کس لئے |

Do not confuse the two aforementioned idiomatic expressions with:

| for this one | اس کے لئے |
| for whom | کس کے لئے |

١۔ میں تمہارے لئے آم لاتا ہوں۔

وہ اُن کے لئے گھر جاتا ہے۔

آپ ہمارے لئے کیا کرتے ہیں؟

میں آپ کے لئے کام کرتی ہوں۔

٢۔ تم گرمی کی وجہ سے بہت سوتی ہو۔

نہیں، میں گرمی کی وجہ سے بالکل نہیں سوتی۔

کام کی وجہ سے آج وہ یہاں نہیں گاتا۔

میں اس لڑکے کی وجہ سے وہاں جاتی ہوں۔

٣۔ میرے ساتھ ایک کتّا ہے۔

ہمارے ساتھ ہمارا دوست ہے۔

کیا، اس کے ساتھ پولیس والا ہے؟

اُن کے ساتھ برما کا صدر ہے۔

٤۔ کیا، وہ تم سے پہلے آتا ہے؟

ان سے پہلے شیلا آتی ہے۔

ہمارے گھر سے پہلے ایک لال مکان آتا ہے۔

وہ بہت کام کی وجہ سے ہم سے پہلے دفتر جاتی ہے۔

٥۔ وہ پڑھنے کے بعد کھیلتا ہے۔

ان کے بعد کون گاتا ہے؟

اس کے بعد ہم گھر جاتے ہیں۔

ٹی۔ وی پر، مہابھارت کے بعد خبریں آتی ہیں۔

٦۔ ہمارے گھر کے اوپر ایک بلّی رہتی ہے۔

اس میز کے اوپر بہت مہنگی گھڑی ہے۔

وہ چھوٹا لڑکا میز کے اوپر ہے۔

اس چھوٹے لڑکے کے اوپر میز ہے!

۷۔ کیا، اِس پلنگ کے نیچے کتابیں ہیں؟

نہیں۔ وہ کتابیں اُس کرسی کے نیچے ہیں۔

وہ میرے گھر کے نیچے رہتا ہے۔

اُن ٹوپیوں کے نیچے کیا ہے؟

۸۔ اس گھر کے سامنے بہت بڑا بازار ہے۔

ان بازاروں کے سامنے ان کا دفتر ہے۔

میرے سامنے دیو ناچتا اور گاتا ہے۔

اس دکان کے سامنے کون رہتا ہے؟

۹۔ ہمارے دفتر کے قریب پھلوں کی دکانیں ہیں۔

اس بازار کے نزدیک ایک ہسپتال ہے۔

ہمارا گھر حیدرآباد کے قریب ہے۔

اِن عمارتوں کے نزدیک ایک بہت بڑا باغ ہے۔

۱۰۔ ہمارے دفتر کے آگے چار باغ ہیں۔

ان باغوں کے آگے کیا ہے؟

لڑکے اِسکول کے آگے کھیلتے ہیں۔

کیا تمہارا گھر میرے گھر کے آگے ہے؟

۱۱۔ اس عمارت کے اندر بہت کمرے ہیں۔

اُس جوتے کے اندر کیا ہے؟

وہ ہر روز اِس کمرے کے اندر ٹی۔وی دیکھتا ہے۔

110

اُس گھر کے اندر کون رہتا ہے؟

۱۲۔ ہمارے گھر کے پاس بہت بڑا بازار ہے۔

ان کے دفتر کے پاس دس کتّے رہتے ہیں۔

آپ کی عمارت کے پاس وہ بڑی دکان ہے، کیا؟

جی نہیں۔ وہ بڑی دکان اس عمارت کے پاس ہے۔

۱۳۔ آپ کس گھر میں رہتے ہیں؟

علی کے ساتھ کون رہتا ہے؟

علی کس کے ساتھ رہتا ہے؟

وہ کس کی دکانیں ہیں؟

Translate the following into Urdu:

1. Ashok comes here every day to eat.

2. With whom does he come?

3. Whose houses are those?

4. Sheila and Sunita go to the club to dance every night, but they don't drink alcohol.

5. Does he bring food for them every day?

6. I buy this car for you (your sake).

7. I go to London every year to watch tennis.

8. With whom do you sing? With crazy Raj?

9. What time is their class every day?

10. We come to Harvard [in order] to study but go to that office [in order] to work.

11. Because of love, there are tears in Nargis' eyes!

6.7 - 6.8 Substitutions

Replace the phrases in brackets with the Urdu equivalents of the English words indicated below.

١۔ وہ (ہمارے لئے) کام کرتے ہیں۔

    you (least formal)

    him

    them

    me

٢۔ (میری) وجہ سے علی نہیں آتا ہے۔

    you (informal)

    us

    them

    that girl

٣۔ کیا، تم (اُن) کے ساتھ پڑھتے ہو؟

    me

    us

    those girls

    those boys

٤۔ وہ (تمہارے) پہلے کھاتا ہے؟

    her

    you (formal)

    the Pakistani president

    that boy

۵۔ (ہمارے) بعد کون آتا ہے؟

me

you (informal)

them

his friend

۶۔ (اِس) کے اوپر کیا ہے؟

that

our house

their thing

their things

۷۔ (پلنگ) کے نیچے ایک کتّا ہے۔

that

window

this

those houses

۸۔ ہم (سیما) کے سامنے نہیں ناچتیں۔

you (formal)

those boys

this building

my brother

۹۔ (اُس) کے باغ کے پیچھے بہت بڑا بازار ہے۔

our

113

their

my

his friend

۱۰۔   تم (میرے) قریب رہتے ہو۔

us

house

that building

this market

۱۱۔   (تمہارے گھر) کے آگے کیا ہے؟

these houses

those houses

that big building

this beautiful market

۱۲۔   (اُس بڑے گھر) کے اندر (دس) کمرے ہیں۔

twenty-five   this big building

seven   my house

twelve   our friend's house

twenty-eight   her office

۱۳۔   (اِس عمارت) کے پاس ایک بہت بڑا بازار ہے۔

these buildings

our office

that big store

114

this poet's house

۱۴۔ وہ (ہمارے) بارے میں کیا کہتا ہے؟

Pakistanis

our friends

that car

Aishwarya Rai and Salman Khan

۱۵۔ آج کل وہاں (کون) ہے؟

whose house

whose things

whose store

whose newspapers

6.9 Pronunciation Drill: Aspirated, Perso-Arabic, and Retroflexive Sounds II

Column 2		Column 1
جھولا		خراب
گھر		اچّھا
جھرّی		غم
جھنڈا		خوشی
تڑپنا		موقع
مژدہ		باغ
بھائی		عادت
بہن		غُنچہ
مدھر		مقبول

115

مدھوبن	مغرور
رادھا	بھاڑ
نٹ کھٹ	پہاڑ
کنھیا	مہاڑی
ابھاگن	ساڑھی
بھارت	گاڑی
بھومی	گنواری
قلم	جھاڑو
نُسخہ	مغل
رقص	شغل
فُغاں	بغل

6.10 گفتگو (Conversation)

ٹیلیفون پر گفتگو

راج: ہلو۔ نمستے جی۔ آپ کون؟

نرگس: راج؟ میں ہوں، نرگس۔ کیا حال ہے؟

راج: سب ٹھیک ہے۔ اچّھا، تم ہر روز اس وقت کیا کرتی ہو؟

نرگس: تم یہ کیوں پوچھتے ہو؟

راج: میں آج تمہارے ساتھ کھانے کے لئے جانا چاہتا ہوں۔

نرگس: نہیں، نہیں۔ میں ہر روز اس وقت سنیل کے ساتھ جاتی ہوں۔

راج: تم سنیل کے ساتھ کیوں جاتی ہو؟

نرگس: کیونکہ میں اس کے ساتھ پڑھتی ہوں اور اس کے بعد ہم باغ میں ٹینیس کھیلتے ہیں۔

116

راج: تم اور سنیل ٹینیس کھیلتے ہو؟ اچّھا! تم کِس باغ میں کھیلتے ہو؟

نرگس: ہم جین پارک میں کھیلتے ہیں۔

راج: اور جین پارک کہاں ہے؟

نرگس: جین پارک یونیورسٹی کے سامنے اور سنیل کے گھر کے پیچھے ہے۔

راج: تو سنیل تمہارا اچّھا دوست ہے! وہ کہاں سے ہے؟

نرگس: راج، یہ کیا ہے؟ سنیل بہت اچّھا لڑکا ہے اور ٹینیس میرا شوق ہے۔

راج: ہاں، ہاں۔ سنیل اچّھا ہے اور میں خراب ہوں۔ اب میں سونے کے لئے جاتا ہوں۔

نرگس: کیا، تم ناراض ہو؟ تم میں کوئی خرابی نہیں ہے۔

راج: نہیں۔ مجھ میں بہت خرابیاں ہیں۔ میں سونے کے لئے جاتا ہوں۔

نرگس: اچّھا! کیا، تم ہمارے ساتھ جانا چاہتے ہو؟

راج: کیا؟! ہاں ٹھیک ہے۔ میں ابھی آتا ہوں۔ تم، میں اور باغ!

نرگس: اور سنیل! راج تم بالکل پاگل ہو۔

راج: ہاں۔ میں تمہاری وجہ سے پاگل ہوں!

نرگس: راج تم تو میرے ساجن ہو۔

راج: اور تم، میری جان!

6.11 Conversation Practice

Andy: Hello, Jane. How are you?

Jane: Fine, thanks. What is this?

Andy: These are apples, bananas, and mangoes. These are for you.

Jane: Thanks so much. Is there a fruit seller's store near your house?

Andy: No. It's in front of my office, behind that big building.

Jane: Do you go to get fruit every day?

Andy: No, I go every week. Why?

Jane: I want to go with you. There is a problem [fault: خرابی] in my car. With whom do you go?

Andy: I go with my friend Ashok. He lives above my apartment.

Jane: Do you want to go with me now?

Andy: Yes, I want to buy oranges as well.

6.12 Songs

۱۔   زندگی اِمتحان لیتی ہے (۲)

لوگوں کی جان (۳) لیتی ہے

دل لگی اِمتحان لیتی ہے (۲)

دل جلوں کی جان (۳) لیتی ہے

دوستی اِمتحان لیتی ہے (۲)

دوستوں کی جان (۳) لیتی ہے

زندگی اِمتحان لیتی ہے

دل لگی اِمتحان لیتی ہے

دوستی اِمتحان لیتی ہے

۲۔   میرا دِل بھی کتنا پاگل ہے

یہ پیار تو تم سے کرتا ہے

پر سامنے جب تم آتے ہو

کچھ بھی کہنے سے ڈرتا ہے

او میرے ساجن، او میرے ساجن

ساجن ساجن، میرے ساجن

میرا دل بھی۔۔۔(دہرائیے)

کتنا اِس کو سمجھاتا ہوں

کتنا اِس کو بہلاتا ہوں

نادان ہے کچھ نہ سمجھتا ہے

دن رات یہ آہیں بھرتا ہے

میرا دل بھی۔۔۔(دہرائیے)

Glossary for Songs

دِل لگی = attachment, friendship, love (f)   نادان = ignorant, foolish

دِل جلا = lover; one with burned heart (m)   آہیں بھرنا = to sigh

بہلانا = to amuse, to cheer, to distract

6.13 Vocabulary

after	کے بعد
angry; upset	ناراض
any; some (adj); someone (noun)	کوئی
to ask	پوچھنا
bad	خراب
because	کیونکہ
because of	کی وجہ سے
bed (m)	پلنگ

before	کے / اسے پہلے
behind	کے پیچھے
beloved, sweetheart (m)	ساجن
building (f)	عمارت
chair (f)	کرسی
clock/watch (f)	گھڑی
to explain, to cause to understand	سمجھانا
fault, blemish, (f)	خرابی
for the sake of, for, in order to	کے لئے
friendship (f)	دوستی
fruit seller (m/f)	پھل والا یا پھل والی
garden (m)	باغ
heat, hot weather (f)	گرمی
in front of, across, facing	کے سامنے، کے آگے
inside	کے اندر
king (m)	راجہ
life, soul; sweetheart; energy (f)	جان
Mahabharata -- Indian epic	مہابھارت
market/bazaar (m)	بازار
to meet	ملنا

near	کے نزدیک، کے قریب، کے پاس
news (f)	خبر
now	اب
on top of	پر، کے اُوپر
post office (m)	ڈاک خانہ
reason (f)	وجہ
regarding	کے بارے میں
to say, to speak	کہنا
to sleep	سونا
test, trial, examination (m)	اِمتحان
therefore	اِس لئے
time (m)	وقت
under	کے نیچے
who	کون
window (f)	کھڑکی
with (in the company of)	کے ساتھ
for what reason, why	کِس لئے (کیوں)

Chapter 7

7.1 Expressing Potentials with سکنا

The verb سکنا (to be able to, or can) is never used by itself. It always needs the stem of another verb before it:

to be able to study   پڑھ سکنا

to be able to eat   کھا سکنا

Note that when conjugating this construction, only the verb سکنا changes. The stem of the verb which is attached to سکنا does not change under any circumstances.

میں ہارورڈ جا سکتا ہوں۔

I can go to Harvard.

وہ کتاب پڑھ سکتے ہیں۔

They can read a book.

کیا، تم ناچ سکتے ہو؟

Can you dance?

Verbs which combine سکنا with the stem of another verb are called compound verbs.

7.2 نہیں with Compound Verbs

In order to form a negative sentence with compound verbs, there are three options:

1.   The particle نہیں precedes the compound verb block:

وہ نہیں پڑھ سکتے۔

2. The particle نہیں is placed between the verb stem and سکنا:

وہ پڑھ نہیں سکتے۔

3. The particle نہیں is placed at the end:

وہ پڑھ سکتے نہیں۔

The gradual shift of the negative particle to the end of the sentence corresponds to an increasing emphasis in negation. Hence example 3 is the most emphatic.

7.3 Further Uses of اور

In addition to being a conjunction meaning "and," اور can also mean "more" and "further."

تم اور کھانا چاہتے ہو؟

Would you like to eat more?

آپ اور گا سکتی ہیں؟

Can you sing more?

7.1-7.3 Reading and Translation Drill

میں اُردو پڑھ سکتا ہوں مگر لکھ نہیں سکتا۔ ۱۔

کیا، تم اُردو لکھ سکتے ہو؟

جی نہیں۔ ہم اُردو نہیں لکھ سکتے۔

وہ سب لوگ اُردو پڑھ سکتے ہیں۔

وہاں گرمی ہے۔ میں وہاں نہیں سو سکتا۔ ۲۔

ہم وہاں مل سکتے ہیں، مگر ناچ نہیں سکتے۔

وہ پشاور جا سکتی ہیں مگر جانا نہیں چاہتیں۔

وہ اُردو سمجھ سکتی ہیں مگر پڑھنا نہیں چاہتیں۔

وہ میرے گھر آ سکتے ہیں مگر آنا نہیں چاہتے۔ ۳۔

میں اور نہیں پی سکتی۔

کیا، تم اور ناچ سکتی ہو؟

نہیں، مگر میں اور گا سکتی ہوں۔

7.4 The Present Continuous Tense

The present continuous tense is formed in Urdu by combining the following components:

the verb stem + the appropriate form of the participle of the verb رہنا : رہا (for masculine

singular subject), رہے (for masculine plural subject), رہی (for feminine singular/plural subject)

+ present tense form of ہونا agreeing with the subject.

Feminine	Singular	Masculine
میں پڑھ رہی ہوں۔	I am studying.	میں پڑھ رہا ہوں۔
تو پڑھ رہی ہے۔	You are studying.	تو پڑھ رہا ہے۔
تم پڑھ رہی ہو۔	You are studying.	تم پڑھ رہے ہو۔
آپ پڑھ رہی ہیں۔	You are studying.	آپ پڑھ رہے ہیں۔
وہ پڑھ رہی ہے۔	He/She is studying.	وہ پڑھ رہا ہے۔

	Plural	
ہم پڑھ رہی ہیں۔	We are studying.	ہم پڑھ رہے ہیں۔
تم پڑھ رہی ہو۔	You are studying.	تم پڑھ رہے ہو۔
آپ پڑھ رہی ہیں۔	You are studying.	آپ پڑھ رہے ہیں۔
وہ پڑھ رہی ہیں۔	They are studying.	وہ پڑھ رہے ہیں۔

To form a negative sentence with this tense, place نہیں before the beginning of the verb block

and drop the ہونا auxiliary unless you want to be emphatic. وہ نہیں پڑھ رہی۔ (She is not

studying).

124

7.4 Reading and Translation Drill

۱۔ میں اخبار پڑھ رہا ہوں۔

وہ خط پڑھ رہے ہیں۔

یہ لڑکی کتاب پڑھ رہی ہے۔

ہم لوگ آج کا اخبار پڑھ رہے ہیں۔

۲۔ کیا، تم کھڑکی کھول رہی ہو؟

نہیں، میں دروازہ کھول رہی ہوں۔

وہ لڑکیاں ڈبّہ کھول رہی ہیں۔

وہ لوگ کمرہ کھول رہے ہیں یا نہیں؟

۳۔ میں آج خط نہیں پڑھ سکتا ہوں کیونکہ میں کتاب لکھ رہا ہوں۔

میں کھا رہی ہوں اور ٹی۔ وی دیکھ رہی ہوں۔

کیا، تم بھی ٹی۔ وی دیکھ رہے ہو؟

گھر میں ایک ریڈیو چل رہا ہے۔

۴۔ کیا آپ کپڑے بدل رہی ہیں؟

نہیں، نہیں۔ میں کچرا اُٹھا رہی ہوں۔

وہ سب کپڑے بدل رہے ہیں۔

تو کپڑے بدل رہی ہے۔

7.5 The Comparative

In Urdu, all comparative and superlative expressions of adjectives are in relative terms. Thus, the comparative is expressed by saying, "x is bigger than y," while the superlative follows the form "x is the biggest of all." The postposition "سے" is used in Urdu in the same sense as "than" and "of" are used in English. The comparative subject appears in the beginning of the sentence

125

or phrase and that which the subject is being compared to follows it with the adjective agreeing with the comparative subject.

adjective agrees with subject	object of comparison	subject
بڑا ہے۔	موہن سے	علی

Ali is bigger (older) than Mohan.

adjective agrees with subject	object of comparison	subject
بڑی ہے۔	علی سے	شیلا

Sheila is bigger (older) than Ali.

Remember that ﺳﮯ is a postposition, so the nouns, pronouns, and adjectives governed by ﺳﮯ will be in the oblique case.

وہ لڑکے علی سے بڑے ہیں۔

Those boys are bigger (older) than Ali.

علی اِن لڑکوں سے بڑا ہے۔

Ali is bigger (older) than these boys.

7.5 Substitutions

۱۔ (یہ سنترہ) اُس سیب سے اچّھا ہے۔

those apples

those oranges

that fruit

these bananas

۲۔ میرا دوست (علی کے دوست) سے ہوشیار ہے۔

that boy

126

that beautiful girl

Harvard's students

Albert Einstein

۳- یہ میز (اُن میزوں) سے مہنگی ہے۔

those windows

those carpets

those pens

that book

7.5 Translation

Translate the following comparative statements:

1. Radha is more beautiful than Sunita.

2. Steve is brighter than Ali.

3. This girl is better than that boy (اچھّی).

4. He is older than me (بڑا).

5. My shoes are more beautiful than the shoes of those girls.

6. Canada is cleaner than the U.S. because there are fewer people and less trash.

7. This picture is better than those pictures.

8. Is your (most formal) room bigger than my room?

9. These apples are more expensive than those apples.

10. Those carpets are cheaper than these carpets.

7.6 The Superlative

In order to form a superlative statement, the pronominal adjective (سب) is used before سے and the rest of the sentence structure remains the same as it would in a comparative sentence.

میرا لڑکا سب سے ہوشیار ہے۔

My son is the brightest (of all).

میری لڑکیاں سب سے ہوشیار ہیں۔

My girls are the brightest (of all).

وہ سب سے بڑا ہے۔

He is the oldest (of all).

7.6 Translation

Translate the following superlative statements.

1. This is the most delicious thing.

2. This is the most expensive carpet.

3. That is the cleanest room.

4. That is my oldest boy.

5. Is he your best friend?

6. Ghalib (غالب) is the world's best poet.

7. My sister is the most beautiful girl.

8. Those are the most difficult books.

9. This picture is good but those pictures are the most beautiful.

10. Our house is the largest.

7.7 Persian Adjectival Elements

It is quite common for Urdu to use the Persian comparative and superlative adjectives. These

adjectives are formed by the addition of the تر suffix (for comparative adjectives) and ترین suffix (for superlative adjectives). The use of تر and ترین suffixes in Urdu is limited, for they can only be attached to adjectives of Persian origin.

good	بہ
better	بہتر
best	بہترین

یہ لڑکی اُس لڑکی سے بہتر ہے۔

This girl is better than that girl.

bad	بد
worse	بدتر
worst	بدترین

وہ بدترین نوکر ہے۔

He is the worst servant.

The Persian adjective پسندیدہ

پسندیدہ is a commonly used Persian adjective meaning "favorite."

ٹام کروز شیلا کا پسندیدہ اداکار ہے۔

Tom Cruise is Sheila's favorite actor.

7.7 Reading and Translation Drill

۱۔ ہارورڈ اسٹینفرڈ سے بہتر ہے۔

یہ پلنگ اُس پلنگ سے بہتر ہے۔

یہ لڑکی اُس لڑکے سے بہتر ہے۔

وہ لڑکے اِن لڑکیوں سے بہتر ہیں۔

کیا، نیپال سری لنکا سے بہتر ہے؟

٢ـ   یہ بہترین ملک ہے۔

فل کالنز بہترین آدمی ہے۔

یہ بہترین چیزیں ہیں، مگر مہنگی ہیں۔

یہ قالین اُس قالین سے بہتر ہے، مگر وہ لال قالین بہترین ہے۔

٣ـ   وہ ملک اِس ملک سے بدتر ہے۔

وہ لڑکیاں بدترین ہیں!

کیا وہ لڑکا اِس لڑکے سے بدتر ہے؟

یہ بدترین کلاس ہے۔

لاہور کی تیزترین منی ٹرانسفر سروس کہاں ہے؟

٤ـ   میرا پسندیدہ اداکار میٹ ڈیمن ہے۔

میری پسندیدہ اداکارہ کرشمہ کپور ہے۔

کیا، آپ کا پسندیدہ ملک امریکہ ہے؟

ہاں۔ کیونکہ میرا پسندیدہ کھلاڑی ٹرائے ایکمن ہے اور وہ امریکہ میں فٹبال کھیلتا ہے۔

7.8 Expressing More or Less

In order to express "x is more than y" in Urdu, the expression سے زیادہ is used. Example :

یہ اُس سے زیادہ ہے۔

This is more than that.

اِس کلاس میں اُس کلاس سے زیادہ لڑکے ہیں۔

In this class there are more boys than in that class.

A similar construction is used to express "x is less than y," but instead of زیادہ, کم is used.

یہ اُس سے کم ہے۔

This is less than that.

130

اِس کلاس میں اُس کلاس سے کم لڑکے ہیں۔

Both زیادہ and کم can be combined with the comparative تر suffix as seen in the following examples:

اِس یونیورسٹی میں زیادہ تر طالبِ علم امریکین ہیں۔

Students in this university are mostly American.

اِس کتاب کی قیمت اُس سے بھی کمتر ہے۔

The price of this book is even less than that.

Note: زیادہ and کم rarely use the ترین suffix to express the superlative.

7.8 Translation

علی: کیا، بوسٹن میں بہت لوگ رہتے ہیں؟

شاہین: نہیں جناب۔ بوسٹن میں نیو یارک سے کم لوگ رہتے ہیں۔

علی: اچّھا! کیا وہاں گرینلینڈ سے بھی کم لوگ رہتے ہیں؟

شاہین: کیا؟ نہیں، نہیں۔ بوسٹن میں گرینلینڈ سے زیادہ لوگ رہتے ہیں۔

علی: آپ بوسٹن میں مکان کا کرایہ کیا دیتے ہیں؟

شاہین: دو کمروں کے مکان کا کرایہ ایک ہزار ڈالر ہے۔

علی: یہ کرایہ بہت زیادہ ہے۔

شاہین: ہاں، مگر نیو یارک سے کم ہے۔

7.8 Reading and Translation Drill

۱۔ میرے گھر کا کرایہ اُن کے گھر کے کرائے سے زیادہ ہے۔

کیا، آپ کے گھر کا کرایہ ہمارے گھر کے کرائے سے زیادہ ہے؟

وہاں کا کرایہ یہاں کے کرائے سے بہت کم ہے۔

کیا، تمہاری دوکان کا کرایہ اِس دوکان کے کرائے سے کم ہے؟

131

۲۔ کیا، دنیا میں سب سے زیادہ لوگ چین میں رہتے ہیں؟

ہندوستان میں امریکہ سے زیادہ لوگ رہتے ہیں۔

کینیڈا میں امریکہ سے کم لوگ رہتے ہیں۔

پاکستان میں سب سے زیادہ لوگ کس شہر میں رہتے ہیں؟ کراچی میں یا لاہور میں؟

7.9 Cardinal Numbers 31-40

۳۱	اِکتِّیس یا اِکتیس
۳۲	بتّیس
۳۳	تینتِیس
۳۴	چونتِیس
۳۵	پینتِیس
۳۶	چھتِیس
۳۷	سینتِیس
۳۸	اڑتِیس
۳۹	اُنتالیس یا اُنچالیس
۴۰	چالیس

7.10 Aggregatives

In order to indicate total plurality in Urdu, the suffix وں is added to the numbers between two

and ten, with the exception of six and nine:

both (special form)	دونوں
all three	تینوں
all four	چاروں
all five	پانچوں

132

all six	چھ کے چھ
all seven	ساتوں
all eight	آٹھوں
all nine	نو کے نو
all ten	دسوں

The numbers six, nine, and numbers larger than ten are expressed in such a construction by being repeated and separated from each other by the postposition کے/کی, depending upon the gender of the noun that follows the numerical adjective.

گیارہ کی گیارہ لڑکیاں or گیارہ کے گیارہ لڑکے, meaning all eleven girls or boys

In order to express indefinite plurality, the suffix یوں or وں is added to the number. Common indefinite plurality adjectives are:

scores of	بیسیوں
hundreds of	سیکڑوں یا سینکڑوں
thousands of	ہزاروں
hundreds of thousands of	لاکھوں
tens of millions of	کروڑوں

ہمارے ساتھ دونوں رہ سکتے ہیں۔

Both can live with us.

وہ تینوں لڑکیاں سندر ہیں۔

All three of those girls are beautiful.

وہاں نو کی نو لڑکیاں ناچتی ہیں۔

All nine girls dance over there.

کورنیل میں سینکڑوں لڑکے پڑھتے ہیں۔

Hundreds of boys study at Cornell.

کورنیل میں سو کے سو لڑکے پڑھتے ہیں۔

All hundred boys study at Cornell.

Note the difference between the last two sentences. The first sentence expresses indefinite

plurality and the second one expresses total plurality.

7.10 Reading and Translation Drill

١۔ ہم دونوں ایم۔ آئی۔ ٹی میں پڑھ رہے ہیں۔

کیا، آپ تینوں اس دکان میں کام کر رہے ہیں؟

بیسیوں لوگ آج یہاں آ رہے ہیں۔

ٹیکساس میں ہزاروں طالبِ علم پڑھ رہے ہیں۔

٢۔ ٹام کروز سینتیس سال کا ہے۔

کیا، مڈونا صرف چالیس سال کی ہے؟

وہ پانچوں عورتیں (women) پینتیس سال کی ہیں۔

کیا، تم دونوں بئیس سال سے یہاں کام کر رہے ہو؟

٣۔ کیا، اس گھر میں پندرہ کی پندرہ لڑکیاں رہ سکتی ہیں؟

ہاں۔ وہاں وہ اٹھارہ کے اٹھارہ لڑکے پڑھتے ہیں۔

چوبیس کے چوبیس طالبِ علم بس میں نہیں جا سکتے۔

پینتیس کی پینتیس تصویریں اچّھی ہیں۔

7.11 The Future Tense

The simple present tense is frequently used to express the immediate future:

میں وہاں جاتا ہوں۔

I go there or I'll go there (immediate future).

The regular future tense is formed by the addition of two suffixes to the verb stem:

1st suffix: وں (1st person singular), ے (2nd, 3rd person singular), یں (1st, 2nd, 3rd person plural), و (2nd person تم).

2nd suffix: گی (feminine singular or plural), گے (masculine plural), گا (masculine singular).

The suffixes used depend on the number and gender of the subject.

The following example will make this more clear:

verb: پڑھنا

stem: پڑھ

Feminine	Masculine	Pronoun Subject
	Singular	
پڑھوں گی	پڑھوں گا	میں
پڑھیگی	پڑھیگا	تو
پڑھو گی	پڑھو گے	تم
پڑھینگی	پڑھینگے	آپ
پڑھیگی	پڑھیگا	وہ/یہ
	Plural	
پڑھینگی/پڑھینگے	پڑھینگے	ہم
پڑھو گی	پڑھو گے	تم
پڑھینگی	پڑھینگے	آپ
پڑھینگی	پڑھینگے	یہ/وہ

There are three verbs that have irregular conjugations in the future tense on account of modifications in their verbal stems: to take, to give, and to be.

لینا – to take

Feminine	Masculine	Pronoun Subject
	Singular	
لوں گی	لوں گا	میں
لے گی	لے گا	تو
لو گی	لو گے	تم
لیں گی	لیں گے	آپ
لے گی	لے گا	یہ/وہ
	Plural	
لیں گی/لیں گے	لیں گے	ہم
لو گی	لو گے	تم
لیں گی	لیں گے	آپ
لیں گی	لیں گے	یہ/وہ

دینا – to give

Feminine	Masculine	Pronoun Subject
	Singular	
دوں گی	دوں گا	میں
دے گی	دے گا	تو
دو گی	دو گے	تم

136

Feminine	Masculine	Pronoun Subject
دینگی	دینگے	آپ
دیگی	دیگا	یہ/وہ

Plural

Feminine	Masculine	Pronoun Subject
دینگی/دینگے	دینگے	ہم
دوگی	دوگے	تم
دینگی	دینگے	آپ
دینگی	دینگے	یہ/وہ

ہونا - to be

Feminine	Masculine	Pronoun Subject

Singular

Feminine	Masculine	Pronoun Subject
ہونگی	ہونگا	میں
ہوگی	ہوگا	تو
ہوگی	ہوگے	تم
ہونگی	ہونگے	آپ
ہوگی	ہوگا	یہ/وہ

Plural

Feminine	Masculine	Pronoun Subject
ہونگی/ہونگے	ہونگے	ہم
ہوگی	ہوگے	تم
ہونگی	ہونگے	آپ
ہونگی	ہونگے	یہ/وہ

Note: The future tense of ہونا can also be used to indicate the suppositional, particularly when it is used as an auxiliary verb. For example, وہ وہاں ہوگا means "He will be there" (future) or "He

137

must be there" (suppositional). وہ لڑکی یونیورسٹی میں پڑھ رہی ہوگی "That girl must be studying at the university." امریکہ کا صدر ہندوستان جا رہا ہوگا "The American President must be going to India." We will discuss the future suppositional in greater detail in chapter 15.

7.11 Reading and Translation Drill

۱۔ میں شام کو کپڑے بدلوں گا۔

کیا، آپ ہر روز کپڑے بدلتے ہیں؟

نہیں، وہ کل کپڑے بدلیں گے۔

ہم اب جوتے بدل لیں گے۔

۲۔ وہ آج غسل کریں گے۔

آپ کب غسل کریں گے؟

تو جمعرات کو غسل کریگا۔

نہیں، میں جمعہ کو غسل کروں گی۔

۳۔ آپ امریکہ کب تک پہنچیں گے؟

میں امریکہ اتوار تک پہنچوں گی۔

وہ پیر کو باسٹن پہنچیگی۔

کیا، وہ منگل کو نیو یارک پہنچیں گے؟

۴۔ میں تم سے پیسے نہیں لوں گا۔

ہم اُن سے وہ پیسے نہیں لیں گے۔

کیا، آپ وہ سبزی (vegetable) لیں گے؟

تو بازار میں کیا لیگا؟

۵۔ وہ اِس سے زیادہ نہیں دیگا۔

کیا، تم اِس سے زیادہ دوگے؟

نہیں، میں بھی اِس سے زیادہ نہیں دونگا۔

وہ سندر لڑکی اِس سے زیادہ دیگی۔

۶۔ تم کل کہاں ہوگے؟

کیا، وہ جنوری میں وہاں ہوگا؟

وہ لڑکیاں اتوار کو باغ میں ہونگی۔

ہم پرسوں گھر میں ہونگے۔

۷۔ میں یہ کام کر سکونگا۔

کیا، تم یہ کتاب پڑھ سکوگے؟

وہ ڈاک خانہ نہیں جا سکیگی۔

ہم گا سکینگے مگر ناچ نہیں سکینگے۔

Translate the following sentences into Urdu:

1. We will go to the cinema tomorrow.

2. What will you (informal) do tonight?

3. Will we be able to eat at your house?

4. Ali will cook tomorrow and we will eat with him.

5. Will Madonna sing on Saturday?

6. Tonight I will read a book and write a letter.

7. Will they buy a newspaper today?

8. He will give a lot of money for this horse.

9. He will not be able to give his house for the party.

10. Where will those beautiful girls be tomorrow night?

11. Sir, your son must be playing tennis right now.

12.   Everyone in that house must be sleeping.

7.12 Pronunciation Drill: Diphthongs

بیل	بیل
سیل	سیل
میں	میں
شے	شے
میل	میل
پھیل	پھیل
پودا	پودا
سودا	سودا
گودا	گودا
رونا	رونا
اور	اور
جور	جور
گور	گور
موت	موت
فوت	فوت

7.13 Response Drill

Answer the following questions.

۱۔   کیا، آپ اُردو سمجھ سکتے ہیں؟

۲۔   ابھی آپ کیا کر رہے ہیں؟

۳۔   کیا، آپ کے دوست آپ سے اچّھا ناچ سکتے ہیں؟

140

۴۔ کیا، آپ کی بہنیں اسکول میں پڑھ رہی ہیں؟

۵۔ آپ کے خیال میں، اس کلاس میں سب سے زیادہ ہوشیار لڑکی کون ہے؟

۶۔ آپ کے خیال میں، اس کلاس میں سب سے زیادہ ہوشیار لڑکا کون ہے؟

۷۔ آپ کے خیال میں، اس دنیا میں سب سے خوبصورت آدمی کون ہے؟

۸۔ آپ کے خیال میں، اس دنیا میں سب سے زیادہ امیر عورت کون ہے؟

۹۔ آپ کا پسندیدہ کھانا کیا ہے؟

۱۰۔ آپ کا پسندیدہ اداکار کون ہے؟

۱۱۔ آپ کے پسندیدہ شاعر کون ہیں؟

۱۲۔ آپ ہر روز صبح کیا کرتے ہیں؟

۱۳۔ آپ کا خاندان کہاں رہتا ہے؟

۱۴۔ آپ کے والد کیا کام کرتے ہیں؟

۱۵۔ آپ کی والدہ کیا کام کرتی ہیں؟

۱۶۔ آپ کے والد کا نام کیا ہے؟

۱۷۔ آپ کی والدہ کا اسمِ شریف کیا ہے؟

۱۸۔ آپ کے نانا اور نانی کہاں رہتے ہیں؟

۱۹۔ کیا، آپ کے دادا اور دادی امریکہ آتے ہیں؟

۲۰۔ دُنیا کی خوبصورت ترین عمارت تاج محل ہے یا وائیٹ ہاؤس؟

۲۱۔ تم آج شام کو کیا کروگے؟

۲۲۔ آپ لوگ اتوار کو کہاں جائینگے؟

۲۳۔ نرگس لاہور کی دکانوں سے کیا خریدیگی؟

۲۴۔ آپ کونسے گریجویئٹ اسکول میں پڑھینگے؟

7. 14 گفتگو (Conversation)

راج: نرگس! کیا حال ہے؟

نرگس: سب ٹھیک ہے۔ تم کیا کر رہے ہو؟

راج: میں اب گھر جا رہا ہوں۔ میں بہت خوش ہوں۔ آج میرے خاندان کے سب لوگ گھر پر ہیں۔

نرگس: ہاں۔ آج تو چھٹی ہے۔

راج: اچّھا۔ کیا، تم میرے ساتھ گھر چلوگی؟

نرگس: ہاں۔ ہاں۔ ضرور۔

(راج کے گھر میں)

راج: نمستے پتاجی۔ ہلو ممی ڈارلنگ۔ تو بہت اچّھی ہے! یہ نرگس ہے۔

نرگس: آداب۔

پتاجی: تمہارا نام بہت سندر ہے۔ کیا یہ پھل کا نام ہے یا پھول کا؟

نرگس: انکل یہ ایک پھول کا نام ہے۔ بہت خوبصورت پھول۔

پتاجی: نرگس تم بھی بہت خوبصورت ہو!

راج: ہاں پتاجی۔ نرگس تو باغ کے ہر پھول سے زیادہ خوبصورت ہے۔

نرگس: راج!!!

ممی ڈارلنگ: بیٹی، تمہارا خاندان کہاں سے ہے؟

نرگس: میرے والد دلّی سے ہیں اور والدہ حیدر آباد سے ہیں۔ مگر اب ہم سب امریکہ میں رہتے ہیں۔

پتاجی: میرے والد ، یعنی راج کے دادا بھی دلّی سے ہیں مگر میری والدہ ،یعنی راج کی دادی لاہور سے ہیں۔ میری بیوی کی ماں، یعنی راج کی نانی بھی لاہور

142

سے ہیں، مگر اُن کے لبّا، یعنی راج کے نانا بنگلور سے ہیں۔

مّی ڈارلنگ: معاف کرو بیٹی! میرے شوہر بہت زیادہ باتیں کرتے ہیں۔ میرے ساس اور سسٹر یعنی راج کی دادی اور دادا بھی بہت زیادہ باتیں کرتے ہیں! اچّھا نرگس، یہ رِشی اور رَوی ہیں۔ یہ دونوں راج کے بھائی ہیں۔ رِشی ہمارا پہلا بیٹا ہے اور رَوی ہمارا دوسرا لڑکا ہے۔ یہ دونوں راج سے بڑے ہیں۔

پتاجی: یہ دونوں بہت ہوشیار ہیں۔ لندن یونیورسٹی میں پڑھ رہے ہیں مگر اِن دِنوں گھر پر ہیں۔

نرگس: اچّھا! آپ لوگ کیا پڑھ رہے ہیں؟

دونوں (ایک ساتھ): میڈِسن۔

نرگس: پڑھائی کے بعد آپ کیا کام کریں گے؟

راج: ڈاکٹر بنیں گے اور کیا ؟! بہت پیسہ بنائیں گے۔

رِشی: نہیں نہیں! ہم غریبوں کی خدمت بھی کریں گے!

راج: ہاں۔ نرگس بھی ڈاکٹر ہے۔ یہ بھی غریبوں کی خدمت کرتی ہے۔

نرگس: اور یہ خوبصورت لڑکی کون ہے؟

مّی ڈارلنگ: یہ ریشما ہے۔ یہ راج کی چھوٹی بہن ہے۔

ریشما: مّی۔ میں چھوٹی نہیں ہوں۔ میں سات سال کی ہوں!

نرگس: اچّھا! آپ تو بہت بڑی ہیں۔ آپ یہ کیا کر رہی ہیں؟

راج: یہ ایک کتاب لکھ رہی ہے۔

نرگس: ریشما آپ تو بہت ہوشیار ہیں۔

ریشما: ہاں! میں کتاب لِکھ سکتی ہوں، گا سکتی ہوں اور ناچ بھی سکتی ہوں۔

نرگس: ارے! آپ تو بہت زیادہ ہوشیار ہیں۔

ریشما: ہاں! میں ان تینوں بھائیوں سے زیادہ ہوشیار ہوں۔ آنرز پروگرام میں ہوں!

نرگس دیدی، کیا آپ میرے ساتھ کھیلینگی؟

نرگس: ہاں، ہاں۔ ضرور۔ تم کیا کھیلنا چاہتی ہو؟

ریشما: میں ٹینیس کھیلنا چاہتی ہوں۔

راج: ہاں، نرگس بھی ہر روز ٹینیس کھیلتی ہے۔ سنیل کے ساتھ!

نرگس: راج! یہ کیا ہے؟ وہ صرف میرا دوست ہے۔

ممی ڈارلنگ: نرگس بیٹی، کھانا تیّار ہے۔

نرگس: ہاں آنٹی، راج ہروقت کہتا ہے کہ آپ بہت اچّھا پکاتی ہیں۔

پتاجی: ہاں! میری بیوی تو سب سے اچّھا پکاتی ہے۔

ممی ڈارلنگ: بس چپ رہو! میں اِس لئے پکاتی ہوں کیونکہ تم نہیں پکا سکتے۔

پتاجی: او ڈارلنگ! کیا، ہم اب کھانا کھانے کے لئے جا سکتے ہیں؟

ممی ڈارلنگ: ہاں، ہاں۔ ضرور! کیوں نہیں؟

راج: نرگس ہم بھی چلتے ہیں۔

7.15 Conversation Practice

Telephone conversation

Reshma: Hello. This is Reshma. Who is speaking?

Mummy darling: Reshma! It's me, your mother! I am speaking from the hospital.

Reshma: Greetings! Mummy darling! What are you doing at the hospital?

Mummy darling: You know that Sunil is in the hospital. He will be here for three days more.

Reshma: When are you coming home?

Mummy darling: I am going to the market first (پہلے) and then I will come home.

Reshma: Can you buy me something from the market?

Mummy darling: What do you want?

Reshma: Oh! Mummy darling! You are the best mother! Can you buy me some sweets and chocolates?

Mummy darling: Reshma! I will not buy you chocolates and sweets! You know that too many sweets are bad for you.

Reshma: In my opinion, they are very good for me. They give me life!

Mummy darling: Absolutely not! I will not buy you trash! I will buy some fruit for you. Fruit is better than sweets. Do you want some mangoes? Mangoes are your favorite fruit.

Reshma: Yes, I want some very sweet mangoes and some sweets also.

Mummy darling: Oh my dear (پیاری) Reshma! My crazy daughter! What shall I do with you?

Reshma: Mummy darling. Will you buy me some sweets?

Mummy darling: OK but you will eat them after dinner.

Reshma: Thank you, Mummy darling. You are the best mother in the world. I love you very much! Bye.

Mummy darling: Bye, my crazy daughter!

7.16 Songs

اچّھا، تو ہم چلتے ہیں ۱)

پھر کب ملو گے؟

جب تم کہو گے

جُمعرات کو؟

ہاں، ہاں، آدھی رات کو

کہاں؟ وہیں جہاں کوئی آتا جاتا نہیں

۲) یاد آ رہی ہے(۲)

تیری یاد آ رہی ہے(۲)

یاد آنے سے

تیرے جانے سے

جان جا رہی ہے

۳) شام ڈھل رہی ہے

تم یاد آ رہی ہو

شام ڈھل رہی ہے

آسمان بھی روتا ہے

میرا غم سُننے کے بعد

شام ڈھل رہی ہے

Glossary for Songs

وہیں = there (emphatic form of وہاں)   ڈھلنا = to decline, sink, fade (as sunset, life, etc.)

جہاں = where (relative pronoun)

7. 17 Vocabulary

athlete/player (m/f)	کھِلاڑی
to bathe	غُسل کرنا ، نہانا
to be able to, can	سکنا
best	بہترین
better	بہتر
both	دونوں

146

box (m)	ڈِبّہ
to change	بدلنا
to cry	رونا
clothes (m)	کپڑے
to come along, to go along, to set out, to walk, to embark	چلنا
to cook	پکانا
door (m)	دروازہ
father (m)	والِد، اَبّا، پِتا، باپ، بابا
father-in-law	سسُر
favorite	پسندیدہ
flower (m)	پھُول
forgive/excuse me	معاف کیجئے/کرو
forty	چالیس
grandfather (maternal)	نانا
grandfather (paternal)	دادا
grandmother (maternal)	نانی
grandmother (paternal)	دادی
grown up, elder person (m/f)	بڑا،بڑی
holiday, vacation (f)	چھٹّی
human being, man, person (m)	آدمی / اِنسان
hundreds of	سیکڑوں / سینکڑوں

hundreds of thousands of	لاکھوں
husband (m)	شوہر، پَتِ (پتی)
less	کَم
letter (m)	خَط
to listen	سُنتا
to be made, built, created;	بَنْنا
to become	
to make, to build, to create	بَنانا
millions of	کروڑوں
money, cash, wealth; coin (m)	پیسا، پیسہ
mother	والدہ، اماں(اَمّی)، ماں، ماتا
mother-in-law	ساس
more	زِیادہ
narcissus (f)	نَرگِس
to open	کھولنا
or	یا
to pick up	اُٹھانا
poor person (m); poor (adj.)	غَرِیب
to reach	پہنچنا
ready	تیّار
rich	امِیر
scores of	بِیسیوں

service (f)	خِدمت، سیوا
sister (f)	دِیدی، باجی، آپا، بہن
a respectful title for sister or	
anybody older to whom one	
wants to show reverence	
shut up; be quiet	چُپ رہو
something; some	کُچھ
sorrow (m)	غم
studies, education (f)	پڑھائی
swift, quick; hot (spicy), fiery,	تیز
sharp	
that is to say, i.e.	یعنی
thirty	تِیس
thought, idea, opinion (m)	خیال
thousands of	ہزاروں
trash (m)	کچرا
wife (f)	پتنی، بیوی
worse	بدتر
worst	بدترین

Chapter 8

8.1 Formal Imperatives (with آپ)

The honorific imperative is used for people who are referred to with the آپ pronoun. It is formed by taking the stem of the verb and adding ـِیے (ie) to it. (In Urdu, the i vowel can be written either as long or short. Thus one may write the imperative of لکھنا as لکھیے or لکھئے.)

Infinitive: کھانا   Stem: کھا   Imperative: کھایِٔے

ملنا   مِل   ملیِٔے

پڑھنا   پڑھ   پڑھیِٔے

In stems that end in ی, a ج is inserted between the stem and ـِیے (ie), e.g., پینا becomes پیجِٔے

Irregular verbs are:

Infinitive: لینا   Imperative: لیجِٔے

دینا   دیجِٔے

کرنا   کیجِٔے

In many situations the use of this imperative conveys the sense of English "please."

Please study.   ۔پڑھیِٔے

Please eat.   ۔کھایِٔے

Translate these sentences using the honorific imperative:

1.   Please eat two apples.

2.   Please read this book.

3.   Please come with me.

4.   Please bring a box with you.

5.   Please look.

6.   Please take more food.

7.   Please work better than this!

8.   Please give a chicken.

9.   Please drink some tea.

10.   Please go home!

A more formal imperative than the aforementioned one is formed by the addition of گا to the

formal imperative. This imperative is only used in situations in which great deference is

implied.

جائیے گا   جانا

پڑھیے گا   پڑھنا

کیجئے گا   کرنا

8.2 Informal Imperatives (with تم)

The imperative used to command those who are referred to in the تم form is formed by the

addition of و to the stem:

جاؤ   جانا

پڑھو   پڑھنا

There are two irregular تم imperatives:

دو   دینا

لو   لینا

Change the following formal imperatives into informal ones:

151

١۔ لکھیئے گا

٢۔ پیجیئے

٣۔ دیکھیئے گا

٤۔ سوئیئے گا

٥۔ کھیلیئے گا

8.3 Least Formal Imperatives (with تو)

The stem of the verb acts as the imperative to be used with the تو form.

کرنا   کر   do

دینا   دے   give

لینا   لے   take

کھانا   کھا   eat

پینا   پی   drink

8.4 Negative Imperatives

In order to form a negative imperative, insert مت or نہ right before the imperative word:

Don't do this (formal)!   یہ مت کیجیئے!

Don't read (formal)!   مت پڑھیئے!

Don't go (informal)!   نہ جاؤ!

Don't come (least formal)!   مت آ!

8.5 The Infinitive as Imperative

The infinitive of a verb can also serve as an imperative. It connotes a neutral or impersonal form

of the imperative in contexts when degrees of formality are not regarded as necessary.

دو سیر گوشت دینا۔

Give two *ser*s of meat.

یہ پانی مت پینا۔

Don't drink this water.

یہاں نہ بیٹھنا۔

Don't sit here.

8.6 Use of مہربانی and ذرا with Imperatives

When we encountered مہربانی in Chapter 1, its implication was one of "thanks." However, when مہربانی is used with the postposition سے, it acts as the adverb "kindly."

مہربانی سے یہ کام کیجئے۔

Kindly do this work/Please do this work.

The expression مہربانی فرماکر or مہربانی کرکے may also be used instead of مہربانی سے as an alternative expression for "please, kindly."

Whereas مہربانی is usually used with formal imperatives, ذرا can act as its counterpart in informal imperative constructions with the connotation of "just" or "please just." Idiomatically its use corresponds to the English expression "would you mind?" The literal meaning of ذرا is "slightly" or "a little bit."

ذرا وہ کتاب دو۔

Please just give that book (informal).

8.6 Reading and Translation Drill

۱۔   مہربانی سے وہ کتاب دیجئے۔

مہربانی سے ہمارے ساتھ چلیئے۔

مہربانی سے یہاں بیٹھیے۔

مہربانی سے یہ خط پڑھیئے۔

۲- ذرا یہ دیکھو۔

ذرا وہاں جاؤ۔

ذرا یہاں آ۔

ذرا پانی پی۔

Fill in the blanks with the appropriate form of the imperative of the verb indicated in the parentheses.

۱- مہربانی سے آپ یہ کتابیں _____ (read)

۲- مہربانی سے وہاں _____ (don't go, formal)

۳- ذرا یہ _____ (read, least formal)

۴- ذرا ہمارے لئے وہ چاول _____ (cook, informal)

۵- ذرا روٹی _____ (give, informal)

۶- پانی _____ (don't drink, informal)

۷- مرچ _____ (don't eat, least formal)

۸- ذرا ایک خط _____ (write, informal)

۹- پچاس سیب _____ (give, formal)

۱۰- پینتالیس کیلے _____ (take, formal)

Summary of Imperative Forms

Impersonal & Least Formal, تو	Informal, تم	Formal, آپ	Infinitive
Less Urgent			
پڑھنا پڑھ	پڑھو	پڑھیے	پڑھنا
کھانا کھا	کھاؤ	کھائے	کھانا

154

کھیلنا	کھیل	کھیلو	کھیلیے	کھیلنا
پینا	پی	پیو	پیجئے	پینا
لینا	لے	لو	لیجئے	لینا
دینا	دے	دو	دیجئے	دینا

<u>Note</u>: Gender is not marked in imperative forms.

8.7 Further Uses of ہونا

We have already encountered ہونا as the "to be" verb and its use in the habitual present tense as an auxiliary verb. ہونا is also used in the sense of "to become, to take place and to happen."

یہاں کیا ہو سکتا ہے؟

What can happen here/What can be done here?

یہاں کیا ہوتا ہے؟

What takes place here?

یہ کیا ہو رہا ہے؟

What is going on?

When ہونا is used with its participle forms, ہوتا، ہوتی، ہوتے , it indicates generalities or statements of fact.

آج کل بہت گرمی ہوتی ہے۔

Nowadays there is (generally) a lot of heat.

نیو یارک میں بہت گندگی ہوتی ہے۔

There is (generally) a lot of filth in New York.

کیا، ہارورڈ میں اچّھے طالبِ علم ہوتے ہیں؟

Are there (generally) good students at Harvard?

کیا، ہندوستان میں کھانا اچّھا ہوتا ہے؟

Is the food in India (generally) good?

8.7 Reading and Translation Drill

۱۔ امریکہ میں چیزیں بہت سستی ہوتی ہیں۔

یہ آم بہترین ہوتے ہیں۔

نہیں، یہ سیب بہتر ہوتے ہیں۔

ایرانی قالین بہترین ہوتے ہیں۔

وہاں گرمی ہوتی ہے یا سردی؟

۲۔ اس گھر میں کیا ہو رہا ہے؟

آج کل دنیا میں کیا ہو رہا ہے؟

یہاں وہ کام نہیں ہو رہا ہے۔

یہ کیا ہو رہا ہے؟

۳۔ لندن میں کیا ہو سکتا ہے؟

کیا، اس گھر میں کام ہو سکتا ہے؟

ان دفتروں میں کام ہو سکتا ہے۔

ہمارے گھر میں کام نہیں ہو سکتا۔

۴۔ کھانا ٹھنڈا ہوتا ہے۔

کھانا ٹھنڈا ہو رہا ہے۔

کھانا ٹھنڈا ہو سکتا ہے۔

کھانا ٹھنڈا نہیں ہوتا۔

۵۔ کیا، یہ دودھ زیادہ گرم ہو سکتا ہے؟

جی نہیں۔ یہ اور گرم نہیں ہو سکتا۔

پانی گرم ہو سکتا ہے۔

پانی ٹھنڈا ہو رہا ہے۔

٦۔ چاول بہت مزیدار ہوتے ہیں۔

روٹی بہت مزیدار ہوتی ہے۔

دال سب سے زیادہ مزیدار ہوتی ہے۔

زیادہ نمک سے کھانا مزیدار نہیں ہوتا۔

٧۔ صحت کے لئے دودھ کوک سے زیادہ اچّھا ہوتا ہے۔

گوشت صحت کے لئے اچّھا نہیں ہوتا۔

بہت مصالحے بھی صحت کے لئے اچّھے نہیں ہوتے۔

کیا، مرچ صحت کے لئے اچّھی ہوتی ہے؟

٨۔ مت شرمائیے۔ اور روٹی لیجئے۔

مت شرمائیے۔ اور بریانی لیجئے۔

مت شرمائیے۔ اور دودھ پیجئے۔

مت شرماؤ۔ اور پاپڑ لو۔

٩۔ بس! یہ بہت زیادہ ہے۔

بس! اب گھر چلو!

بس! زیادہ مرچ صحت کے لئے ٹھیک نہیں۔

بس! اور مت پیجئے۔

١٠۔ سبزی گوشت سے زیادہ مزیدار ہوتی ہے۔

دودھ پانی سے مہنگا ہوتا ہے۔

نمبو پیاز سے زیادہ مہنگے ہوتے ہیں۔

کیا، دہی دودھ سے سستا ہوتا ہے؟

8.8 The Past Participles of تھا - ہونا

The verb ہونا has two past participles, each of which is associated with a special meaning and function. We will discuss the تھا participle here and the ہوا participle in Chapter 12. The past participle تھا and its various forms, تھے (masculine plural), تھی (feminine singular), and تھیں (feminine plural), are used for "was, were." It is declined as follows:

Feminine	Translation	Masculine	Pronoun
تھی	I was	تھا	میں
تھی	You were	تھا	تو
تھی	She/he was	تھا	یہ/وہ
تھیں	We were	تھے	ہم
تھیں	You were	تھے	آپ
تھیں	They were	تھے	یہ/وہ
تھیں	You were	تھے	تم

Examples:

وہ کل رات کو کہاں تھے؟

Where were they last night?

میں دس سال پہلے طالبِ علم تھا۔

Ten years ago I was a student.

وہ چیز میز پر تھی۔

That thing was on the table.

کل صبح آٹھ بجے لڑکیاں اسکول میں تھیں۔

Yesterday morning at eight o'clock the girls were in school.

تھا and its variants are also used as auxiliary verbs in various past tense constructions. They function exactly like ہے in the present tense. Examples:

وہ کام کرتا تھا۔

He used to work.

وہ کام کر رہا تھا۔

He was working.

وہ کام کر سکتی تھی۔

She was able to work.

8.8 Reading and Translation Drill

۱۔ آپ چار سال پہلے کہاں تھے؟ راولپنڈی میں یا اسلام آباد میں؟

کیا، دو سال پہلے تم طالبِ علم تھے؟

نہیں، میں دو سال پہلے ڈاکٹر تھا۔

دس سال پہلے وہ لڑکی کہاں تھی؟

۲۔ تو کل کہاں تھا؟

کیا، تم کل باغ میں تھے؟

نہیں، ہم کل دفتر میں تھے۔

وہ لڑکیاں بھی ہمارے ساتھ دفتر میں تھیں۔

۳۔ یہ چھری زیادہ تیز نہیں تھی۔

کل رات سالن میں مرچ تیز تھی۔

کیا، آپ کے لئے کھانا زیادہ تیز تھا؟

بچپن میں اُن کی بیٹیاں بہت تیز تھیں۔

آپ بچپن میں سبزی خور تھے یا گوشت خور؟

Translate the following sentences into Urdu:

1.   Were you a doctor 20 years ago?

2.   He was a very bright student many years ago.

3.   Rita Hayworth was our favorite actress.

4.   Were you at Sheila's house with your friends last week?

5.   Last week Raj was working in the restaurant. Now he is not there.

8.9 The Past Habitual Tense

The past habitual tense is formed in a manner similar to the present habitual tense except that the present form of the auxiliary verb ہونا is replaced by its corresponding past form.

Present habitual:

میں پڑھتا ہوں۔   I study.

وہ وہاں کام کرتا ہے۔   He works there.

Past habitual:

میں پڑھتا تھا۔   I used to study.

وہ وہاں کام کرتا تھا۔   He used to work there.

This tense is used to denote regular or habitual actions in the past. The conjugation pattern is as follows:

Feminine	*Masculine*	*Pronoun*
پڑھتی تھی	پڑھتا تھا	میں
پڑھتی تھی	پڑھتا تھا	تو
پڑھتی تھی	پڑھتا تھا	وہ/یہ
پڑھتی تھیں	پڑھتے تھے	ہم

پڑھتی تھیں	پڑھتے تھے	تم
پڑھتی تھیں	پڑھتے تھے	آپ
پڑھتی تھیں	پڑھتے تھے	وہ/یہ

8.9 Reading and Translation Drill

١۔ میں سات سال پہلے وہاں پڑھتا تھا۔

کیا، تم اُن کے دفتر میں کام کرتے تھے؟

وہ ہمارے ساتھ گاتے تھے۔

ایک زمانے میں وہ بہت اچّھا گاتی تھی۔

٢۔ ہم اُن کے ساتھ کبھی کبھی کھیلتے تھے۔

ایک زمانے میں تم اچّھا ناچتے تھے۔

آپ ہر وقت کیا یاد کرتی تھیں؟

میں بچپن کے دِن یاد کرتی تھی۔

٣۔ بیماری کی وجہ سے وہ نہیں کھیلتے تھے۔

شور کی وجہ سے ہم نہیں پڑھ سکتے تھے۔

اُن کی وجہ سے ہم کام نہیں کرتے تھے۔

وہ تمھاری وجہ سے روتے تھے۔

٤۔ میں گرمی کی وجہ سے کھانا نہیں پکا سکتا ہوں۔

ہم سردی کی وجہ سے گھر کے باہر نہیں نکلتے ہیں۔

بارش کی وجہ سے وہ باہر نہیں کھیلتا تھا۔

کیا، تم کام کی وجہ سے کھانا نہیں کھاتے تھے؟

٥۔ کیا، آپ بچپن میں تیز چیزیں کھاتی تھیں؟

ایکسیڈنٹ سے پہلے وہ عورت گاڑی بہت تیز چلاتی تھی۔

میری وہ گاڑی تو آپ کی گاڑی سے بھی زیادہ تیز چل سکتی تھی۔

وہ تیز دھوپ کی وجہ سے مکان کے اندر کام کرتی تھی۔

8.10 The Past Continuous Tense

The past continuous tense is used to describe actions that were in progress at a particular time in the past. Again, this tense is formed in the same way as the present continuous tense, except that the present form of ہونا is replaced by its past counterpart.

Present continuous:

میں پڑھ رہا ہوں۔	I am studying.
وہ کام کر رہا ہے۔	He is working.

Past continuous:

میں پڑھ رہا تھا۔	I was studying.
وہ کام کر رہا تھا۔	He was working.

The conjugation pattern is as follows:

Feminine	*Masculine*	*Pronoun*
پڑھ رہی تھی	پڑھ رہا تھا	میں
پڑھ رہی تھی	پڑھ رہا تھا	تو
پڑھ رہی تھی	پڑھ رہا تھا	وہ/یہ
پڑھ رہی تھیں	پڑھ رہے تھے	ہم
پڑھ رہی تھیں	پڑھ رہے تھے	تم
پڑھ رہی تھیں	پڑھ رہے تھے	آپ
پڑھ رہی تھیں	پڑھ رہے تھے	وہ/یہ

8.10 Reading and Translation Drill

۱۔ اُس وقت وہ عورتیں کتابیں پڑھ رہی تھیں۔

اُس وقت آپ کیا کر رہے تھے؟

اُس وقت میں ٹیلیفون پر بات کر رہا تھا۔

کیا، اُس وقت ہوائی جہاز بمبئی سے دلّی جا رہا تھا؟

۲۔ ایک بوڑھا آدمی اِسکول کے لڑکوں کے لئے کھانا پکا رہا تھا۔

باورچی مہمانوں کے لئے بریانی پکا رہا تھا۔

آپ کی لڑکیاں بہت شرارت کر رہی تھیں۔

پولیس چور کو پکڑ رہی تھی۔

۳۔ پیاس کی وجہ سے بچّے رو رہے تھے۔

امریکہ میں بھوک کی وجہ سے کتنے لوگ مر رہے تھے؟

بیماری کی وجہ سے کبیر کچھ بھی نہیں کھا رہا تھا۔

گرمی کی وجہ سے وہ بیمار ہوتی تھی۔

۴۔ پچھلے ہفتے، جمعرات دوپہر کو، عورتیں بازار جا رہی تھیں۔

پیر کی صبح وہ طالبِ علم اسکول جا رہا تھا۔

اتوار کی رات کو سب گھروالے سو رہے تھے۔

منگل کی شام کو ہم دوستوں کے ساتھ ہندوستانی فلموں کے گیت سن رہے تھے۔

کل تیز ہوا چل رہی تھی۔

8.11 Cardinal Numbers 41-50

۴۱	اِکتالیس
۴۲	بیالیس
۴۳	تینتالیس

چوالیس	۴۴
پینتالیس	۴۵
چھیالیس	۴۶
سینتالیس	۴۷
اڑتالیس	۴۸
اُنچاس	۴۹
پچاس	۵۰

8.12 Pronunciation Drill: Doubling of Consonants

پتّہ	پتہ
کتّھا	کتھا
بتّا	بتا
کتّا	کتا
پتّا	پتا
ڈبّا	ڈبا
گدّا	گدا
رسّا	رسا
مدّا	مدا
جھبّا	جھبا
صفّاک	صفا
غدّار	غدر
سجّاد	سجدہ
غسّال	غُسل

164

رزّاق   رِزق

سچّا   اچّھا

کچّا   لجّا

8.13 گفتگو (Conversation)

(راج کے گھر میں، کھانے پر)

مّمی: نرگس بیٹی، تم یہاں بیٹھو۔

نرگس: جی نہیں۔ آنٹی آپ یہاں بیٹھیئے۔

پتاجی: نہیں، نہیں۔ وہ ہر وقت یہاں بیٹھتی ہے، میرے پاس!

مّمی: ریشما! تو کہاں جا رہی ہے؟ یہاں بیٹھ۔

ریشما: نہیں۔ میں نرگس دیدی کے پاس بیٹھنا چاہتی ہوں۔

راج: او ہو! یہ کیا ہو رہا ہے؟

پتاجی: ہاں، ہاں۔ کھانا ٹھنڈا ہو رہا ہے۔ تم لوگ بیٹھو۔

رِشی: نرگس، کیا تم پانی پینا چاہتی ہو یا دودھ؟

راج: نہیں۔ نرگس لسّی پیئے گی۔

رشی: لسّی! لسّی گھر میں نہیں ہے۔ ہاں، البتّہ دہی ہے۔ کیا، دہی کھاؤ گی؟

مّمی: بیٹی، یہ تمہارا گھر ہے، مت شرماؤ۔ اچّھا، یہ چاول ہیں، یہ روٹی، یہ مُرغی کا سالن، یہ سبزی، یہ گوشت کی بریانی، یہ پاپڑ اور یہ ہے آم کا اچار۔ تم سبزی خور تو نہیں؟

نرگس: نہیں آنٹی میں ہر چیز کھاتی ہوں۔ یہ تو بہت اچّھی چیزیں ہیں۔ مگر میں کھانے سے پہلے پیاز اور نمک کھاتی ہوں۔

راج: کیا؟! مّمی، روٹی دیجیئے۔ میں بھی آج روٹی کے ساتھ پیاز کھاؤں گا۔

165

پتاجی: ہاں! تمہاری ماں بہت اچّھی ممی ہے اور وہ بہت اچّھا پکاتی ہے۔ مگر آج اِس مُرغی کے سالن میں مرچ کم ہے۔

ممّی: تم اچار لو۔ اچار میں بہت زیادہ مرچ ہے۔ یہ نمبو کا اچار ہے۔ اور وہ آم کا ہے۔

پتاجی: نرگس، تم بچپن میں کہاں رہتی تھیں؟

نرگس: میں بچپن میں راجستھان میں رہتی تھی۔ ہمارے رشتہ دار دِلّی، لکھنو، اور بنارس میں بھی تھے۔

پتاجی: کیا، تمہارے والد فوج میں تھے؟

نرگس: جی نہیں۔ وہ آرکیٹیکٹ تھے اور راجستھان کے ایک شہر، جئے پور، میں کام کرتے تھے۔ میں وہاں بورڈنگ اِسکول میں تھی۔

پتاجی: ہاں، راجستھان بہت خوبصورت جگہ ہے مگر وہاں بہت گرمی ہوتی ہے۔

نرگس: جی ہاں، مگر گرمیوں کے موسم میں ہم کشمیر جاتے تھے۔ کشمیر بہت ٹھنڈی جگہ ہے۔ یہ بریانی تو بہت مزیدار ہے۔ اس میں کیا ہے؟

ممّی: اس میں چاول، بکری کا گوشت، دہی، پیاز، نمک اور دو تین مصالحے ہیں۔

رشی: ریشما، کیا تم میرے لئے کوک لا سکتی ہو؟

ممّی: گھر میں کوک نہیں ہے۔ تم دُودھ پیو۔ یہ صحت کے لئے اچھا ہے۔ کوک صحت کے لئے اچھی نہیں۔ ریشما، یہ تم کیا کھا رہی ہو؟

ریشما: مٹھائی

روی: تم بالکل پاگل ہو۔ کھانے سے پہلے مٹھائی کھا رہی ہو؟

ریشما: تم بھی پاگل ہو۔

ممّی: ریشما، نہیں۔ روی تم سے بڑا ہے۔ اچّھا، یہاں آؤ۔ دیکھو، یہ مزیدار مُرغی کا سالن، سبزی اور روٹی کھاؤ۔

ریشما: نہیں! میں مِٹھائی کھانا چاہتی ہوں۔

نرگس: ریشما، تم اور میں کھانے کے بعد مِٹھائی کھا سکتی ہیں۔

ریشما: دیدی آپ بہت اچھی ہیں۔ آپ ہمارے گھر سے مت جائیے۔

راج: ہاں۔ میں بھی نرگس سے یہ کہہ رہا ہوں!

(سب لوگ ہنستے ہیں۔)

پتاجی: تم تو ایک پاگل عاشق ہو۔

راج: ہاں عاشقی ہی میرا کام ہے!

نرگس: راج!!

8.14 Conversation Practice

Ali: Sunita, you sit here. Reshma, you sit over there, and I'll sit by you.

Sunita: Is the food (generally, ہوتا ہے) good here?

Reshma: Yes, it is (generally) very good. I was here last week. The chicken curry and biriyani are delicious.

Sunita: But I don't eat meat. I am vegetarian.

Ali: You can eat lentils, bread, and yogurt. Lentils are (generally) very good.

Reshma: Yes, they are also good for your health.

Waiter: What do you people want to eat and drink? Would you like to eat papad?

Ali: No, we will drink lassi and we will eat chicken curry, biriyani, rice, lentils, vegetable curry, and yogurt.

Sunita: Also, give us (ہم کو) some onions and pickles. Are the pickles very hot?

Reshma: A lot of red peppers are not good for your health. Ali also eats a lot of spices.

Waiter: In our pickles there are no red peppers. Would you like some bread with your food?

Ali: Yes, we will take both bread and rice.

8.15 Songs

۱)

میری جان کچھ بھی کیجیئے

چاہے جان میری لیجیئے

پر دل ہمیں کو دیجیئے

کبھی یاد ہمیں بھی کیجیئے

کبھی نام ہمارا لیجیئے

سپنوں میں آیا کیجیئے

۲)

سانسوں کی ضرورت ہے جیسے زندگی کے لئے

بس ایک صنم چاہیئے عاشقی کے لئے

جام کی ضرورت ہے جیسے بے خودی کے لئے

ہاں ایک صنم چاہیئے عاشقی کے لئے

بس ایک صنم چاہیئے عاشقی کے لئے۔

۳)

آنکھوں میں آنکھوں میں آنکھوں میں ہو آنکھوں میں

آنکھوں میں تیرا ہی چہرہ

دھڑکن میں تیری ہی یادیں

کرتی ہیں دیوانہ

ہائے کہاں گئیں وہ راتیں

وہ میٹھی میٹھی سی باتیں

168

کرتی تھیں جو دیوانہ

Glossary for Songs

ہمیں کو = emphatic form of ہم (see ch. 12) "only to me/us"

بے خودی = selflessness; being beside oneself; ecstasy, madness (f)

ہمیں = special object form of ہم (see ch. 9)

جام = goblet, cup (usually of wine) (m)

آیا کیجیے = keep on constantly coming

چہرہ = face (m)

جیسے = just as

میٹھا = sweet

صنم = idol; beloved, sweetheart (m)

گئیں = past tense (feminine plural) of verb جانا

8.16 Vocabulary

airplane (m)	ہَوائی جہاز
although	البتّہ، اگرچہ
army (f)	فوج
to catch, apprehend	پکڑنا
chicken (f)	مُرغی
child (m)	بچّہ
childhood (m)	بچپن
cold (adjective)	ٹھنڈا
cold (noun, f)	سردی، ٹھنڈ
cook (m)	باورچی
curry (m)	سالن
chicken curry	مُرغی کا سالن

meat curry	گوشت کا سالن
vegetable curry	سبزی کا سالن
to die	مرنا
dream (m)	سپنا
enough!	بس
fear (m/f)	ڈر
to fear	ڈرنا
to fear x	x سے ڈرنا
fifty	پچاس
guest (m/f)	مہمان
health (f)	صحت
hot	گرم
hunger (f)	بھوک
knife (f)	چھری
to laugh	ہنسنا
last, past, previous; back; latter	پچھلا
lemon/lime (m)	نمبو، لیموں
lentils (f)	دال
lover (m)	عاشق
being a lover (f)	عاشقی
meat (m)	گوشت
meat eater (m/ f)	گوشت خور

milk (m)	دُودھ
mischief (f)	شرارت
necessity (f)	ضرُورت
necessity/need for x	x کی ضرورت
noise, uproar, disturbance (m)	شور
onion (f)	پیاز
out, outside	باہر، کے باہر
papad (crispy appetizers) (m)	پاپڑ
pepper (f)	مِرچ
pickles (hot) (m)	اچار
please, kindly (with آپ forms)	مہربانی سے، مہربانی کرکے
	مہربانی فرماکر
(with تم forms)	ذرا
relatives, family members (m)	رِشتہ دار
rice (m pl)	چاول
rice w/ meat or vegetables (f)	بریانی
salt (m)	نمک
to scream, yell	چیخنا
season (m)	موسم
to be shy, recitent	شرمانا
sick, ill (adj.); sick person (m/f)	بیمار
sickness, illness (f)	بیماری

to sit	بیٹھنا
song (m)	گیت، گانا، نغمہ
to speak, to talk, converse	بات کرنا
spices (m)	مصالحہ/مسالا
sunshine, heat of sun (f)	دھوپ
time, age; world; fortune (m)	زمانہ
thief (m)	چور
thirst (f)	پیاس
vegetable (f)	سبزی
vegetarian (m/f)	سبزی خور / شاکاہاری
woman (f)	عورت
yogurt (m)	دہی

Chapter 9

The postposition کو in Urdu has several uses. We will systematically discuss the most important uses in this chapter.

9.1 کو as a Temporal Marker

As we have seen in previous chapters, days of the week and most of the times of the day are marked by کو to mean "on," "in," and "at."

میں ہر پیر کو اسکول جاتا ہوں۔

I go to school every Monday.

کیا، وہ شام کو سنیما جاتے ہیں؟

Does he go to the cinema in the evening?

Note that among the times of the day only صبح "morning" does not use the postposition کو.

9.1 Reading and Translation Drill

۱۔ میں اس اتوار کو ٹینیس کھیل سکتا ہوں۔

کیا، تم منگل کو میرے ساتھ ٹینیس کھیل سکتے ہو؟

نہیں، میں منگل اور بدھ کو بہت مصروف ہوں۔

ہم لوگ جمعرات کو کھیل سکتے ہیں۔

۲۔ کیا، آپ ہر روز صبح دفتر جاتے ہیں؟

وہ ہر روز دو پہر کو دفتر جاتے ہیں۔

وہ لڑکیاں رات کو کھانا نہیں کھا سکتیں۔

وہ لڑکے آج شام کو مُرغی کی بریانی اور دال پکا سکتے ہیں۔

Translate the following sentences into Urdu:

1. We can play tennis on Saturday because we are busy on Friday.

2. My friend drinks wine every evening.

3. Can you read books every morning?

4. What are you (informal) doing tonight?

5. Why are both of you going to school on Sunday?

9.2 کو as a Direct Object Marker

When the direct object of an Urdu sentence is animate or specific, then کو marks such an object.

میں علی کو بھیجتا ہوں۔

I send Ali.

(subject -- direct object -- object marker کو -- verb)

میں اُس لڑکے کو بھیجتا ہوں۔

I send that boy.

(subject -- direct object -- object marker کو -- verb)

Although it is necessary to use کو with a direct object that is animate, we can see in the example

below that کو can also mark a direct object when that object is inanimate but needs to be

emphasized. If no emphasis is intended, then کو is not employed after inanimate objects.

آپ اِس قالین کو خریدیئے۔

You buy this carpet. (*emphasis on object*)

(subject -- inanimate direct object -- object marker کو -- verb)

آپ یہ قالین خریدیئے۔

You buy this carpet. (*object not emphasized*)

174

(subject -- inanimate direct object -- verb)

9.2 Reading and Translation Drill

١۔ میں علی کو کھانے پر بُلاتا ہوں۔

کیا، تم اُس دوست کو کھانے پر بُلا رہے ہو؟

ہم اُن دوستوں کو کھانے پر نہیں بُلا سکتے۔

وہ لڑکیاں میرے دوست کو کھانے پر بُلا رہی ہیں۔

٢۔ میں شام کو یہ کتاب بھیج سکتا ہوں۔

کیا، تم راشِد کو بھیج سکتے ہو؟

نہیں۔ ہم راشِد کو نہیں بھیج سکتے۔

میں اُس کے بھائی کو بھیج رہی ہوں۔

٣۔ یہ کتابیں اچّھی ہیں۔ آپ اِن کو خریدیئے

کیا، آپ اِن تصویروں کو خریدنا چاہتے ہیں؟

نہیں۔ ہم اُن خوبصورت تصویروں کو خریدنا چاہتے ہیں۔

یہ قالین بہت مہنگی ہے۔ ہم اِس قالین کو نہیں خرید سکتے۔

9.2 Substitutions

١۔ میں راج کو بلاتی ہوں۔

that beautiful girl

those clever boys

your friend's brother

his friend

٢۔ وہ پھل والے کو بھیجتا ہے۔

that vagabond

those famous actors

our daughter

your (least formal) doctor

٣۔ کیا، آپ اِن کتابوں کو بیچتے ہیں؟

those newspapers

the best book

these big expensive houses

his red shoes

9.3 کو as an Indirect Object Marker

When a sentence has both a direct and an indirect object, only the indirect object is marked by کو.

He gives a book to Ali.

(subject-- verb--direct object--indirect object)

The above word order is the usual order in English in which the direct object precedes the indirect object. In Urdu is the word order is reversed, with the indirect object usually preceding the direct object.

وہ علی کو کتاب دیتا ہے۔

(subject -- indirect object marked by کو -- direct object -- verb)

If the sentence has temporal and locative elements then they are placed between the indirect and direct objects.

وہ علی کو شام کو وہاں کتاب دے سکتا ہے۔

In the evening, he can give Ali the book there.

(subject-- indirect object marked by کو -- temporal phrase -- locative phrase --direct object -- verb)

This order may slightly change depending upon the element of the sentence that needs to be especially emphasized.

شام کو وہ علی کو وہاں کتاب دے سکتا ہے۔

By placing شام کو at the beginning of the sentence, the temporal element is emphasized.

9.3 Reading and Translation Drill

١۔ میں سنیل کو پیسے دیتا ہوں۔

کیا، آپ مجھ کو پیسے دے سکتے ہیں؟

مہربانی سے راج کو پیسے دیجیئے۔

شیلا اور رما کو پیسے دو۔

٢۔ کیا، تم علی کو اخبار دے رہی ہو؟

نہیں، میں علی کو وہ اچّھی کتابیں دے رہی ہوں۔

کیا، آپ زاہد کو روٹی دے سکتے ہیں؟

ہم اُن ہوشیار لڑکوں کو مٹھائی دے سکتے ہیں۔

٣۔ وہ اِن لڑکیوں کو شام کو اسکول میں کتابیں دیتے ہیں۔

وہ غریبوں کو ہر دو پہر کو دِلّی بازار میں روٹیاں دیتے ہیں۔

میں اُن غریبوں کو ہر دو پہر کو دِلّی بازار میں روٹیاں دے سکتا ہوں۔

وہ ہمارے دوست کو ہر روز ہسپتال میں دوائی دیتے ہیں۔

Translate the following sentences into Urdu:

1.   He gives me money every Monday.

2.   Can you give the poor money tonight?

3.   They give food to my friends every Thursday.

4.   What can you give us?

5.   I can give you the world.

9.4 پسند -- کو in Verbal and Adjectival Constructions

In Urdu the logical subject of certain verbal and adjectival constructions is sometimes marked by

کو . پسند "pleasing" is a predicate adjective used in constructions in which the logical subject in

English is marked by کو . The verb (ہے or ہیں) agrees with the grammatical subject in Urdu.

علی کو یہ کتاب پسند ہے۔

Ali likes this book. (Literally: This book is pleasing to Ali.)

(کتاب = grammatical subject in Urdu, علی = logical subject in English)

مجھ کو یہ چیزیں پسند ہیں۔

I like these things. (Literally: These things are pleasing to me.)

(چیزیں = grammatical subject in Urdu, میں = logical subject in English marked by کو)

In the sentences above, the verb agrees with the grammatical subjects in Urdu (کتاب and چیزیں)

and not with the logical subjects in English. In the past tense, the auxiliary تھا, in its appropriate

forms, replaces ہے following the same rules of agreement.

مجھ کو یہ پھل پسند تھا۔

I liked this fruit.

(verb تھا agreeing with پھل = grammatical subject in Urdu)

لڑکے کو کتاب پسند تھی۔

The boy liked the book.

(verb تھی agreeing with کتاب = grammatical subject in Urdu)

مہمانوں کو سبزیاں پسند تھیں۔

The guests liked the vegetables.

(verb تھیں agreeing with سبزیاں = grammatical subject in Urdu)

9.4 Reading and Translation Drill

ا۔   مجھ کو یہ عمارتیں بہت پسند ہیں۔

کیا، آپ کو وہ دوکانیں پسند ہیں؟

اِن کو یہ گھر پسند نہیں۔

ہم کو وہ کتابیں بہت پسند ہیں۔

۲۔   مجھ کو سیر کرنا بہت پسند ہے۔

کیا، آپ کو لتا منگیشکر کی آواز پسند ہے؟

ہاں، ہم کو لتا منگیشکر کی آواز مڈونا کی آواز سے زیادہ پسند ہے۔

اُن کو وہ اخبار اِن اخباروں سے زیادہ پسند ہے۔

۳۔   مینا کو بازار کا اچار پسند نہیں تھا۔

پنکج کو زیادہ باتیں کرنا پسند نہیں تھا۔

ملّار کو بدترین لوگ کیوں پسند تھے؟

عابد کو کشمیری لڑکیاں بہت پسند تھیں!

Translate the following sentences into Urdu:

1.   I like Madonna very much.

2.   Some people like tea more than coffee.

3.   Do you (least formal) like these big buildings?

4.   I like *biriyani* very much but I can't eat rice.

5.   I don't like meat, but I like sweets very much.

6.   Did Reshma like the Chinese food?

7.	When Ravi was in India, he did not like watching Indian movies.

8.	He is my favorite actor but he cannot sing well. His voice is not very good.

9.5 کو in Infinitive + ہے Construction

کو marks the logical subject of "the infinitive + ہے " construction which conveys that something "has to be," "is necessary," or "must be done."

علی کو پڑھنا ہے۔

Ali has to study.

رحیم کو جانا ہے۔

Rahim has to go.

At times, the verbal infinitive may have an object. In such a situation, in some dialects of Urdu-Hindi the infinitive agrees with that object:

علی کو کتاب پڑھنی ہے۔

Ali has to read the book.

In the above sentence, the verbal infinitive پڑھنا has been declined to پڑھنی because کتاب, the object of پڑھنا, is feminine. In order to make a negative sentence, نہیں is used.

علی کو نہیں پڑھنا ہے۔

Ali doesn't have to study/read.

علی کو پڑھنا نہیں ہے۔

Ali doesn't have to study/read (*emphatic*).

In the past and future tenses, the verb ہے is replaced by the auxiliary تھا or ہوگا:

رحیم کو گھر جانا تھا۔

Rahim had to go home.

رحیم کو گھر جانا ہوگا۔

Rahim will have to go home.

علی کو کتاب پڑھنی تھی۔

Ali had to read the book.

In the last sentence, the verb پڑھنی تھی agrees with the gender of its object کتاب

9.6 Infinitive as the Subject

In the "infinitive + ہے " construction, the infinitive can also act as the subject of the sentence.

پڑھنا ہے۔

It is necessary to study/studying is necessary.

If an adjective is inserted between the infinitive and ہے, then the adjective becomes the

predicate of the infinitive.

پڑھنا اچّھا ہے۔

It is good to study/studying is good.

In the past and future tenses, the auxiliaries تھا and ہوگا replace ہے:

پڑھنا اچّھا تھا۔

It was good to study/ studying was good.

پڑھنا اچّھا ہوگا۔

It will be good to study/studying will be good.

9.5-9.6 Reading and Translation Drill

۱۔   مجھ کو آج بہت پڑھنا ہے۔

کیا، تم کو آج بہت پڑھنا ہے؟

ہم کو کل بہت لکھنا ہے۔

181

کیا، اُن کو یہ کتابیں پڑھنی ہیں؟

۲۔ تجھ کو یہ خط لکھنے ہیں۔

میں یہ کام نہیں کر سکتی۔ مجھ کو وہ کام کرنا ہے۔

ہاں، اُس کو یہ پچاس اخبار پڑھنے ہیں۔

میں بہت مصروف ہوں، مگر مجھ کو وہاں جانا ہے۔

۳۔ کیا، آپ کو کل شام کو گانا ہے؟

نہیں، مجھ کو کل صبح گانا ہے۔

آپ کو کل رات کو کہاں جانا ہے؟

اُن کو کل دو پہر کو یہاں آنا ہے۔

۴۔ کل روی کو اُردو کی کلاس کے لئے ایک مضمون لکھنا تھا۔

پچھلے سال اس شاعر کو کتنی غزلیں لکھنی تھیں؟

پچھلے ہفتے ایلیکس کو نیویارک جانا تھا۔

ہسپتال میں رہنے کے لئے اس بیچارے بیمار کو کتنے پیسے دینے ہونگے؟

Translate the following sentences into Urdu:

1. I have to write these three essays (papers) by tomorrow.

2. Do you have to read your friend's letters at this time of the night?

3. I have to go to school on Sunday.

4. What do they have to do tomorrow afternoon?

5. She doesn't have to cook.

6. What did you have to do all day yesterday?

9.7 چاہئے کو in Constructions

چاہئے constructions are similar to "the infinitive + ہے " construction in that the logical subject in such constructions is also marked by کو. چاہئے is an impersonal verb form that may be preceded by either a noun or a verbal infinitive. In case of a noun, the construction means that the noun is desired, wanted, or needed by the logical subject. For example,

جم کو ایک کتاب چاہئے۔

Jim wants a book.

(logical subject "Jim" marked by کو)

اِس دُنیا میں سب کو پیار چاہئے۔

In this world everyone needs love.

(logical subject "everyone" marked by کو)

If the object desired is plural, then چاہئے may be optionally nasalized:

کیا، آپ کو یہ کپڑے چاہئیں؟

Do you want these clothes?

In the past tense, the چاہئے construction uses the past auxiliary تھا. Since the logical subject is marked by کو, the past auxiliary will agree in number and gender with the desired object.

Examples:

راج کو ایک سیب چاہئے تھا۔

Raj wanted an apple. (the auxiliary تھا agreeing with سیب)

نرگس کو کچھ ساڑیاں چاہئے تھیں۔

Nargis wanted some saris. (the auxiliary تھیں agreeing with ساڑیاں)

In order to convey the sense that something "ought to" or "should be" done, a verbal infinitive is placed before چاہئے. The logical subject continues to be marked by کو, which cuts off agreement between it and the impersonal چاہئے:

علی کو پڑھنا چاہیئے۔

Ali ought to study/read.

چھوٹی بچّی کو ابھی سونا چاہیئے۔

The little girl ought to sleep now.

In some dialects of Urdu-Hindi, the verbal infinitive is made to agree in number and gender with its object, if it has one:

علی کو کتاب پڑھنی چاہیئے۔

Ali ought to read the book.

(پڑھنا verb) agreeing with its object (کتاب)

دوکاندار کو یہ پھل بیچنے چاہیئیں۔

The shopkeeper ought to sell these fruits.

(بیچنا verb) agreeing with its object (پھل)

In the past tense, تھا is added at the end of the sentence. This auxiliary will agree in number and gender with any object of the verbal infinitive. Examples:

علی کو پڑھنا چاہیئے تھا۔

Ali ought to have/should have studied.

دوکاندار کو یہ پھل بیچنے چاہیئے تھے۔

The shopkeeper ought to have/should have sold these fruits.

چاہیئے constructions may be put into the negative by using the particle نہیں. Placing نہیں toward the end of the sentence increases the emphasis of the negation. Example:

کالج کے طالبِ علم کو شراب نہیں پینا (پینی) چاہیئے!

کالج کے طالبِ علم کو شراب پینا (پینی) نہیں چاہیئے!

A college student should not drink alcohol!

9.7 Reading and Translation Drill

۱۔ مُجھ کو وہاں جانا چاہیۓ۔

تم کو یہ کام کرنا چاہیۓ۔

آپ کو ہر روز اخبار پڑھنا چاہیۓ۔

تم کو کچرے کے ساتھ نہیں کھیلنا چاہیۓ!

۲۔ اُن کو یہاں آنا چاہیۓ، مگر وہاں بہت کام کرنا ہے۔

ہم کو یہ کتابیں پڑھنی چاہئیں مگر ہم بہت مصروف ہیں۔

آپ کو دوپہر کو نہیں کھیلنا چاہیۓ۔

مجھ کو وہ جگہ پسند نہیں مگر وہاں جانا ہے۔

۳۔ یہ قالین بہت سُندر ہے۔ کیا تم کو یہ قالین چاہیۓ؟

نہیں، ہم کو وہ پھول چاہیۓ۔

مجھ کو چاول، گوشت اور دہی چاہیۓ۔

اُن لڑکیوں کو پھل، مٹھائی اور پھول چاہئیں۔

۴۔ اُس آدمی کو پانچ قمیضیں چاہیۓ تھیں۔

پارٹی کے بعد ریشما کو جلدی گھر جانا چاہیۓ تھا۔

مائیکل کو اِتنی بریانی نہیں کھانی چاہیۓ تھی۔

زمیندار کو غریب لوگوں سے زیادہ کرایہ نہیں لینا چاہیۓ تھا۔

Translate the following sentences into Urdu:

1. He ought to write these papers (essays) now.

2. We ought to eat but we have to go there.

3. Sunil ought not to have fallen in love with Nargis!

185

4.   Both these houses are expensive. Would you like to buy them?

5.   I would like some salt, onions, and bread.

6.   We ought to wash our clothes..

7.   The guest wanted some more alcohol.

8.   Sheila's brother wants five shirts.

9.   The patient (sick person) ought to have drunk this medicine.

10.   Rahim should have sold this beautiful carpet yesterday.

9.8 کو with Abstract Possessions

کو marks the possessor of abstract nouns such as "tiredness" (تھکن), "happiness" (خوشی),

"worry" (فکر), "leisure" (فرصت) and so on. In this construction, the verb agrees with the abstract

noun being possessed since the logical subject in English is marked with کو. We will discuss this

further in Chapter 11 when we consider expressions of possession.

مجھ کو تھکن ہے۔

I am tired.

کیا، آپ کو فرصت ہے؟

Do you have free time?

ہم کو بہت فِکر ہے۔

We are very worried.

سنیل کو پیسوں کی ضرورت تھی۔

Sunil needed money (lit. Sunil had the need for money).

In the last example above, the past tense auxiliary تھی is in the feminine agreeing with the

abstract noun ضرورت.

۱۔ کیا، تم کو آج بہت تھکن ہے؟

اُس کو آج بہت تھکن ہے، کیا؟

میں ٹینس نہیں کھیل سکتا کیونکہ مجھ کو بہت تھکن ہے۔

ہم وہاں نہیں جا رہے ہیں کیونکہ ہم کو تھکن ہے۔

۲۔ کل میرا خاندان آ رہا ہے۔ مجھ کو بہت خوشی ہے۔

کیا، تم کو بھی بہت خوشی ہے؟

سینڈریلا کو بھی بہت خوشی تھی کیونکہ وہ بھی پارٹی میں جا رہی تھی۔

اُس لڑکے کو خوشی ہے کیونکہ آج وہ بہت مٹھائی کھا سکتا ہے۔

۳۔ ہاں، بیچارے بیمار طالبِ علم کو بہت فکر ہے۔

آپ خاموش کیوں ہیں؟ کیا، آپ کو فکر ہے؟

ہاں، آج مجھ کو بہت فکر ہے۔

اُس پاگل لڑکی کو بالکل فکر نہیں تھی۔

۴۔ میں نہیں کھیل سکتا۔ مجھ کو فرصت نہیں۔

کل اُن کو بہت فرصت تھی۔ آج وہ بہت مصروف ہیں۔

ہم نیو یارک جا رہے ہیں کیونکہ ہم کو فرصت ہے۔

کیا، آپ کے دوستوں کو پچھلے ہفتے فرصت تھی؟

۵۔ ولیم کو کس چیز کی ضرورت تھی؟

کیا، ہندوستان جانے کے لئے امریکنوں کو ویزا کی ضرورت ہے؟

پچھلے پیر کو اکبر کو فرصت کی بہت ضرورت تھی۔

انیتا کو یہاں آنے کی کیا ضرورت تھی؟!

Translate the following sentences into Urdu:

1.   My friends can play tomorrow because they have free time (leisure).

2.   I cannot work because I am very tired.

3.   Are you (informal) happy today?

4.   No. I am worried because tomorrow evening I have to go to school.

5.   I have some free time today and I ought to play tennis.

6.   The patient needed the best doctor (lit. had need of the best doctor).

7.   Did you need more books from the library last night? (lit. did you have the need for more

books from the library last night?)

9.9 Special Object Forms

When certain pronouns in the oblique case are combined with کو, they generally have a special

form:

مجھ کو	مجھے
تجھ کو	تجھے
تم کو	تمہیں
اِس کو	اِسے
اُس کو	اُسے
ہم کو	ہمیں
اِن کو	اِنہیں
اُن کو	اُنہیں
کس کو	کسے
کن کو	کنہیں

188

The use of these special forms is considered preferable in idiomatic Urdu.

مجھ کو کام کرنا ہے۔

مجھے کام کرنا ہے۔

I have to work.

Both these sentences are grammatically correct, but the second sentence is more idiomatic. Note that the combination of pronouns and postpositions is only possible when the postposition کو immediately follows the pronouns.

9.9 Reading and Translation Drill

۱۔   مجھے آج وہاں جانا ہے۔

تجھے اُس سے مِلنا چاہیئے۔

تمہیں بہت پڑھنا ہے۔

کیا، آپ کو یہ پھل لینے ہیں؟

۲۔   کل کِسے کام کرنا ہے؟

پرسوں کنہیں کام کرنا ہے؟

مجھے بہت بُخار ہے، مگر میں سو نہیں سکتا کیونکہ مجھے وہاں جانا ہے۔

تجھے کھانسی ہے، مگر اُسے بُخار ہے۔

۳۔   ہمیں اُسے شراب نہیں دینی چاہیئے!

اُنہیں کیا پسند ہے؟ کافی یا چائے؟

اُنہیں یہ کتاب اِسے دینی نہیں چاہیئے۔

کل رات کو مجھے گھر جلدی جانا تھا۔

۴۔   اُسے یہ کام کرنے کی فرصت نہیں تھی۔

کیا! انہیں آپ سے بات کرنے کی فرصت نہیں ہے!

189

ہمیں ایک ٹھنڈی کوکا کولا چاہیئے۔

اس بات کے بارے میں تمہیں نرگس کی والدہ سے پوچھنے کی ضرورت تھی۔

Translate the following sentences into Urdu using the special object form.

1.   He has a lot of work but he has to go there.

2.   Do you (informal) have free time? We don't have free time.

3.   To whom will you (least formal) give this book?

4.   I will send him in the evening.

5.   Do you (informal) have a cough?

6.   I should have gone home last night! I am very sick today.

9.10 Stem + کے/کر

When two actions are performed consecutively by the same subject, the sentence is formed in this manner:

stem of the infinitive of the first verb + کے/کر + conjugated form of second verb.

The enclitics کر or کے divide the two actions and can be used interchangeably unless the first verb is کرنا or a complex verb formed with کرنا. If this is the case then only the enclitic کے can be used.

میں ناچ کر گاتا ہوں۔

Having danced, I sing.

(subject -- verb 1 stem -- enclitic -- verb 2)

The second verb is conjugated and agrees with the subject.

میں کام کر کے ٹی۔ وی دیکھتا ہوں۔

Having done work, I watch T.V.

The "stem + کر" construction occurs in one of the common Urdu phrases used to express "please." Instead of using مہربانی سے for "please" or "kindly," the phrase مہربانی کرکے (lit. "having done a kindness") may be used. In formal Urdu, the verb فرمانا (lit. "to order, to command") is sometimes used instead of کرنا, resulting in the phrase مہربانی فرما کر (lit. "having commanded a kindness") being employed as a very polite equivalent of the English "please."

مہربانی سے بچّے کا سیٹ بیلٹ باندھیئے!

مہربانی کرکے بچّے کا سیٹ بیلٹ باندھیئے!

مہربانی فرماکر بچّے کا سیٹ بیلٹ باندھیئے!

Please fasten the child's seat belt.

Combine the two sentences in the following manner and then translate them into English:

Example:

میں کھانا کھاتا ہوں۔ میں گھر جاتا ہوں۔

میں کھانا کھا کر گھر جاتا ہوں۔

Having eaten the food, I go home.

۱۔ وہ اخبار پڑھتا ہے۔ وہ خط لکھ سکتا ہے۔

۲۔ ٹینس کھیلو۔ دودھ پیئو۔

۳۔ شام کو کام کیجیئے۔ رات کو سنیما دیکھیئے۔

۴۔ ہماری لڑکیاں گاتی ہیں۔ ہماری لڑکیاں ناچ سکتی ہیں۔

۵۔ تم ٹی۔وی دیکھتے ہو۔ تم سو سکتے ہو۔

۶۔ بیچاری غریب لڑکی کچرا اُٹھا رہی تھی۔ بیچاری غریب لڑکی کچرا کھا رہی تھی۔

۷۔ عورت بازار سے سبزی خریدتی ہے۔ عورت سبزی پکائیگی۔

۸۔ پاکستان کے صدر اِس کمرے میں تشریف لائینگے۔ پاکستان کے صدر اُس بڑی کرسی پر

تشریف رکھیںگے۔

9.10 Reading and Translation Drill

۱۔ میں کام کر کے وہاں جاتا ہوں۔

وہ کام کر کے کھیلتا ہے۔

کیا، تم کام کر کے پڑھتی ہو؟

نہیں، میں پڑھ کے کام کرتی ہوں۔

۲۔ میں گوشت پکا کر کھاتا ہوں۔

وہ سبزیاں پکا کر نہیں کھا سکتا۔

کیا، تو کام کر کے نہیں کھا سکتا؟

ہم آئیس کریم خرید کر کھا رہے ہیں۔

۳۔ کیا، تم ہر روز گا کر سوتی ہو؟

نہیں، میں ہر رات پڑھ کر سوتی ہوں۔

کیا، وہ ہر پیر کو ٹینیس کھیل کر کام کرتے ہیں؟

نہیں، وہ کام کر کے ٹینیس کھیل رہے ہیں۔

۴۔ مہربانی فرما کر یہ کام کیجئے۔

مہربانی فرما کر ہمارے گھر تشریف لائے۔

مہربانی فرما کر یہاں بیٹھیئے۔

مہربانی فرما کر تشریف رکھیئے۔

مہربانی فرما کر اُن کو کھانا دیجئے۔

9.11 Noun-Verb Agreement in Urdu

In Urdu, if there are several inanimate nouns, the number-conjugation of the verb will depend on

the last object in the series.

192

مجھ کو چاول، دال، اور روٹی بہت پسند ہے۔

I like rice, dal, and bread.

The end verb is ہے instead of ہیں because روٹی is singular. If the series of nouns has animate

beings, then the verb will be in the plural:

مجھ کو علی، راشد، روی اور گیتا بہت پسند ہیں۔

I like Ali, Rashid, Ravi, and Gita very much.

9.11 Reading and Translation Drill

ا۔   آج کھانے میں گوشت، روٹی، چاول اور مرغی کا سالن ہے۔

کیا، آپ کے گھر میں دہی اور روٹی ہے؟

مجھے برگر، پیزا اور کوک بہت پسند ہے۔

اُس کو بریانی اور مٹھائیاں بہت پسند ہیں۔

Translate the following sentences into Urdu:

1.   Sheila likes Matt Damon, Brad Pitt, and Tom Cruise. Which actors do you like?

2.   Please give Neil and Dimple apples, oranges, and milk.

3.   Do you (least formal) like chicken curry and rice?

4.   Do you (informal) like Lata Mangeshkar and Muhammad Rafi? -- Who are they?

5.   We don't like Amitabh Bachchan. Our favorite actor is Shahrukh Khan.

6.   Mallar liked that blue shirt.

7.   Abid has to buy some pens and books from the store.

9.12 Cardinal Numbers 51-60

اکاون   ۵۱

باون   ۵۲

ترپن	۵۳
چوّن	۵۴
پچپن	۵۵
چھپّن	۵۶
ستاون	۵۷
اٹھاون	۵۸
اُنسٹھ	۵۹
ساٹھ	۶۰

9.13 Expressing Time with the Enclitic کر/کے

The verb بجنا, "to strike," is used in Urdu to express time in phrases that are equivalent to the English "o'clock." In order to express *complete hours*, the past participles of بجنا - بجا/بجے are used. بجا is only used for 1, and بجے for all other numbers.

It's one o'clock.   ایک بجا ہے۔

It's eleven o'clock.   گیارہ بجے ہیں۔

For expressions indicating minutes past the hour, بجنا is combined with the enclitic کر/کے.

In order to say 8:10, one would say "having struck 8, it is 10 minutes."

8:10   آٹھ بج کر دس منٹ ہیں۔

5:20   پانچ بج کے بیس منٹ ہیں۔

In this construction, کر/کے are added to the stem of بجنا and then followed by the number of minutes. *To express minutes before the hour,* the postposition میں is used instead of کر/کے with the verb بجنا. The postposition میں puts the infinitive بجنا into the oblique.

9:40   دس بجنے میں بیس منٹ ہیں۔

(literally: There are twenty minutes in the striking of ten.)

To state that something will occur or take place at a certain time, the postposition پر is used for "at," when a specific number of minutes is mentioned. With other time expressions involving complete hours (or fractions of hours), the postposition is generally not explicitly used but implied. Consequently the past participle of بجنا is used in its oblique form, i.e., بجے. Example:

ٹرین دس بجے نکلیگی۔

The train will depart at ten o'clock.

ٹرین ایک بجے روانہ ہوگی۔

The train will depart at one o'clock.

(Note: past participles in above two examples are in the implied oblique)

ہوائی جہاز دس بج کر پانچ منٹ پر پہنچ رہا ہے۔

The airplane is arriving at five minutes past ten.

ہوائی جہاز دس بجنے میں پانچ منٹ پر پہنچ رہا ہے۔

The airplane is arriving at five minutes to ten.

To express a.m. or p.m., the time of the day is stated with کو if appropriate:

دوپہر کو دو بجے آئیے!

Come at two p.m. (lit. two o'clock in the afternoon)!

Sometimes the possessive کے may also be used in this construction instead of کو:

رات کے دس بجے تو کہاں جا رہا تھا؟

Where were you going at ten o'clock at night (at 10 p.m.)?

To express exact time, the word ٹھیک is used before the time expression:

ہماری چھوٹی بیٹی ہر صبح ٹھیک چار بجے جاگتی ہے۔

Our little daughter wakes every morning at exactly 4 o'clock.

9.13 Reading and Translation Drill

۱۔ میں دس بج کر بیس منٹ پر سوتا ہوں۔

وہ سات بج کر پانچ منٹ پر آ سکتا ہے۔

کیا، تم گیارہ بج کر بیس منٹ پر جا سکتی ہو؟

نہیں، مجھ کو گیارہ بج کر بیس منٹ پر کام کرنا ہے۔

۲۔ آٹھ بجنے میں دس منٹ پر ملازم اسکول میں تھا۔

کل صبح ٹھیک نو بجنے میں پچیس منٹ پر امیت کو وہاں کیوں جانا ہوگا؟

اسکول بس ہر روز ٹھیک سات بجنے میں بیس منٹ پر بچّوں کو لینے کے لئے آتی ہے۔

میں آپ کے دفتر ٹھیک ایک بجے پہنچوں گی۔

امریکہ میں گرمیوں کے مہینوں میں رات کو آسمان پر تارے دیرے سے نکلتے ہیں۔

۳۔ میرے خیال میں بارش کی وجہ سے ہوائی جہاز وقت پر دلّی نہیں پہنچے گا۔

میرے خیال میں پی۔ آئی۔ اے کا ہوائی جہاز دیر سے آئیگا۔

ایر انڈیا کے افسر کے خیال میں ہوائی جہاز گیارہ بجنے میں چھبّیس منٹ پر کلکتہ سے روانہ ہوگا۔

مہربانی فرما کر آپ لوگ ٹھیک چار بج کر دس منٹ پر ہسپتال کے سامنے مجھ سے ملیئے!

۴۔ آپ جمعرات کو یہاں سے کتنے بجے نکلینگے؟

میں حیدر آباد کے لئے صبح پانچ بیس کی ریل گاڑی سے روانہ ہونگا۔

کل رات حسین بیمار تھا۔ اس کے لئے ہم رات کے دو بجے ہسپتال میں تھے۔

کیا، تم لوگ میرے گھر تین بجے تک پہنچ سکتے ہو؟

یہ آل انڈیا ریڈیو ہے۔ اس وقت رات کے گیارہ بج رہے ہیں۔

Write out the following times in Urdu:

1.	1:00	11.	11:39 p.m
2.	2:10	12.	12:40 a.m.
3.	3:17	13.	1:43
4.	4:20 p.m.	14.	2:47 a.m.
5.	5:22 a.m.	15.	3:49 p.m.
6.	6:24	16.	4:51 p.m.
7.	7:25	17.	5:52 a.m.
8.	8:28 p.m.	18.	6:54 p.m.
9.	9:32	19.	7:55
10.	10:37	20.	8:58 p.m.

Translate the following passage into English:

میرا نام سیما ہے۔ میں کورنیل میں پڑھتی ہوں۔ کورنیل بہت خوبصورت یونیورسٹی ہے۔ مجھ کو کورنیل بہت پسند ہے۔ میرا خاندان بھی نیو یارک میں رہتا ہے۔ میرے والد صاحب پروفیسر ہیں اور میری والدہ گھر میں کام کرتی ہیں۔ میرے ماں باپ ہر سال پاکستان جاتے ہیں مگر میں اُن کے ساتھ نہیں جا سکتی کیونکہ میں اِسٹوڈنٹ ہوں اور میں ہر وقت مصروف رہتی ہوں۔ مجھے آج بھی بہت پڑھنا ہے۔ پڑھ کر ایک مضمون لکھنا ہے۔ مضمون لکھ کر میں دیوی کے گھر جاؤں گی ۔ دیوی میری سہیلی ہے۔ وہ بھی کورنیل میں پڑھ رہی ہے۔ وہ ہندوستان سے ہے۔ وہ اِس وقت کام کر رہی ہے۔ کام کر کے وہ میرے لئے کھانا پکائے گی۔ وہ بہت مزیدار کھانا بناتی ہے۔ ہم دونوں کو دال اور روٹی بہت پسند ہے۔ ہم ہر روز شام کو کھانا کھا کر ٹینیس کھیلتی ہیں۔ ٹینیس کھیلنے کے بعد، ہم دونوں ٹی۔ وی دیکھتی ہیں۔ میرا پسندیدہ پروگرام فرینڈز ہے۔ اچّھا، اب مجھے جانا ہے۔ خدا حافظ۔

9.14 گفتگو (Conversation)

ممّی:	نرگس بیٹی، کیا، تم چائے پینا چاہتی ہو؟
نرگس:	جی نہیں۔ مگر مجھے ہاتھ دھونے ہیں۔
راج:	نرگس دیکھو، غسل خانہ اُدھر ہے۔
پتاجی:	راج، کل شام کو تم کیا کر رہے ہو؟ کیا، تم کو فرصت ہے؟
راج:	جی پتاجی۔ مجھ کو فرصت ہے۔ کل دو پہر کو ہمیں بہت کام کرنا ہے۔
پتاجی:	مجھ کو حسین کے لئے پھل خریدنے ہیں۔ وہ ہسپتال میں ہے۔
ممّی:	ہاں۔ مجھے بھی وہاں جانا چاہئیے۔ وہ بیچارہ بیمار ہے۔ ریشما، کیا، تم ہسپتال جا کر حسین بھائی کو یہ مٹھائی دے سکتی ہو؟
ریشما:	ممّی، مجھے بہت تھکن ہے۔ میں اب سونا چاہتی ہوں۔
نرگس:	کیا، تم میرے ساتھ کھیلنا نہیں چاہتی ہو؟
ریشما:	ہاں، ہاں! میں سو کر کھیل سکتی ہوں۔
نرگس:	یہ مٹھائی بہت مزیدار ہے۔ مجھ کو سب مٹھائیاں بہت پسند ہیں۔ ریشما، اِدھر آؤ۔ تھوڑی مٹھائی کھاؤ۔
ریشما:	جی نہیں دیدی۔ میں اب سونا چاہتی ہوں۔
راج:	نرگس، کیا تم ٹی۔ وی دیکھنا چاہتی ہو؟
نرگس:	کیا وقت ہے؟
راج:	نو بج کر دس منٹ ہیں۔
ممّی (نرگس سے):	تم صبح کب اُٹھتی ہو؟
نرگس:	میں سات بجے اُٹھتی ہوں۔
ممّی:	اچّھا نرگس۔ اب تم بیٹھو۔ میں تو جاتی ہوں۔

نرگس: اچّھا آنٹی۔ خدا حافظ۔ اب مجھے بھی جانا چاہئیے۔ کل صبح مجھے بہت کام کرنا ہے۔

راج: میں تمہارے ساتھ چلتا ہوں۔ کیا تم پندرہ منٹ اور بیٹھ سکتی ہو؟ مجھے گئے کو کھانا دینا ہے۔

نرگس: کیوں؟ پندرہ منٹ کے بعد کیا اِرادہ ہے، راج؟

راج: بولو! تم کو مجھ سے پیار ہے؟

نرگس: راج!

9.15 Conversation Practice (1)

Create a dialogue with at least 8-10 sentences, using the following words and constructions:

تھکن

فُرصت

فِکر

خوشی

پسند

infinitive + ہے

infinitive + چاہئیے

verbal stem + کر

9.15 Conversation Practice (2)

Anil: Hello, Madhu, how are you?

Madhu: Fine, thanks. What are you doing here? Do you come to work even on Sunday?

Anil: No, I don't come every Sunday, but I have to do a lot of work today. Having done my work, I can play tennis with Ashwin.

Madhu: Yes, I also don't have a lot of free time. Having done this work, I have to cook. There is no food in the house.

Anil: Would you like to play tennis with Ashwin and me? Playing tennis is good for health. We play tennis at five o'clock.

Madhu: I like tennis very much but I ought to study. Can I play with both of you tomorrow?

Anil: Yes, we can play tomorrow. I have to go. I am meeting Ashwin at ten minutes to five at his house.

Madhu: Take these. These are very good sweets.

Anil: These sweets are very good. Can I give them to Ashwin?

Madhu: No, you eat these. I can make more for Ashwin tomorrow.

9.16 Songs

۱)
تو چیز بڑی ہے مست مست

تو چیز بڑی ہے مست

نہیں تجھ کو کوئی ہوش ہوش

اُس پر جوبن کا جوش جوش

نہیں تیرا، نہیں تیرا کوئی دوش دوش

مدہوش ہے تو ہر وقت وقت

تو چیز بڑی ہے مست مست

عاشق ہے تیرا نام نام

دِل لینا تیرا کام کام

میری بانہیں مت تھام تھام

بدنام ہے تو بد مست مست

200

تو چیز بڑی ہے مست مست

٢) او باغوں میں بہار ہے؟ (ہے)

کلیوں پہ نکھار ہے؟ (ہے)

او تم کو مجھ سے پیار ہے؟

(نا نا نا نا۔۔۔۔)

اے باغوں میں بہار ہے؟

بولو تم کو اقرار ہے؟ (ہاں ہے)

پھر بھی انکار ہے؟ (ہاں ہے)

او تم کو مجھ سے پیار ہے؟(نا نا نا نا۔۔۔۔)

اے باغوں میں بہار ہے؟

بولو کیا دل بیقرار ہے؟ (ہے)

مجھ پہ اعتبار ہے؟ (ہاں ہے)

جینا دشوار ہے؟ (ہے، ہے)

آج سوموار ہے؟ (ارے بابا ہے!)

تم کو مجھ سے پیار ہے؟ (ہے، ہے۔۔نا نا نا نا۔۔۔۔۔)

٣) تم سے ملنے کی تمنا ہے

پیار کا ارادہ ہے

اور ایک وعدہ ہے جانم

جو کبھی ہم ملے تو زمانہ دیکھیگا اپنا پیار۔۔۔او میرے یار!

201

Glossary for Songs

ہوش = understanding, awareness (m)

کلی = flower bud (f)

جوبن = youthfulness; adolescence (m)

نکھار = glow, shine; freshness (m)

جوش = fervor, zeal, ardor (m)

اِقرار = consent, agreement (m)

دوش = fault, blemish (m)

اِنکار = refusal, denial (m)

مدہوش = intoxicating; stupefying; perplexing

بے قرار = restless, uneasy, anxious

بانہہ = arm; sleeve (f)

اِعتبار = confidence, trust (m)

تھامنا = to hold; to seize

تمنّا = desire, wish (f)

بدنام = disreputable, infamous

وعدہ = promise (m)

بہار = spring season (f)

جانم = my beloved (Persian)

9.17 Vocabulary

to call/invite	بُلانا
to come out, to arise; to depart	نِکلنا
to depart, to set out	روانہ ہونا
cough (f)	کھانسی
to enter (formal Urdu)	تشریف لانا
essay/composition (m)	مضمُون
fever; wrath; steam (m)	بُخار
girlfriend (for girls)	سہیلی
hand (m)	ہاتھ
happiness (f)	خُوشی
hour (m)	گھنٹا

in that direction/in this direction	اُدھر/ اِدھر
intention (m)	اِرادہ
intoxicating	مست
late	دیرسے
leisure; free time (f)	فُرصت
medicine (f)	دوا، دوائی
pleasing	پسند
poor thing/fellow (f/m)	بیچارہ/بیچاری
quiet/silent	خاموش
to sell	بیچنا
to send	بھیجنا
shirt (f)	قمِیض
to sit down (formal Urdu)	تشریف رکھنا
sixty	ساٹھ
some, few; scanty, little; less	تھوڑا
stroll, walk, tour (f)	سیر
to stroll, to take a walk, to tour	سیر کرنا
tiredness (f)	تھکن
voice, sound, noise (f)	آواز
to wake up/rise	اُٹھنا/جاگنا
to wash	دھونا
worry (f. or m.)	فِکر

Chapter 10

10.1 The Verb جاننا, "To Know"

The verb جاننا, the generic form of the verb "to know," is used in the following instances:

1. When the subject desires to express familiarity/acquintance with a person.

2. When the subject expresses knowledge about a general fact or an area/field or a skill.

When جاننا is used in cases in which its object is animate or specific, then the object is marked by کو. Remember that کو is a postposition and nouns/pronouns marked by it will be in the oblique.

میں سلمان کو جانتا ہوں۔

(subject -- object -- object marker کو -- verb)

I know Salman.

میں اِس لڑکے کو جانتا ہوں۔

(subject -- object -- object marker کو -- verb)

I know this boy.

میں اُردو اور ہندی جانتا ہوں۔

I know Urdu and Hindi.

In the last example, Urdu and Hindi are inanimate objects, so they are not marked by کو.

Important note: The verb جاننا should not be confused with the verb جانا "to go." The stem of جاننا is جان while that of جانا is جا. Thus میں جانتا ہوں means "I know" while میں جاتا ہوں means "I go." Similarly, میں جانوں گا means "I will know" and میں جاؤں گا means "I will go."

10.1 Reading and Translation Drill

۱- میں صرف سلمان خان کو جانتا ہوں۔

کیا، آپ ٹام کروز کو جانتے ہیں؟

نہیں۔ مگر میری بہنیں ٹام کروز کو جانتی ہیں۔

وہ بل کلنٹن کو جانتے ہیں، کیا؟

۲- ہم عربی نہیں جانتے مگر اُردو/ہندی جانتے ہیں۔

کیا، وہ تمھارا نام جانتے ہیں؟

جی نہیں۔ وہ میرا نام نہیں جانتے۔

کیا، وہ سب لوگ انگریزی جانتے ہیں؟

۳- کیا، ہم آپ کے والد صاحب کا اسمِ شریف جان سکتے ہیں؟

اُن کے پیار کی قیمت دینا کیا جانیگی؟

کون جانتا ہے کہ پچھلی جمعرات کو کیا تاریخ تھی؟

بچپن میں، یہ بوڑھی عورت اِن سب چیزوں کے نام جانتی تھی!

10.1 Substitutions

۱- میں (اُن لڑکوں) کو جانتا ہوں۔

these girls

that beautiful girl

your brother

his family

۲- کیا، وہ (تم) کو نہیں جانتے تھے؟

these players/athletes

those students

our daughters

this clever girl

۳۔ ہم (اُردو) نہیں جانتے، مگر (انگریزی) جانتے ہیں۔

| Hindi | German |

| Gujarati | Bengali |

names of these people   their names

this famous poet   that clever boy's name

10.2 معلوم ہونا Construction

معلوم ہونا, or "to be known," is a complex verbal formation, formed with the predicate adjective معلوم and the auxiliary verb ہونا. In comparison to جاننا, the construction معلوم ہونا is used in a restricted context. It primarily denotes knowledge of one specific fact or a group of ascertainable facts such as:

1.   times of the day

2.   prices of things

3.   names of people, etc.

جاننا, being a more expansive verb "to know," can often replace معلوم ہونا, but the reverse is usually not possible. In معلوم ہونا constructions, the logical subject in English is marked by کو:

کیا، آپ کو وقت معلوم ہے؟

Do you know the time?

(Note: Although آپ is the logical subject in English, in Urdu it is actually the grammatical object, and وقت is the grammatical subject, with which the verb ہونا agrees. The literal translation of the example above is: "Is the time known to you?")

کیا، اُس کو اُن کے نام معلوم ہیں؟

Does he know their names?

In the example above, the verb ہونا is in the plural because the grammatical subject in Urdu (نام)

is plural.

مجھ کو اِس چیز کی قیمت معلوم نہیں۔

I don't know the price of this thing.

In the past tense, the appropriate form of the auxiliary تھا is used:

مجھے معلوم تھا کہ انھیں فکر تھی۔

I knew that he was worried.

Similar to the معلوم ہونا construction, but perhaps more colloquial, is one that employs the word

پتا, meaning "trace, clue, hint; address." It too is used with the verb ہونا with the logical subject

in English being marked by کو to indicate knowledge of a specific fact or piece of information.

آپ کو پتا ہے کہ شالیمار باغ کہاں ہے؟

Do you know where is the Shalimar garden?

جناب، مجھے پتا نہیں!

Sir, I don't know.

پتا may also be used with the verb چلنا, with the logical subject in English marked by کو, as the

verb "to come to know."

ہمیں اس بات کے بارے میں کب پتا چلیگا؟

When will we (come to) know about this matter?

10.2 Reading and Translation Drill

١۔ کیا، تمہیں میرے گھر کا پتا معلوم ہے؟

جی نہیں۔ ہمیں آپ کے گھر کا پتا نہیں معلوم۔

اُسے امیتابھ بچّن کے گھر کا پتا معلوم ہے، کیا؟

تمہارے گھر کا پتا کسے معلوم تھا؟

٢۔ اُن طالبِ علموں کو کل کی تاریخ نہیں معلوم تھی۔

کیا، آپ کو آج کی تاریخ معلوم ہے؟

مجھ کو آپ کی سالگرہ کی تاریخ معلوم ہے۔

کیا، آپ کو ہمارے امتحان کی تاریخ معلوم ہے؟

٣۔ ہم کو اِن قالینوں کی قیمت معلوم ہے۔

کیا، تجھ کو اِس دوائی کی قیمت معلوم تھی؟

مجھ کو اُن کتابوں کی قیمتیں معلوم ہیں۔

اُن کو اِس چائے کی قیمت نہیں معلوم۔

٤۔ کیا، آپ کو امیتابھ بچّن کی بیوی کا نام معلوم ہے؟

جی ہاں، مجھ کو معلوم ہے۔ اُن کا نام جیہ بہادُری ہے۔

کیا، تم کو امریکہ کے صدر کا نام معلوم ہے؟

نہیں، مگر مجھ کو ہندوستان کے صدر کا نام معلوم ہے۔

٥۔ کیا، آپ کو پتا نہیں کہ وہ بیچارہ بہت غریب تھا۔

کیا، اس کے ساجن کو پتا ہے کہ وہ ہر وقت اُس کو یاد کرتی ہے اور سوتی نہیں؟

ہم لوگوں کو پتا ہے کہ مجنون ایک مشہور مست عاشق تھا۔

مجھے کیا پتا تھا، میری سہیلی صرف سبزی کھائیگی۔

میری ممی کو راج کے بارے میں سب کچھ پتا تھا۔

10.3 The Verb آنا and Knowledge of Learned/ Acquired Skills

We have already encountered آنا in its meaning "to come." آنا is also used in constructions in

sentences that denote the knowledge of a learned/acquired skill. In such a construction, the

logical subject in English is marked by کو, thus becoming an object in Urdu. The verb agrees

with the grammatical subject in Urdu or the logical object in English:

مجھ کو اُردو آتی ہے۔

I know Urdu.

کیا، آپ کو سرود بجانا آتا ہے؟

Do you know how to play sarod?

In the first sentence, the verb is feminine because its grammatical subject (Urdu) is feminine. In

the second sentence, the verb is masculine because its grammatical subject, the infinitive سرود

بجانا, "to play sarod," is a verbal noun in the masculine. Note that the grammatical subject of آنا

can either be a proper noun, اُردو, or a verbal noun, بجانا. Sometimes, the agreement of the verb

will vary depending on the definition of the grammatical subject:

کیا، آپ کو گاڑی چلانا آتا ہے؟

Do you know how to drive a car?

The grammatical subject in the sentence above is گاڑی چلانا, "driving a car," hence the verb is in

the masculine.

کیا، آپ کو گاڑی چلانی آتی ہے؟

Do you know how to drive a car?

In the second example, since گاڑی is feminine, the infinitive چلانا can take on a feminine ending,

and in that case so will the verb آنا. In the past tense, the appropriate form of the auxiliary تھا is

209

used.

راج کو ناچنا آتا تھا۔

Raj used to know how to dance.

10.3 Reading and Translation Drill

١-   مجھے تیرنا آتا ہے۔

کیا، تجھے گانا آتا ہے؟

جی ہاں، مجھے گانا آتا ہے۔

اُسے ٹینس کھیلنا آتا ہے۔

٢-   اُن لڑکوں کو پکانا آتا ہے۔

اِن لڑکیوں کو کام کرنا آتا ہے۔

اُس کے لڑکے کو گاڑی چلانی نہیں آتی۔

تمہیں سکوٹر چلانا آتا ہے، کیا؟

٣-   اُسے ناچنا نہیں آتا۔

ہمیں گانا نہیں آتا۔

کیا، اِنہیں اُردو آتی ہے؟

نہیں۔ اُنہیں صرف انگریزی آتی ہے۔

10.3 Substitutions

١-   ہمیں (گانا) آتا ہے۔

how to dance

how to swim

how to cook

how to eat

۲۔ نرگس کو (لکھنا) (آتا ہے۔)

will know   how to read this book

used to know   how to cook Indian food

used to know   a little Chinese

will know   how to make yogurt

10.3 Translations

Translate the following into idiomatic Urdu:

1.   Do you know my favorite actor?

2.   I know who Javed Akhtar is, but I don't know him (personally). He is a poet, isn't he?

3.   Excuse me, sir, do you know where is the post office?

4.   My grandmother (maternal) used to know the famous actor Dilip Kumar.

5.   I know that Amitabh Bacchan is taller than you (informal).

6.   Does Nargis know how to make spaghetti with Indian spices?

10.4 The Verb پوچھنا, "To Ask"

When پوچھنا "to ask" is used in Urdu, the indirect object is followed by a سے:

میں اُس سے پوچھتا ہوں۔

I ask him.

(subject -- indirect object -- marker سے -- verb)

میں اُس عورت سے پوچھوں گی۔

I will ask that woman.

(subject -- indirect object -- marker سے--- verb)

The direct object, if animate or specific, is followed by کے بارے میں. If the object is not

211

animate or specific, the use of کے بارے میں is optional.

میں اُس سے علی کے بارے میں پوچھ رہا ہوں۔

I am asking him about Ali.

(subject -- indirect object -- marker سے -- animate direct object -- object marker کے بارے میں

-- verb)

میں اُس سے یہ بات (اِس بات کے بارے میں) پوچھتا تھا۔

I used to ask him about this matter.

(subject -- indirect object -- marker سے -- inanimate direct object -- verb)

10.4 Reading and Translation Drill

١۔ وہ مجھ سے اُس بوڑھے آدمی کا نام پوچھتا ہے۔

وہ تم سے اُن لڑکوں کے نام پوچھتا ہے۔

وہ اُن لڑکوں سے تمھارا نام پوچھتا ہے۔

ہم اُن لڑکیوں سے تمھارا نام نہیں پوچھتے۔

٢۔ تم ہم سے اُن کا پتا پوچھتے ہو؟

نہیں، میں اُس اچھی لڑکی سے اُن کا پتا پوچھتی ہوں۔

آپ کس سے اُن کا پتا پوچھ رہے ہیں؟

میں اِن ہوشیار لڑکوں سے اُن کا پتا پوچھ رہی ہوں۔

٣۔ تم یہ سوال وزیرِ اعظم کے بچّے سے کیوں پوچھ رہے ہو؟ وہ سچ نہیں بولے گا۔

جناب، آپ میرے دل کی باتیں مجھ سے نہ پوچھیئے!

وہ ہوشیار عورت پاکستان کے صدر سے ایک مشکل سوال پوچھے گی۔

شاہ رُخ جی، کیا ہم آپ سے پیار کے بارے میں دو تین سوال پوچھ سکتے ہیں؟

212

10.4 Substitutions

ا۔   (راج) سے پوچھیئے۔

That girl

These boys

My brother

Your clever friend

ٹ۔   میں (زاہد) سے (علی) کے بارے میں پوچھتا ہوں۔

that girl	your brother
that boy	these doctors
that vagabond's home	my father
Imran Khan's address	that athlete

10.5 The Verb ملنا with سے and کو

The meaning of certain verbs changes depending upon the postposition with which they are used.

1) ملنا + postposition سے to mark the object means "to meet":

میں علی سے ملتا ہوں۔

I meet (with) Ali.

وہ اُن لڑکیوں سے ملتے ہیں۔

They meet (with) those girls.

In the above sentences, the object (of meeting) is marked with سے.

2) ملنا + postposition کو to mark its logical subject in English means "to get, obtain, find":

وہاں مجھ کو خدا ملتا ہے۔

213

I find God there.

اُس کو وہ چیزیں ملتی ہیں۔

He gets those things.

آپ کو یہ کتابیں کہاں ملتی ہیں؟

Where do you get these books?

In the above sentences, the logical subject in English, that is the person/thing who is getting, obtaining, or finding something is marked by کو. Note that the verb in all the sentences agrees with the things that are being obtained or found.

10.5 Reading and Translation Drill

١۔   ہم عمران خان سے ملنا چاہتے ہیں۔

کیا، تم امریکہ کے صدر سے ملنا چاہتے ہو؟

نہیں، میں امریکہ کے صدر سے ملنا نہیں چاہتا مگر ہندوستان کے وزیرِ اعظم سے ملنا چاہتا ہوں۔

میں اُن خوبصورت لڑکیوں سے ملنا چاہتی ہوں۔

٢۔   کیا، ہم بولیوڈ میں شاہ رُخ خان سے مل سکتے ہیں؟

نہیں، آپ وہاں اُس سے نہیں مل سکتے۔

ہم بھی اُن ڈاکٹروں سے مل رہے ہیں۔

آپ اُن مشہور شاعروں سے کب ملیں گے؟

٣۔   کیا، ہم کو بازار میں یہ سندر چیزیں ملتی ہیں؟

آپ کو پاکستان میں ہر چیز مل سکتی ہے۔

آج کل یہاں کیا ملتا ہے؟

آجکل یہاں کچھ بھی نہیں ملتا۔

214

۴۔ معاف کیجئے، اُس خوبصورت لڑکی کو آنکھوں کا کاجل کہاں ملیگا؟

معاف کیجئے، ہمیں تاج محل ہوٹل میں دو کمرے ملینگے؟

معاف کیجئے، میری اِس سہیلی کو چائے کب ملیگی؟

معاف کیجئے، نرگس جی، اِس مست عاشق سے ملیئے۔ وہ آپ سے بہت پیار کرتا ہے!

Translate into Urdu:

1.   We are meeting those boys today.

2.   Can I meet that famous professor?

3.   They get all those beautiful things in India.

4.   What can you (informal) get in Canada?

5.   Those girls want to meet Shahrukh Khan.

6.   Where will I find medicine for this illness?

7.   Raj used to get sweets from this famous sweet shop.

10.6 The Verb کہنا with سے and کو

When the verb کہنا means "to tell," the person to whom something is being said or told is usually marked by سے.

میں اُن سے کہتا ہوں۔

I tell them.

میں اُن سے ایک بات کہتا ہوں۔

I tell them a thing.

When the object of کہنا is marked by کو, then it means to call the object something, usually something negative, but not necessarily so.

لوگ آپ کو کیا کہتے ہیں؟

What do people call you?

لوگ آپ کے ہونٹوں کو یاقوت کہتے ہیں۔

People call your lips rubies.

اِس چیز کو انگریزی میں کیا کہتے ہیں؟

What is this thing called in English?

10.6 Reading and Translation Drill

۱۔ میں اُن سے یہ باتیں کہتا ہوں۔

وہ مجھ سے یہ سب چیزیں کہتا ہے۔

راج نرگس کو دیکھ کر غزل کہتا ہے۔

آپ اُس سے کیا کہتے ہیں؟

کیا تم مجھ سے دِل کی باتیں کہوگے؟

۲۔ اِن چیزوں کو انگریزی میں کیا کہتے ہیں؟

کیا، شاعر کو انگریزی میں "poet" کہتے ہیں؟

کیا، لوگ آپ کو آوارہ کہتے ہیں؟

جی نہیں، لوگ مجھ کو آوارہ نہیں کہتے۔ آسمان کا تارا کہتے ہیں۔

۳۔ آپ ڈاکٹر سے کیا کہہ رہے تھے؟

تو مجھے اُلّو کہتا ہے؟! تو سب سے بڑا اُلّو ہے!

پاکستان کے صدر ہندوستان کے وزیرِ اعظم سے کیا کہہ سکتے ہیں؟

انگریزی میں نرگس کے پھول کو کیا کہتے ہیں؟

مجھے کچھ بھی کہو! پاگل کہو، مست کہو مگر میں تم سے پیار کرتا ہوں۔

Translate the following sentences into Urdu:

1.   Why are you telling me these things?

2. Tell him, "don't go there."

3. What is "love" in Urdu?

4. What does he tell your friends?

5. What does he call your friends?

10.7 Indefinite Pronouns and Adjectives

کوئی can be used as a pronoun or an adjective and, depending on context, may mean "someone, anyone, any; approximately."

وہاں کوئی کھیل رہا ہے۔

Somebody is playing over there.

When کوئی is used as a pronoun in an affirmative sentence, then it means somebody, anybody, or a particular person. کوئی as a pronoun subject is usually singular, hence the verb remains singular too. When کوئی is used with نہیں, then it means nobody.

وہاں کوئی نہیں تھا۔

Nobody was over there.

کوئی may also be used as an adjective, as in the following sentence:

کیا، کوئی آدمی آ رہا ہے؟

Is some man coming?

آپ کو لائبریری سے کوئی کتاب چاہیئے؟

Do you need any book from the library?

The oblique form of کوئی is کسی.

آپ کسی سے اس بات کے بارے میں پوچھیئے۔

You ask someone concerning this matter.

217

Before specific numbers کوئی may also be used as an adjective meaning "some, approximately."

In this case its oblique form is the same as the nominative:

اس قمیض کی قیمت کوئی تین سو روپے تھی۔

The price of this shirt was approximately three hundred rupees.

ان پچاس سیب میں کوئی چار یا پانچ خراب ہوں گے۔

Among these fifty apples, approximately four or five will be rotten.

Note: Following idiomatic usage, the noun سیب in the second sentence does not adopt its plural oblique form because a specific number -- پچاس -- precedes it.

کچھ can also be used as an indefinite pronoun or adjective. Depending on context, it may mean "something, anything; somewhat; some, any; a little."

وہاں کچھ ہے۔

There is something over there.

کچھ as an adjective means some or a few.

وہاں کچھ لڑکے کھیل رہے تھے ۔

There were some boys playing over there.

When کچھ is used with نہیں it means "nothing."

وہاں کچھ نہیں ہے۔

There is nothing over there.

When used with بھی it means "anything at all, anything whatsoever; nothing at all."

ممی ڈارلنگ آپ کو بازار سے کچھ بھی چاہیئے؟

Mummy darling, do you want anything at all from the market?

۱۔ کیا، کوئی گھر میں ہے؟

کیا، کوئی وہاں جا رہا ہے؟

نہیں، وہاں کوئی نہیں جا سکتا۔

یہ کام کوئی بھی نہیں کر سکتا ہے۔

۲۔ ذرا دیکھو! کوئی بچّہ ہماری گاڑی پر ناچ رہا ہے!

کیا، یہاں کوئی لڑکی پڑھتی ہے؟

نہیں، یہاں کوئی لڑکی نہیں پڑھتی۔

کوئی بھی لڑکا وہاں نہیں جا سکتا تھا۔

۳۔ کیا، آپ یہ باتیں کسی سے پوچھ سکتے ہیں؟

نہیں، ہم یہ باتیں کسی سے نہیں پوچھ سکتے۔

کسی ڈاکٹر کو اُس بیمار آدمی کے گھر جانا چاہیئے۔

یہاں بہت کام ہے۔ آج کسی کو کام کرنا ہے۔

۴۔ اُن کے گھر میں کچھ اچّھی چیزیں ہیں۔

کیا، آپ کے مکان میں کچھ سندر چیزیں ہیں؟

نہیں، ہمارے مکان میں کچھ بھی نہیں ہے۔

میں کچھ لڑکوں سے اِس کے بارے میں پوچھنا چاہتی ہوں۔

ریشما تو کیا کر رہی ہے؟ کچھ بھی نہیں ممی ڈارلنگ!

۵۔ نرگس ایک کمرے میں کسی سے میٹھی میٹھی باتیں کر رہی تھی!

یہ نہیں ہو سکتا! میں جانتی ہوں کہ اُس کمرے میں کوئی نہیں تھا!

دیوالی کے پروگرام میں کوئی دو سو لوگ تھے۔

اگلے مہینے پاکستان سے کوئی تین ہزار لوگ دُبئی کے لئے روانہ ہونگے۔

۶۔ گرمیوں میں اکثر اس ہوٹل میں کوئی نہیں ہوتا ہے۔

راج کی بلّی چیتا اکثر بیمار رہتی ہے۔

دلّی میں ہوائی آلودگی(air pollution) کی وجہ سے کچھ لوگوں کی طبیعت اکثر خراب رہتی ہے۔

دفتر کے اکثر لوگ آپ کی پارٹی میں نہیں آ سکینگے مگر کوئی بات نہیں!

Translate into idiomatic Urdu:

1.   Do you need some work?

2.   The poor boy is so sick on account of love that he eats nothing at all.

3.   Can anyone take (use verb لے جانا) this child to the hospital? He is somewhat sick.

4.   Is there any need (ضرورت) to go to Delhi?

5.   I think that at night you will not be able to get any taxis from the hotel.

6.   Because of air pollution, I will not stay in Los Angeles.

10.8 Fractions and Mass Measurements

Fractions

Fractions used to express quantity in Urdu are as follows:

quarter	پاؤ
half	آدھا/آدھ
3/4	پون
1 1/4	سوا
numeral + 1/4	numeral + سوا
1 1/2	ڈیڑھ
2 1/2	ڈھائی

numeral + 1/2   numeral + ساڑھے

(except for 1 1/2 and 2 1/2, see above)

Note: آدھا and پون are only used as adjectives with nouns and not with numerals.

پونے [lit. quarter less than] is used before numerals to mean three quarters.

پونے دو کیلو آم

1 3/4 kilo mangoes [lit. quarter less than two].

پونے چار گز کاٹیئے۔

Please cut 3 3/4 yards [lit. quarter less than four].

مجھے آدھی روٹی چاہیئے۔

I want half a bread.

ہمیں پون پیالی چائے چاہیئے ۔

We want 3/4 cup of tea.

Note: پونے and ساڑھے can only be used with numerals and not with nouns.

مجھے ساڑھے پانچ کیلو سیب چاہیئے ۔

I want 5 1/2 kilos of apples.

کیا، اُن کو پونے دو کیلو گوشت چاہیئے؟

Do they want 1 3/4 kilos of meat?

Review of Fractions from 1 - 4

1/4	پاؤ	1 1/4	سوا	2 1/4	سوا دو	3 1/4	سوا تین
1/2	آدھ، آدھا	1 1/2	ڈیڑھ	2 1/2	ڈھائی	3 1/2	ساڑھے تین
3/4	پون	1 3/4	پونے دو	2 3/4	پونے تین	3 3/4	پونے چار
1	ایک	2	دو	3	تین	4	چار

Note: Numbers larger than four follow the same pattern to express fractions as for the numeral 3.

Mass Measurements

In the previous chapters we have seen that mass nouns in Urdu (پانی) are treated as singular entities just like their English counterparts:

یہ پانی اچّھا ہے۔

This water is good.

Similar logic is followed for other nouns like سبزی (vegetables).

یہ سبزی اچّھی ہے۔

This vegetable is good.

The above sentence expresses the opinion that a specific type of vegetables, in mass quantity, is good. If you want to express that more than one kind of vegetables are good, then سبزی should be expressed in plural form:

یہ سبزیاں اچّھی ہیں۔

These vegetables (different kinds) are good.

As far as specific measurements are concerned, the words used to express measurements immediately precede the thing that is being measured.

ایک پیالی چینی۔

One cup (of) sugar.

دو چمچے نمک۔

Two spoons (of) salt.

Note that Urdu disposes of any possessive postpositions that are the equivalent of the English

"of."

10.9 Telling Time in Fractions

12:45	پون بجا ہے۔
1:00	ایک بجا ہے۔
1:15	سوا بجا ہے یا سوا ایک بجا ہے۔
1:30	ڈیڑھ بجا ہے۔
1:45	پونے دو بجے ہیں۔
2:00	دو بجے ہیں۔
2:15	سوا دو بجے ہیں۔
2:30	ڈھائی بجے ہیں۔
2:45	پونے تین بجے ہیں۔
3:00	تین بجے ہیں۔
3:15	سوا تین بجے ہیں۔
3:30	ساڑھے تین بجے ہیں۔

The pattern is regular from 3:30 to 12:30.

As we have seen in Chapter 9, the past participle of بجنا (بجا/بجے) is used as the Urdu equivalent of o'clock. As long as the base number is 1, time is expressed as بجا, that is, in the singular.

Note that 30 minutes past the hour is expressed through ساڑھے except in the case of 1:30 (ڈیڑھ) and 2:30 (ڈھائی). To express am or pm, times of the day such as صبح, دوپہر, شام, and رات are used.

1:45 pm	دوپہر (کے) پونے دو بجے۔

Write out the following times in Urdu:

5:45 pm, 6.30 am, 7:15 am, 12:45 am, 2:30 am, 2:45 pm, 1:15 pm, 8:00 am, 1:30 am, 11:45 pm

10.9 Reading and Translation Drill

۱۔ مجھ کو پاؤ کیلو چاول چاہئے۔

کیا، آپ کو آدھ کیلو چینی چاہئے؟

جی نہیں، مجھ کو پون کیلو چینی چاہئے۔

ہم کو سوا دو کیلو پیاز چاہئے۔

۲۔ سنئے، کیا یہاں ڈیڑھ کیلو مرچ مل سکتی ہے؟

معاف کیجئے، آپ کو یہاں ڈیڑھ کیلو مرچ نہیں مل سکتی۔ یہ مٹھائی کی دکان ہے!

میں ساڑھے پانچ کیلو پھل خریدنا چاہتا ہوں۔

کیا، آپ بھی ساڑھے پانچ کیلو پھل خریدنا چاہتے ہیں؟

۳۔ اُن لڑکیوں کو پونے آٹھ کیلو سیب چاہئے۔

ہمیں آدھ کیلو سبزی چاہئے۔

کیا، تمہیں چار پیالی دودھ چاہئے؟

نہیں، مجھے صرف چار چمچے دودھ چاہئے۔

Answer the following questions in complete Urdu sentences:

۱۔ آپ ہالی ووڈ میں کس کو جانتے ہیں؟

۲۔ کیا، آپ سنسکرت جانتے ہیں؟

۳۔ کیا وقت ہے؟

۴۔ کیا، آپ کو امریکہ کے صدر کا نام معلوم ہے؟

۵۔ کیا، آپ کے دوست کو اِلزبیتھ ٹیلر کے گھر کا پتا معلوم ہے؟

۶۔ کیا، آپ کو گاڑی چلانی آتی ہے؟

۷۔ کوئی آپ کو آلّو بنا سکتا ہے؟

224

٨۔ کیا، آپ کو تیرنا آتا ہے؟

٩۔ آپ جارج بُش سے کیا پوچھنا چاہتے ہیں؟

١٠۔ آپ بولی ووڈ میں کس سے ملنا چاہتے ہیں؟

١١۔ آپ یونیورسٹی میں کیا پڑھتے ہیں؟

١٢۔ اُردو میں "student" کو کیا کہتے ہیں؟

١٣۔ کیا، آپ کسی کے ساتھ رہتے ہیں؟

١٤۔ آپ ہر روز ڈھائی بجے کیا کرتے ہیں؟

١٥۔ آج کیا تاریخ ہے؟

10.10 Cardinal Numbers 61-70

٦١   اِکسٹھ

٦٢   باسٹھ

٦٣   تِرسٹھ (تریسٹھ)

٦٤   چونسٹھ

٦٥   پینسٹھ

٦٦   چھیاسٹھ

٦٧   سرسٹھ (سڑسٹھ)

٦٨   اڑسٹھ

٦٩   اُنہتّر

٧٠   ستّر

پتاجی (ممّی سے): میری جان! کیا مجھے اور مٹھائی مِل سکتی ہے؟

ممّی: نہیں۔کیا، آپ کو معلوم نہیں کہ مٹھائی آپ کی صحّت کے لئے خراب ہے؟

پتاجی: او ہو! ہاں، مجھے یہ تو معلوم ہے۔ مگر میں کیا کر سکتا ہوں؟ مٹھائی مجھ کو بہت پسند ہے۔

نرگس: کیا، انکل بیمار ہیں؟

ممّی: نہیں، یہ بیمار نہیں ہیں۔ چار سال پہلے تمہارے انکل بہت مٹھائی کھاتے تھے اور اُس کی وجہ سے اُن کی طبیعت خراب رہتی تھی۔ دِن رات ہم ہسپتال میں گزارتے تھے۔ میں گھر کا کچھ بھی کام نہیں کر سکتی تھی۔ اِن کے ڈاکٹر صاحب اب بھی کہتے ہیں کہ مٹھائی دِل کے لئے اچھی نہیں اور اُنہیں مٹھائی نہیں کھانی چاہیئے۔

نرگس: ہاں، یہ تو سچ ہے۔ آپ کے ڈاکٹر کون ہیں؟

پتاجی: اُن کا نام انوپ سنگھ ہے۔ کیا، تم اُن کو جانتی ہو؟

نرگس: ہاں، ہاں، میں اُن کو اور اُن کی بیوی کو اچھی طرح جانتی ہوں۔ وہ دونوں بہت اچھّے انسان ہیں۔ کیا، اُن کو معلوم ہے کہ میں راج کی دوست ہوں؟

ممّی: نہیں، یہ اُن کو نہیں معلوم۔ اچھّا بیٹی، کیا تم کو گانا آتا ہے؟

نرگس: جی؟ میری آواز اچھی نہیں، میں بچپن میں گاتی تھی مگراب میں اچھّا ناچتی ہوں اور مجھے کتھک بہت پسند ہے۔

پتاجی: واہ! کیا، تم ابھی ہمارے سامنے ناچ سکتی ہو؟

نرگس: انکل آج نہیں مگر کل میرا پروگرام ہے اور آپ لوگ اُس میں آ سکتے ہیں۔

ممّی: کل تو ہم مصروف ہیں۔ میری سہیلی بہت بیمار ہے۔ اُس سے ملنا ہے۔ اچھّا بیٹی، گھر میں مٹھائی بہت ہے۔ تم یہ مٹھائی ہسپتال میں کسی کو دے سکتی ہو؟

نرگس: آنٹی ہسپتال میں کوئی بھی مٹھائی نہیں کھائے گا۔

(راج گھر میں آتا ہے)

راج: نہیں، نہیں، تم رادھا کو مٹھائی دے سکتی ہو۔ رادھا بھی بہت میٹھی ہے!

نرگس: بس راج۔ اب مجھے جانا ہے۔ تم رادھا کو مٹھائی دے سکتے ہو اور اس کی
میٹھی میٹھی باتیں ہر وقت سن سکتے ہو!!

ممّی: یہ رادھا کون ہے؟ کیا، تمہاری سہیلی ہے؟

نرگس: یہ آپ راج سے پوچھئے۔ اُس کو رادھا بہت پسند ہے۔ دیکھو راج! ساڑھے
گیارہ بجے ہیں۔ کل صبح مجھ کو کام کرنا ہے۔

راج: اچّھا، اچّھا، تم ناراض کیوں ہو؟ رادھا میٹھی نہیں۔ تم سب سے زیادہ میٹھی
ہو۔ اب بیٹھو گی؟

نرگس: نہیں۔ نہیں بیٹھوں گی راج! اچّھا، آنٹی، انکل، میں اب جانا چاہتی ہوں۔
اِجازت چاہتی ہوں۔ ہم پھر ملیں گے۔

ممّی + پتاجی: خدا حافظ بیٹی۔

راج: چلو میں بھی تمہارے ساتھ چلتا ہوں۔

نرگس: نہیں۔ رادھا کے پاس جاؤ!

10.12 Conversation Practice

Anil: Hello Usha. This is my friend Seema. We are going to buy *paan* for Seema's mother.

Usha: Yes, I know Seema. She studies with me.

Seema: How are you, Usha?

Usha: Fine, thanks. Anil, do you know how to drive a car?

Anil: No, I don't. But Seema knows how to drive a car. Where do you have to go?

Usha: I have to go to Shehla's house. She is very ill. But her house is very far and the bus always (ہمیشہ) leaves late.

Seema: I know Shehla. She is a good friend of mine. Can we come along with you to Shehla's house?

Usha: Of course. I have to buy some fruits for Shehla. Can we all go to the fruitseller's shop?

Anil: Do you know the address of the fruitseller's shop?

Usha: Yes, it is near that big hospital.

Anil: OK, let's go after half an hour. Seema and I will be here with the car at 4:30 pm. Be ready!

10.13 Songs

۱) مجھے کچھ کہنا ہے
مجھے بھی کچھ کہنا ہے
پہلے تم! پہلے تم!
دیکھو جس طرح لکھنؤ کے دو نوابوں کی
گاڑی پہلے آپ (x۴) کر کے نکل گئی تھی
اِس طرح ہماری پہلے تم (x۴) میں یہ
مستی بھری رُت نہ چلی جائے
اچّھا میں کہتی ہوں۔۔۔۔اکثر کوئی لڑکی اس حال میں
کسی لڑکے سے سولہویں سال میں
جو کہتی ہے وہ مجھے کہنا ہے۔
اکثر کوئی لڑکا اس حال میں کسی لڑکی سے
سولہویں سال میں جو کہتا ہے، وہ مجھے کہنا ہے۔
اکثر کوئی لڑکی۔۔۔اکثر کوئی لڑکا۔۔۔اکثر کوئی لڑکی۔۔۔اس حال میں۔۔۔

228

۲)	ایک پیار کا نغمہ ہے
موجوں کی روانی ہے
زندگی اور کچھ بھی نہیں
تیری میری کہانی ہے
کچھ پا کر کھونا ہے
کچھ کھو کر پانا ہے
جیون کا مطلب تو آنا اور جانا ہے
دو پل کے جیون سے ایک عمر چرانی ہے
زندگی اور کچھ بھی نہیں۔۔۔۔

Glossary for Songs

موج = wave (f)
روانی = flow, flux, going (f)
جیون = life, existence; livelihood (m)

نواب = a lord, prince, governor (m)
رُت = season (f)
مستی بھری رُت = season filled with intoxication
نغمہ = song, melody (m)

10.14 Vocabulary

address; hint, clue, trace (m)	پتا
to come to know; to find out	پتا چلنا
air, wind (f)	ہَوا
aerial	ہَوائی
air pollution (f)	ہَوائی آلودگی
to be/become upset, angry	ناراض ہونا
birthday (f)	سالگرہ

229

to call (something a name) (use with کو)	کہنا
cup (f)	پیالی
date/history (f)	تاریخ
to drive	چلانا
to drive a car	گاڑی چلانا
to find	پانا
generally, often; most; many	اکثر
half	آدھ/آدھا
(numeral + half)	ساڑھے
kilogram	کیلو
to know	جاننا، معلوم ہونا
life, lifetime; also age (f)	عُمر
to lose	کھونا
manner, style (f)	طرح
minister (government) (m/f)	وزیر
prime minister (m/f)	وزیرِ اعظم
nobody	کوئی نہیں
nothing	کچھ نہیں
one and a quarter	سَوا
one and a half	ڈیڑھ
owl; fool; stupid (m)	اُلّو

permission (f)	اِجازت
to give permission (to leave)	اِجازت دینا
to play (an instrument)	بجانا
price, cost (f)	قیمت
purpose, intent; motive (m)	مطلب
quarter	پاؤ
question (m)	سوال
numeral less than a quarter (m)	پونے
seventy	سَتّر
somebody/anybody; some	کوئی
something/anything	کچھ
speech, word; thing (abstract);	بات
matter; affair (f)	
to spend time, to pass time	گُزارنا
spoon; sycophant (colloquial)(m)	چمچہ
to steal	چُرانا
sugar (f)	چینی
sweet	میٹھا
to swim	تیرنا
temperament, health (f)	طبیعت
three-quarters	پون
true (adj.); truth (m)	سچ

two and a half ڈھائی

Chapter 11

11.1 The Interrogative کیسا

The meaning of کیسا depends upon its location in the sentence. When کیسا appears before the noun it is modifying, it can be translated as "what kind of." When کیسا appears before the verb it can be translated as "how." Its oblique form کیسے is often used adverbially.

وہ کیسی لڑکیاں ہیں؟

What kind of girls are those?

وہ کیسے لڑکے تھے؟

What kind of boys were those?

آپ کی بیٹی کیسی ہے؟

How is your daughter?

وہ آپ سے کیسے ملیگا؟

How will he meet you?

Note that کیسا, when not being used adverbially, acts as a marked adjective and agrees in number and gender with the noun it modifies.

11.1 Reading and Translation Drill

۱۔ یہ کیسی سبزی ہے؟

یہ کیسا شہر ہے؟

وہ کیسے لوگ تھے؟

وہ کیسی قالینیں تھیں؟

233

۲۔ آپ کے والد صاحب کیسے ہیں؟

اُس لڑکی کی صحت کیسی ہے؟

اُن کے دوست کیسے تھے؟

تمہارا کتّا کیسا تھا؟

۳۔ تمہیں یہ بات کیسے معلوم تھی؟

آپ اِس پُرانی کنگھی سے کیسے کنگھی کریںگے۔

وہاں ریڈیو چل رہا ہے! کتنا شور ہے! مریض کیسے آرام کر سکیں گے؟

ہمیں اس بات کا مطلب کیسے معلوم ہوگا؟

11.2 The Interrogative کتنا

کتنا, "how much, how many," like کیسا, acts like a marked adjective and agrees in gender and

number with the noun it modifies.

آپ کی کلاس میں کتنی لڑکیاں ہیں؟

How many girls are in your class?

ہسپتال میں کتنے مریض تھے؟

How many patients were there in the hospital?

اُن کا گھر کتنا بڑا ہے؟

How big is their house?

کتنا can also be used in an exclamatory manner.

اُن کا گھر کتنا بڑا ہے!

Their house is so big!

11.2 Reading and Translation Drill

ا۔ آپ اس دوکان سے کتنی پیالیاں خریدنی چاہتے ہیں؟

آج ویلیم کو کتنے کپڑے دھونے ہیں؟

تمہارا مکان کتنا بڑا ہے؟

تیرے کتنے دوست ہیں؟

۲۔ یہ شہر کتنا خوبصورت ہے!

وہ لڑکیاں کتنی سُندر ہیں!

ٹام کروز کتنا اچّھا اداکار ہے!

آپ کتنے خراب ہیں!

۳۔ ریشما کتنی میٹھی باتیں کر رہی ہے!

اُس فیکٹری (کارخانے) میں کتنی عورتیں کام کرتی تھیں؟

ایک ہوشیار طالبِ علم ایک سال میں کتنی کتابیں پڑھ سکتا ہے؟

اتنا کم مرغی کا سالن کتنے مہمان کھا سکیں گے؟

11.3 Expressing "To Have"

Urdu does not have the verb equivalent of the English "to have." Instead, Urdu uses three different constructions to convey the corresponding meaning of the English "to have." These constructions depend on the nature of the object possessed.

1. *Expressing human relationships, legal ownership, and parts of the body.*

In such a construction, the possessive adjectives or possessive postpositions کا، کے، کی are used with the logical subject in English. The appropriate form of the verb ہونا (in present, past, or future tenses) agrees with the object being possessed. For example:

میرے دو لڑکے ہیں۔

I have two boys.

(possessive adjective -- object of possession -- verb)

235

میری دس اُنگلیاں ہیں۔

I have ten fingers.

بیچارے لڑکے کا کوئی نہیں ہے۔

The poor boy has no one.

اُس آدمی کا ایک گھر تھا۔

That man had a house.

اگلے سال حسین کی بھی بیوی ہوگی۔

Next year Hussein too will have a wife.

11.3 Reading and Translation Drill (1)

١۔ ہمارے دس دوست ہیں۔

اُن کے چار بھائی ہیں۔

اُس کی دو بہنیں ہیں۔

میری پانچ سہیلیاں ہیں۔

٢۔ تیری دو آنکھیں ہیں۔

ہماری ایک ناک ہے۔

رادھا کے دو ہاتھ ہیں۔

میرے لمبے بال ہیں۔

٣۔ کیا، تمہارا بڑا گھر ہے؟

کیا، تمہاری کوئی اولاد ہے؟

اُن کے دو پیر ہیں۔

ارے! آپ نہیں جانتے کہ اُس عورت کے تین شوہر ہیں!

٤۔ اُن کے پندرہ مکان تھے۔

کیا، آپ کی زمین تھی؟

ہماری بیس دوکانیں تھیں۔

کیا، اُس کے کوئی رشتہ دار تھے؟

2.   *Expressing possession of material, movable objects.*

In order to express possession of material, movable objects, the postposition کے پاس or "near"

is used with nouns or pronouns representing the logical subject in English. The verb ہونا, in all

its tenses, agrees with the object being possessed. Note that several pronouns adopt their

possessive forms when used with کے پاس. For example کے پاس + میں = میرے پاس

اُس عورت کے پاس بہت پیسے ہیں۔

That woman has a lot of money.

(logical subject in English -- کے پاس -- object of possession -- verb)

کیا، آپ کے پاس یہ چیزیں ہیں؟

Do you have these things?

میرے پاس صرف دو کتابیں تھیں۔

I only had two books.

کیا، کل تمہارے پاس دکان میں مٹھائی ہو گی؟

Tomorrow you will have sweets in the shop?

11.3 Reading and Translation Drill (2)

ا۔   کیا، آپ کے پاس بہت ڈالر ہیں؟

جی نہیں، میرے پاس ایک بھی ڈالر نہیں۔

اُن کے پاس بہت پیسے ہیں۔

ہم غریب ہیں۔ ہمارے پاس ایک بھی پیسہ نہیں۔

٢۔ اُن کے پاس تین ہوائی جہاز ہیں۔

ہمارے بھائی کے پاس یہ گاڑی ہے۔

اُن کی بہن کے پاس وہ اچّھی کتاب ہے۔

میرے والد کے پاس وہ خوبصورت قلم ہے۔

٣۔ دوکاندار کے پاس چینی نہیں تھی۔

بس میڈم! مجھے اور کھانا نہیں چاہیئے! میرے پاس بہت چاول ہیں!

چور کے پاس کچھ بھی پیسے نہیں تھے۔ صرف کچرا تھا!

تیرے پاس بہترین چائے ہے۔ تو کہاں سے خریدتی ہے؟

3. *Expressing abstract possessions.*

As already discussed in Chapter 9, the postposition کو is used with the subject in order to convey abstract possessions.

مجھے بہت کام ہے۔

I have a lot of work.

اُس کو بُخار ہے۔

He has fever.

ہمیں فِکر تھی۔

We were worried.

اُنہیں بالکل فُرصت نہیں تھی۔

They did not have any free time at all.

نہ سونے کی وجہ سے اُن کو تھکن ہے۔

On account of not sleeping, they are tired (lit. they have tiredness/fatigue).

کیا، آپ کو اِس چیز کی ضرورت ہے؟

Do you need this thing? (Do you have the necessity of this thing?)

Note: ضرورت is feminine, hence the possessive particle preceding it will always be کی. The expression is x کی ضرورت ہونا, to have need of x.

11.3 Reading and Translation Drill (3)

١۔ آج ہمیں بہت کام ہوگا۔

جمعرات کو اُن کو کام ہوگا۔

کیا، آپ کو پیر کو بہت کام ہے؟

نہیں، پیر کو مجھے بہت کام نہیں۔

٢۔ اُس لڑکی کو بُخار تھا۔

ہمارے لڑکے کو بہت بُخار ہے۔

میرے دوست کو بُخار ہے۔

اُن کی سہیلی کو بُخار ہے۔

٣۔ کیا، اُس کو کھانسی تھی؟

ہمیں بہت کھانسی تھی۔

اُن لڑکوں کو کھانسی ہے۔

اُس کے دوست کو کھانسی ہے۔

٤۔ اُن طالبِ علموں کو زُکام ہے۔

کیا، آپ کو زُکام تھا؟

نہیں، مجھ کو زُکام نہیں تھا۔

ہمیں بُخار ہے اور ہمارے دوستوں کو زُکام ہے۔

٥۔ اُنہیں اِس بات کی بہت فِکر تھی۔

اُس لڑکے کو ہماری بہت فِکر ہے۔

239

مجھے اِس بات کا بہت غم تھا۔

ہمارے لڑکوں کو اُس کا بہت غم تھا۔

Translate the following sentences into Urdu:

1.   I have three brothers and one sister.

2.   Do you (formal) have two eyes?

3.   Bill Gates has a lot of money. People say he is the richest man in the world.

4.   We will have a lot of free time. We should not spend it (گزارنا) in doing useless things.

5.   They have a lot of work, but they ought to go there.

6.   Nargis will also need (ضرورت) to have her teeth examined.

7.   The patient doesn't have a fever but has a cough.

8.   Do you have a need for a lot of love in your life?

9.   I was very worried about these things.

10.   Excuse me, sir. Do you sell combs? I don't have one; I want to buy a good comb.

11.   The landlord in this village has a lot of land and money, but he does not help the poor.

11.4 The Possessive Adjective اپنا

When the subject of the sentence is also the possessor of a noun in that sentence, then the

declinable possessive adjective اپنا is used:

میں اپنے پروفیسر سے ہر روز ملتا ہوں۔

I meet my (own) professor every day.

وہ اپنی لڑکی سے ملتی ہے۔

She meets with her (own) daughter.

مجھے اپنا کام کرنا چاہئے۔

I ought to do my (own) work.

ہمارے لڑکے اپنے دوستوں کے ساتھ فٹبال کھیلیں گے۔

Our boys will play football with their (own) friends.

Note: اپنا immediately precedes the possessed object and agrees in number and gender with the possessed object. اپنا is also used to emphasize the possessor/owner of nouns. In such circumstances, اپنا follows the possessive noun or adjective:

یہ اُس کی اپنی چیز ہے۔

This is his (very own) thing.

وائیٹ ہاؤس پریزیڈنٹ کا اپنا گھر نہیں، امریکن لوگوں کا گھر ہے۔

The White House is not the president's (own) house, it is the house of the American people.

11.4 Reading and Translation Drill

۱- میں اپنی گاڑی چلا رہا تھا۔

وہ اپنی کتاب پڑھ رہے تھے۔

کیا، تم وہاں اپنا کام کر سکتے تھے؟

اُن کی وجہ سے ہم اپنا گھر صاف نہیں کر سکتے تھے۔

۲- کیا، آپ اپنی لڑکی کو ہارورڈ بھیجنا چاہتے تھے؟

ہم اپنے لڑکوں کو برکلی بھیجنا چاہتے ہیں۔

وہ اپنے نوکر کو بازار بھیج سکتا ہے۔

تم اپنے طالبِ علموں کو اردو کی مفید کتابیں خریدنے کے لئے کہاں بھیجو گے؟

۳- یہ میرا اپنا گھر نہیں۔

کیا، یہ تمہاری اپنی گاڑی ہے؟

ہم کو ہمارے اپنے قلم پسند تھے۔

اُن کو اُن کی اپنی کتابیں پسند نہیں تھیں۔

11.5 The Reflexive Pronoun خود

خود is a reflexive pronoun that refers back to the subject of the sentence in a manner similar to

that of the English "self" or "selves."

میں خود پڑھتا ہوں۔

I myself study.

وہ خود وہاں جاتے ہیں۔

They themselves go there.

11.5 Reading and Translation Drill

۱۔   یہ کام میں خود کر رہا تھا۔

کیا، آپ خود وہاں رہ سکتے تھے؟

ہم تو سبزی خور ہیں۔ ہم خود شاکاہاری کھانا پکائینگے۔

اُن کو خود جانا چاہیئے۔

۲۔   اُس کو خود پڑھنا ہے۔

یہ کتابیں وہ خود پڑھ سکتا ہے۔

تم خود بھی بیکار باتیں کرتے ہو۔

بل کلنٹن خود بھی یہاں رہتے ہیں۔

۳۔   بچّوں کی والدہ خود رو رہی تھیں۔

راج خود چور کو پکڑیگا۔

پاکستان کے صدر خود یہاں تشریف لائینگے۔

یہاں کا راجہ خود بہار میں اس خوبصورت باغ میں سیر کرتا تھا۔

242

Translate the following sentences into English:

1.   We will eat with our friends tomorrow.

2.   This is his (very own) idea.

3.   Madonna herself is singing tonight.

4.   Do you (informal) yourself study at Princeton?

5.   I used to go to India with my family every December.

6.   We do not cook meat in our house.

7.   Do you yourself know how to play the piano?

8.   Abid himself was helping Nilofer.

9.   Their life was so busy that they themselves could not rest.

10.   In his childhood, the old man had his (very own) hair and teeth.

11.   Please stop (prevent) your children from playing with the flowers in the garden.

11.6 Noun + والا

When the suffix والے/والی/والا is attached to an oblique noun, it frequently signifies the doer, seller or user of that noun. In the case of place names, a construction with والا indicates the resident of a place. Several of these expressions with this suffix have idiomatic meanings that are also listed here.

Feminine	*English*	*Masculine*
پھل والی	fruit seller	پھل والا
سبزی والی	vegetable seller	سبزی والا
جوتے والی	shoe seller	جوتے والا
تانگے والی	tonga driver	تانگے والا

گاؤں والی	villager	گاؤں والا
گھر والی	wife, husband	گھر والا
کام والی	one who does work, servant	کام والا
دلّی والی	a Delhi resident	دلّی والا

یہاں بہت پھل والے رہتے ہیں۔

Many fruit sellers live here.

آپ کی گھر والی کیا کرتی ہے؟

What does your wife do?

اخبار والا روز ہمارے گھر آتا تھا۔

The newspaper man used to come to our house every day.

In some instances, the addition of the والا suffix to a noun may result in an adjective:

مجھے دودھ والی چائے پسند ہے۔

I like tea with milk.

11.7 Adjective + والا

The suffix والا can be added to adjectives in order to avoid ambiguity or to lay emphasis. In such an instance والا, like the adjective to which it is attached, will agree with the noun it is modifying.

مجھے وہ لال والی ٹوپی دیجیے۔

Please give me that red hat.

You would say this if you are pointing to the red hat as opposed to hats of other colors.

11.8 Postposition or Adverb + والا

The addition of the والا suffix to an adverb or postposition transforms it into an adjective or a noun.

کیا، وہ اُوپر والے کمرے میں رہتا ہے؟

Does he stay in the upstairs room?

وہ باہر والی لڑکی ہے۔

She is the girl who was/is outside.

اُوپر والا ہم کو ہر وقت دیکھتا ہے۔

God (lit. The One Above) watches us all the time.

مجھے نیچے والی ساڑی دکھائیے۔

Please show me the sari that is underneath.

11.6-11.8 Reading and Translation Drill

۱۔   وہ پھل والا وہاں جائیگا۔

ہم گاؤں والے ہیں۔ ہم کو وہاں کا پتا نہیں معلوم۔

یہاں سب کام والے ہیں، بیکار نہیں۔

میں اُوپر والے سے ڈرتا ہوں۔

۲۔   یہ امریکہ والے بہت ہوشیار ہوتے ہیں۔

کیا، پاکستان والے سندر ہوتے ہیں؟

گاؤں والے اچّھے ہوتے ہیں، کیا؟

شہر والے اچّھے نہیں ہوتے۔

۳۔   مجھے وہ کالی والی پتلون پسند ہے۔

کیا، آپ کو یہ لال والی ساڑی پسند ہے؟

ہمیں وہ سفید والی کتاب دیجیئے۔

یہ نیلا والا گھر اچّھا ہے۔

۴۔ وہ اندر والی دوکان میں کام کر رہا ہے۔

کیا، تم اُوپر والے کمرے میں رہ سکوگے؟

وہ بات باہر والی لڑکیوں کو معلوم تھی۔

تم نیچے والی کھڑکی بند کرو۔

۵۔ شرمیلا پرسوں والا اخبار پڑھ رہی تھی۔

پولیس والے یہاں والے چوروں کو اچّھی طرح جانتے تھے۔

کیا آپ کو معلوم ہے کہ سامنے والا گھر کس کا تھا؟

میں آپ کی بیٹی کے لئے وہ چھوٹی والی کرسی ابھی لاتا ہوں۔

11.9 Oblique Infinitive + والا

When the suffix والا is attached to the oblique infinitive it can be used in two different ways. In the first usage it indicates the performer of the action of the infinitive.

پھل بیچنے والے وہاں رہتے ہیں۔

The fruit sellers live over there.

آپ کی کام کرنے والی کہاں جا رہی ہے؟

Where is your worker going?

Note that والا will decline according to the number and gender of the performer of the action of the infinitive. In the second usage the oblique infinitive used with the والا suffix is used to denote immediate future or actions about to happen or take place. In such cases, the conjugated form of ہونا follows the والا suffix. The suffix will agree in number and gender with the subject.

میں ہندوستان جانے والا ہوں۔

I am about to go to India.

وہ کام کرنے والی ہے۔

She is about to work.

Note: In the last example above there is ambiguity in meaning. The sentence can be translated either as "She is about to work" or "She is a worker."

If the oblique infinite + والا construction is part of a phrase, it is best translated in English as a relative clause, beginning with "who," "which," or "that" as may be appropriate:

اس ہوائی جہاز میں بنگلا دیش جانے والے لوگ تھے۔

In this airplane there were people who were going to Bangladesh.

اس کے خیال میں گوشت کھانے والے آدمی کی صحت بہت اچّھی نہیں ہوتی۔

He thinks that the health of a person who eats meat is generally not good.

11.9 Reading and Translation Drill

١۔   یہاں سبزی بیچنے والے آتے ہیں۔

کیا، آپ اُس کپڑے بیچنے والے کو جانتے ہیں؟

اب اخبار خریدنے والے آئینگے۔

کیا، پڑھنے والے لڑکے کھیل سکتے ہیں؟

٢۔   میں کھانا پکانے والا ہوں۔

وہ لڑکیاں جانے والی ہیں۔

ہمارا دوست آنے والا ہے۔

کیا، تم سونے والے ہو؟

٣۔   ابھی شیلا آپ کو ٹیلیفون کرنے والی تھی۔

بہت زیادہ شراب پینے والے آدمیوں کو یہاں سے نکالو!

زیادہ سوال پوچھنے والا وہ طالبِ علم آج کلاس میں نہیں تھا۔

دیر سے آنے والے لوگوں کو یہاں تشریف رکھنا چاہیئے۔

247

Translate into Urdu:

1. He is a Delhi resident and he doesn't like Mumbai. He ought to go back.

2. That fruit seller will not be able to sell shoes.

3. I am about to buy that white hat. Do you like it?

4. His family has money and they are about to go to Las Vegas.

5. Many workers will not be able to go to work tomorrow because they have the flu.

6. They are about to sell their beautiful house in Lahore.

7. There is a lot more heat and sunshine in the big room that is upstairs.

8. The woman who drives the red car used to live in that big red house.

9. The train from New York will be arriving late. It is about to leave New York now.

11.10 Cardinal Numbers 71-80

۷۱	اِکہتّر
۷۲	بہتّر
۷۳	تہتّر
۷۴	چوہتّر
۷۵	پچھتّر
۷۶	چھہتّر
۷۷	ستہتّر (ستّر)
۷۸	اٹھتّر
۷۹	اُنیاسی (اُناسی)
۸۰	اسّی

248

11.11 گفتگو (Conversation)

راج: تم کیسی ہو؟ کیا، تم اپنے دوستوں کے ساتھ سنیما نہیں جا رہی ہو؟

نرگس: نہیں راج۔ آج میری طبیعت خراب ہے۔ مجھے بہت کھانسی اور بُخار ہے۔ کل رات کو میرے پیٹ میں درد بھی تھا۔

راج: کیا، تم ہسپتال چلنا چاہتی ہو؟

نرگس: ہاں مگر آج مجھے بہت کام ہے۔ کل جاؤنگی۔

راج: تم کتنی پاگل ہو! کل تو میں تمہارے ساتھ نہیں چل سکونگا۔ آج میرے پاس گاڑی ہے اور مجھے فرصت بھی ہے۔

نرگس: ہاں، ہاں، میں خود جانا چاہتی ہوں۔ مگر مجھے فرصت نہیں۔ بہت کام ہے۔

راج: تم اِس حالت میں کام کرنے والی ہو؟ میں کچھ سننا نہیں چاہتا۔ ہمیں اب ہسپتال جانا ہے! کیا، تمہارا کوئی دوست آج کام کر رہا ہے؟

نرگس: مجھے نہیں معلوم۔ اچّھا مجھ کو وہ کالے والے جوتے دو۔

(راج اور نرگس ہسپتال جاتے ہیں۔)

راج: یہ نیا ہسپتال کتنا سُندر ہے! یہاں کتنے مریض رہ سکتے ہیں؟

نرگس: کوئی دو سو۔ اچّھا، یہاں گاڑی روکو۔ میں زیادہ دور نہیں چل سکتی۔

راج: ٹھیک ہے۔ میں تمہارے پیچھے آتا ہوں۔

(راج اور نرگس، ڈاکٹر کے دفتر میں۔)

ڈاکٹر: نمستے نرگس جی۔ کیا حال ہے؟

نرگس: میری طبیعت دو دن سے ٹھیک نہیں۔ کھانسی، بُخار اور پیٹ میں بھی درد ہے۔

ڈاکٹر: میرے خیال میں فلو ہے۔ کیا، آپ کو کل رات کو درد کے ساتھ دست آ

رہے تھے؟

نرگس: ہاں۔ پیٹ میں بہت درد تھا۔ اب ذرا بہتر ہے۔

ڈاکٹر: اچّھا۔ آپ اپنے خون، پاخانے اور پیشاب کا معائنہ کرائیے۔ آج کل شہر میں اسٹوماک فلو چل رہا ہے۔ آپ کو اچھی طرح آرام کرنا چاہیے۔

نرگس: یہ تو بہت مشکل ہوگا ۔ مجھے بہت زیادہ کام کرنا ہے۔

ڈاکٹر: کل دو انگریز میرے ہسپتال میں تھے۔ اُن کے پیٹ میں بھی بہت درد تھا۔وہ بہت پریشان تھے۔مگر آج وہ بالکل ٹھیک ہیں اور اِس وقت ٹینس کھیل رہے ہیں۔ میں آپ کو بھی ایک اچّھی دوائی دونگا۔ آپ خود ڈاکٹر ہیں اور جانتی ہیں کہ یہ خطرناک بات نہیں ہے۔ آپ کل تک بالکل ٹھیک ہو جائینگے۔ مگر پیشاب، پاخانے اور خون کا مُعائنہ ضرور کرائیے۔

راج: ہاں، ڈاکٹر صاحب۔ مُعائنہ کرانا ہے۔ اِن کو کھانے میں کیا کھانا چاہیے؟

ڈاکٹر: نیمبو کا شربت اورکیلے پیٹ کے درد کے لئے اچّھے ہوتے ہیں۔ لوگ کہتے ہیں کہ چاول اور دہی بھی مُفید ہیں۔ بُخار کم ہونے کے لئے ٹائیلنول لیجیے۔

نرگس: شکریہ ڈاکٹر صاحب۔ ہم پھر ملینگے۔

ڈاکٹر: نرگس جی، آرام کیجیے۔زیادہ کام مت کیجیے۔

نرگس: اچّھا، میں آرام کرونگی۔

11.12 Conversation Practice

Doctor: How are you doing today?

Anil: I have a stomach ache and severe cough. I also have a fever. Since yesterday I have

diarrhea.

Doctor: Please open your mouth. Does it hurt here?

Anil: Yes, a lot!

Doctor: I think you have the flu. I'll give you medicine. Drink a lot of water and get (literally, take) rest. Drink very little milk for two or three days. It is not very good for your stomach.

Anil:	Do you have a daughter?

Doctor: Yes, her name is Reena. Do you know her?

Anil:	Yes, she is in my class. Sometimes both of us study in the library.

Doctor: You ought to come to our house sometime. I have two sons and you can play tennis

with them. When will you be able to come?

Anil:	Thanks. Can I come to your house Friday evening? Are you busy at that time?

Doctor: No, no. We are free. Eat dinner with us. What would you like to eat? My wife is from

Hyderabad. She cooks Hyderabadi food very well.

Anil:	I like Indian food very much, but I don't eat meat. Also I don't like very hot food.

Doctor: We also don't eat meat. We are vegetarians. Don't worry. My wife only puts a little

pepper in our food. So we'll meet you Friday evening. Get (literally, take) a lot of rest.

Anil:	Thank you and good-bye. We'll meet again.

11.13 Songs

۱)	اچّھا تو ہم چلتے ہیں
	پھر کب ملو گے؟
	جب تم کہو گے
	جمعرات کو؟
	ہاں، ہاں، آدھی رات کو
	کہاں؟ وہیں جہاں کوئی آتا جاتا نہیں
	تو آؤ پاس بیٹھیں پل دو پل

251

آج نہیں کل

کیوں کیوں؟

آج نہیں کل

یہ تو ایک بہانہ ہے

واپس گھر بھی جانا ہے

کتنی جلدی یہ دن ڈھلتے ہیں!

ہائی! ٹاٹا۔۔۔اچّھا تو ہم چلتے ہیں۔

۲) یہ دوستی، ہم نہیں توڑینگے

توڑینگے دم مگر تیرا ساتھ نہ چھوڑینگے

ارے، میری جیت تیری جیت

تیری ہار میری ہار

سن اے میرے یار

تیرا غم میرا غم

میری جان تیری جان

ایسا اپنا پیار

جان پہ بھی کھیلینگے

تیرے لئے لے لینگے

سب سے دُشمنی

یہ دوستی۔۔۔

۳) میرے من کی گنگا

252

اور تیرے من کی جمنا کا

بول رادھا بول سنگم ہوگا کہ نہیں

ـــــ نہیں! کبھی نہیں!

ـــــ جا! جا!

ـــــ جاؤ نہ! کیوں ستاتے ہو! ہوگا ہوگا ہوگا!

<u>Glossary for Songs</u>

بہانہ = excuse (m)	دُشمنی = enmity (f)
ڈھلنا = to fade, to sink, to decline	من = heart, soul, spirit; mind; intellect (m)
توڑنا = to break	گنگا = River Ganges (f)
چھوڑنا = to abandon, to give up	جمنا = River Jumna (f)
جیت = victory (f)	سنگم = union, confluence (m)
ہار = loss (f); also necklace (m)	ستانا = to tease, to torment

11.14 Vocabulary

to become well	ٹھیک ہو جانا
blood (m)	خُون
cold (illness) (m)	زُکام
comb (f)	کنگھی
to comb	کنگھی کرنا
condition (f)	حالت
to cough	کھانسنا
cough (f)	کھانسی
dangerous	خطرناک

253

to have diarrhea	دست آنا
ear (m)	کان
eighty	اسّی
examination (medical), investigation (m)	مُعائنہ
to have something examined (medically)	مُعائنہ کرانا
finger (f)	اُنگلی
flu (m)	نزلہ (فلو)
to go back, return	واپس جانا
hair (m)	بال
help (f)	مدد
to help	مدد کرنا
to help x	x کی مدد کرنا
land (f)	زمین
landlord (m)	زمیندار/مکان مالک
leg (m)	پَیر
mouth, face (m)	مُنھ اِمُنہ
nose (f)	ناک
offspring, children (f)	اولاد
pain (m)	درد
patient (m/f)	بیمار / مریض

to pour, to place, to put	ڈالنا
to be reduced	کم ہونا
to reduce	کم کرنا
rest (m)	آرام
to rest	آرام کرنا
self (reflexive); oneself	خُود
servant (m)	نَوکر
sherbet (beverage) (m)	شربت
stomach (m)	پیٹ
to stop, to prevent	روکنا
teeth (m)	دانت
thief (m)	چور
toilet/excrement/stool (m)	پاخانہ
town/city (m)	شہر
until	تک
urine (m)	پیشاب
useful, profitable	مُفید
useless/unemployed	بیکار
worried	پریشان

Chapter 12

12.1 Simple Past Tense

The simple past tense indicates an action that has been completed.

1.   I went home.

2.   I saw the movie.

In order to form the simple past tense in Urdu, it is essential to know whether the verb is transitive or intransitive. Intransitive verbs are those that cannot have objects such as verbs of motion. Transitive verbs, on the other hand, have objects (for example, the verb "saw" in # 2 above). In addition, there are a few verbs that are transitive in English but their Urdu counterparts are treated as intransitive. A notable instance is the verb لانا "to bring." In the same vein, there are a few transitive verbs in Urdu whose English conterparts are intransitive. The chart below should make these distinctions clear.

Common Intransitive Verbs

to forget	بُھولنا	to come	آنا
to bring	لانا	to go	جانا
to be afraid of / fear x	x سے ڈرنا	to speak / talk to x	x سے بولنا
to fight with x	x سے لڑنا	to live	جینا
to cry	رونا	to live	رہنا
to smile	مُسکرانا	to get up	اُٹھنا
to reach	پہنچنا	to rise / to awake	جاگنا

to be constructed/ become	بننا	to climb	چڑھنا
to bathe	نہانا	to meet x	x سے ملنا
to dance	ناچنا		

Intransitive when object is not expressed and transitive when the object is expressed:

to lose	ہارنا
to win	جیتنا
to understand	سمجھنا

Common Transitive Verbs

to say	کہنا	to open	کھولنا
to ask	پوچھنا	to buy	خریدنا
to do	کرنا	to sell	بیچنا
to see	دیکھنا	to sing	گانا
to eat	کھانا	to wash	دھونا
to drink	پینا	to dry x	x کو سکھانا
to keep	رکھنا	to work	کام کرنا
to read	پڑھنا	to clean	صاف کرنا
to write	لِکھنا	to fix/repair	ٹھیک کرنا

Note: Urdu has a substantial number of verbs created by adding a "verbalizer" (usually کرنا and ہونا) to an adjective or noun to create a verb. For example, the Urdu equivalent of the verb "to work" is created by adding the verb کرنا to the noun کام ; the verb "to clean" is similarly created by adding کرنا to the adjective صاف . While constructions with کرنا result in the creation of transitive verbs, those with ہونا produce intransitive verbs, for example, صاف ہونا "to be

257

clean."

12.2 The Simple Past Tense of Intransitive Verbs

To form the simple past tense of intransitive verbs, the past participle is used. The past

participle is formed in the following way:

verb stem + ا (masculine singular subject)

verb stem + ے (masculine plural subject)

verb stem + ی (feminine singular subject)

verb stem + یں (feminine plural subject)

Examples:

ناچنا "to dance"

stem: ناچ

Feminine Singular	Masculine Singular	Pronoun
ناچی	ناچا	میں
ناچی	ناچا	تو
ناچی	ناچا	یہ/وہ

Feminine Plural	Masculine Plural	Pronoun
ناچیں	ناچے	ہم
ناچیں	ناچے	تم
ناچیں	ناچے	آپ
ناچیں	ناچے	یہ/وہ

If the stem of the verb ends in ا, or و, then the consonant ی is inserted for the masculine singular

past participle.

لانا "to bring"		سونا "to sleep"
stem: لا		stem: سو

لایا	Masculine Singular	سویا
لائے	Masculine Plural	سوئے
لائی	Feminine Singular	سوئی
لائیں	Feminine Plural	سوئیں

If the stem of the verb ends in ی then it is shortened in the masculine forms. No additional ی is added for the formation of the feminine past tense.

جینا "to live"

stem: جی

جیا	Masculine Singular
جیئے	Masculine Plural
جی	Feminine Singular
جییں	Feminine Plural

12.1-12.2 Reading and Translation Drill

۱۔   میں وہاں سے آیا۔

وہ لڑکے امریکہ سے آئے۔

وہ خوبصورت لڑکی اِس دوکان سے آئی۔

ہماری بہنیں ابھی آئیں۔

۲۔   وہ آدمی مجھ سے کیا بولا؟

وہ عورتیں ہم سے نہیں بولیں۔

کیا، تو اُن سے وہ بات بولی؟

259

ہماری لڑکی آپ سے کیا بولی؟

٣۔ آپ اُس گھر میں کب تک رہے؟

ہم وہاں دس بجے تک رہے۔

سیما اُس شہر میں کبھی نہیں رہی۔

احمد اُس مُلک میں صرف دو سال تک رہا۔

٤۔ تو لاہور سے میرے لئے کیا لائی؟ کچھ نہیں!

اُس کی والدہ بازار سے یہ پھل لائیں۔

کیا، آپ میری کتابیں لائیں؟

روم سروِس والا ہمارے لئے دو پیالی چائے لایا ۔

12.3 The Case of جانا "To Go"

An important intransitive verb, جانا, has an irregular pattern of conjugation.

Masculine Singular	Feminine Singular
میں گیا	میں گئی
تو گیا	تو گئی
تم گئے	تم گئیں
آپ گئے	آپ گئیں
وہ گیا	وہ گئی

Masculine Plural	Feminine Plural
ہم گئے	ہم گئیں
تم گئے	تم گئیں
آپ گئے	آپ گئیں
وہ گئے	وہ گئیں

12.3 Reading and Translation Drill

١۔ میں دو سال پہلے پاکستان گیا۔

ہماری لڑکیاں کل لاہور گئیں۔

تمہاری سہیلی کہاں گئی؟

وہ لڑکے ابھی اُس باغ میں گئے۔

٢۔ کل شام کو آپ کہاں گئے؟

ہم اُن کے ساتھ نیو یارک گئیں۔

ہمارا ہوائی جہاز پانچ گھنٹے میں بوسٹن سے سین فرنسیسکو گیا۔

نوکر سبزی خریدنے کے لئے بازار گیا۔

٣۔ نیپال کے فنکار پرسوں اپنے وطن گئے۔

صاحب، آگرہ کی ٹرین تو دس بجے گئی۔

ہم اپنا سامان لے کر ہوائی اڈّے گئے مگر ہوائی جہاز وہاں نہیں تھا۔

بھاری سامان اُٹھا کے بوڑھی عورتیں بازار سے اپنے گھر گئیں۔

زیادہ بارش کی وجہ سے روی سینما نہیں گیا۔

12.4 The Case of ہونا "To Be, To Happen, To Become"

The verb ہونا mean to be, to happen, or to become. The past participle forms of ہونا when it means "to be" are تھیں، تھی، تھے، تھا . The past participle forms of ہونا when it means "to become" or "to happen" are :

	Singular	Plural
Masculine	ہوا	ہوئے
Feminine	ہوئی	ہوئیں

Study the examples below illustrating constructions meaning "I became happy," "You became happy," and so on:

Feminine	Masculine
میں خوش ہوئی۔	میں خوش ہوا۔
تو خوش ہوئی۔	تو خوش ہوا۔
تم خوش ہوئیں۔	تم خوش ہوئے۔
آپ خوش ہوئیں۔	آپ خوش ہوئے۔
وہ/یہ خوش ہوئی	یہ/وہ خوش ہوا۔
ہم خوش ہوئیں۔	ہم خوش ہوئے۔
تم خوش ہوئیں۔	تم خوش ہوئے۔
آپ خوش ہوئیں۔	آپ خوش ہوئے۔
وہ/یہ خوش ہوئیں۔	یہ/وہ خوش ہوئے۔

Other examples of the use of ہونا are:

وہاں کام ہوا۔

Work took place there.

یہاں تماشا ہوا۔

A spectacle happened here.

12.4 Reading and Translation Drill

۱۔ میں وہاں سے اُٹھی۔

وہ خوبصورت لڑکیاں وہاں سے اُٹھیں۔

مہارانی ایلیزابیتھ اپنی کرسی سے کب اُٹھیں؟

تو یہاں سے کیوں اُٹھا؟

۲۔ ہمارا دوست اُس پیڑ پر چڑھا۔

262

وہ بہادر فنکار اپنا کام کرنے کے لئے قُطب مینار پر چڑھا۔

تیری سہیلی ہمالیہ پر کب چڑھی؟

ہم پانچ سال پہلے اُس پہاڑ پر چڑھے۔

۳۔ تم آج صبح کب جاگے؟

وہ عورتیں ابھی نہیں جاگیں۔

ہمارا وطن ابھی نہیں جاگا۔

کیا بُلبُل کے گیت کی وجہ سے گُل کے دل میں پیار جاگا؟

۴۔ سنیل اور علی وہاں کبھی نہیں گئے۔

کل شام کو میں بازار گیا۔

وہ اُن لڑکیوں کے ساتھ سنیما گئی۔

آپ اُس مسجد میں جُمعہ کو گئے؟

۵۔ میں بُدھ کو نہایا۔

کیا، تم آج صبح نہائے؟

وہ لڑکے چار دِن سے نہیں نہائے۔

وہ لڑکیاں کب نہائیں؟

۶۔ ہم دلّی آج صبح پہنچے۔

تم لندن کب پہنچے؟

وہ لڑکی وہاں نہیں پہنچی۔

کیا، راجیش اُن کے گھر پہنچا؟

۷۔ یہ سُن کر وہ لڑکا بہت رویا۔

اُس آدمی کی کہانی سُن کر وہ لڑکیاں بہت روئیں۔

ایلٹن جان کا گانا سُن کر شاہزادہ چارلز بہت روئے۔

کیا، وہ سب لوگ یہ کتاب پڑھ کر روۓ؟

۸۔ وہ نئی عمارت کب بنی؟

اُس دعوت میں کیا کیا بنا؟

شان کانزی اُس فِلم میں جیمز بانڈ بنا۔

اُس پُرانے گھر کے پاس چار نۓ گھر بنے۔

۹۔ وہ شرمندہ ہوئی۔

وہ شریر لڑکی اپنی والدہ کے سامنے شرمندہ ہوئی۔

ہمارے دوست اپنے والد کے سامنے شرمندہ ہوۓ۔

اُن کا دوسرا لڑکا اپنی اِس حرکت پر شرمندہ ہوا۔

۱۰۔ ہمارے بھائی ہماری اِس حرکت پر ناراض ہوۓ۔

نرگس کی والدہ اُن لڑکوں کی اُس حرکت پر ناراض ہوئیں۔

میرے خیال میں، وہ لڑکا ناراض نہیں ہوا۔

جارج واشنگٹن کے والد اُن کی اِس حرکت پر ناراض ہوۓ۔

۱۱۔ غالب کی شاعری سن کر وہ بہت خوش ہوۓ۔

میرابائی کے بھجن سن کر وہ انگریز بہت خوش ہوا۔

پریم چند کی کہانی پڑھ کر وہ ہوشیار لڑکیاں خوش ہوئیں۔

شیکسپیئر کا وہ ڈرامہ دیکھ کر برکلی کے طالبِ علم خوش نہیں ہوۓ۔

۱۲۔ میں وہاں جا کر بہت بیمار ہوا۔

کیا، وہ عورتیں امریکہ میں بیمار ہوئیں؟

بوڑھا پھل والا بیمار ہوا۔

ہمارے دوست لندن میں بیمار ہوۓ۔

۱۳۔ چور کو دیکھ کر راج پریشان ہوا۔

وہاں پہنچ کر وہ لڑکیاں بہت پریشان ہوئیں۔

ہمارے ماں باپ ہماری وجہ سے پریشان ہوئے۔

چور کو دیکھ کر ہم زیادہ پریشان نہیں ہوئے۔

Translate into Urdu:

1. Having seen my friend, I became very happy.

2. Did you and your brother become ill in India?

3. Those girls became worried after seeing that thief.

4. Did those bright students go to London?

5. What time did you (formal) wake up yesterday morning?

6. Did that man get up from there?

7. Those naughty boys climbed that mango tree.

8. Did they take a bath in this house?

9. I reached Mumbai this morning but my friends reached Mumbai last night.

10. What happened in Raja's house yesterday afternoon?

11. I became very embarrassed in front of my family.

12. I don't think he became upset yesterday.

12.5 Relatives and Correlatives

Relatives and correlatives are used to create clauses that frequently join two sentences which have a common noun, pronoun, adjective, or adverb. These clauses agree in number and gender with each other. The relative clause usually precedes the correlative clause but this order is quite flexible.

(جو) آدمی گا رہا ہے، (وہ) کون ہے؟

correlative   relative

Who is the man who is singing?

(وہ) کون ہے (جو) گا رہا ہے؟

relative   correlative

Who is that who is singing?

(جہاں) آپ کا دل ہے (وہاں) آپ کا گھر ہے۔

Your home is where your heart is.

The following chart lists the common sets of interrogatives, relatives, and correlatives:

Interrogative	Correlative of Proximity	Correlative of Distance	Relative
کیا/کون	یہ	وہ	جو
oblique: کن/کس	oblique: اِس/اِن	oblique: اُس/اُن	oblique: جس/جن
who/what?	this/these	that/those	who/that/which
کب	اب	تب	جب
when?	now	then	when
کب سے	اب سے	تب سے	جب سے
since/from when?	from now	since then	from the time when
کب تک	اب تک	تب تک	جب تک
until when?	until now	until then	as long as
کہاں	یہاں	وہاں	جہاں
where?	here	there	where
کِدھر	اِدھر	اُدھر	جِدھر

in which direction? (whither?)	in this direction (hither)	in that direction (tither)	in which direction (whither)
کِتنا	اِتنا	اُتنا	جِتنا
how much/how many?	this much/this many	that much/that many	as much/as many/the extent to which
کیسا	ایسا	ویسا	جیسا
how, what kind of, in what manner?	like this, in this manner	like that, in that manner	that which, of such kind

12.5 Reading and Translation Drill

۱۔ جب تم برکلی میں پڑھ رہی تھیں، تب میں ٹیکساس میں پڑھ رہا تھا۔

جب آپ ناچ رہے تھے، تب میں گا رہی تھی۔

جب وہ پکا رہا تھا، تب میں گھر صاف کر رہا تھا۔

جب ہم سو رہے تھے، تب وہ ورزش کر رہا تھا۔

۲۔ جہاں ہم ورزش کر رہے تھے، وہاں اور کوئی ورزش نہیں کرتا تھا۔

جہاں ہم پڑھ رہے تھے، وہاں وہ کھیل رہا تھا۔

جدھر ہم جا رہے تھے، اُدھر اور کوئی نہیں تھا۔

جدھر تو جا رہا ہے، اُدھر ہم نہیں جانا چاہتے۔

۳۔ جتنا کھانا میں کھا رہا ہوں، اُتنا تم کو کھانا چاہیئے۔

جتنی روٹیاں میں کھا رہی ہوں، اُتنی روٹیاں تم کو کھانی چاہئیں۔

جتنے لڑکے وہاں کھیل رہے ہیں، اُتنے تو میرے گھر میں بھی کھیل سکتے ہیں۔

جتنی لڑکیوں سے تم پوچھ رہے ہو، اُتنی لڑکیوں سے میں نہیں پوچھ سکتی۔

۴۔ جس جگہ آپ کام کر رہے تھے، وہ بہت خطرناک تھی۔

جو جانور اِدھر آ رہا تھا، وہ بہت خطرناک تھا۔

جن لڑکیوں کو آپ پسند کرتے تھے، وہ اب یہاں کام نہیں کر رہی ہیں۔

جو چیز آپ کو پسند ہے، وہ خطرناک چیز ہے۔

۵۔ جو چیزیں آپ کو پسند ہیں میں وہ لاؤنگا۔

جس جگہ آپ جانا چاہتے ہیں، وہ جگہ ٹھیک نہیں۔

جن چیزوں کو آپ خریدنا چاہتے ہیں، وہ بہت مہنگی ہیں۔

جو لڑکا یہاں پڑھتا ہے، اُس کا نام علی ہے۔

پیار کرنے والے کبھی ڈرتے نہیں۔ جو ڈرتے ہیں وہ پیار کرتے نہیں۔

۶۔ جہاں میں پڑھتا ہوں، وہاں ایک مشہور لڑکی بھی پڑھتی ہے۔

جہاں ہم گاتے ہیں، وہاں وہ پڑھتی ہے۔

جدھر تم جا رہے ہو، اُدھر ایک خوبصورت عمارت ہے۔

ہمارا گھر اُدھر ہے، جدھر وہ لڑکے کھیل رہے ہیں۔

۷۔ جتنے پیسے میں چاہتا ہوں، اُتنے پیسے وہ نہیں دے سکتے۔

جتنا خوبصورت تاج محل ہے، لال قلعہ اُتنا خوبصورت نہیں۔

جتنی اچّھی چیزیں فلوریڈا میں ملتی ہیں، اُتنی اچّھی چیزیں یہاں نہیں ملتیں۔

جتنا وقت اُن کے پاس ہے، اُتنا وقت ہمارے پاس نہیں ہے۔

۸۔ جیسا آپ پکاتے ہیں، ہم ویسا نہیں پکا سکتے۔

جیسا کھانا آپ چاہتے ہیں، میں ویسا کھانا پکاؤنگی۔

جیسی چیزیں آپ کے پاس ہیں، میں ویسی چیزیں خریدنا چاہتا ہوں۔

جیسے طالبِ علم ہماری یونیورسٹی میں پڑھتے ہیں، ویسے طالبِ علم دوسری یونیورسٹیوں میں نہیں پڑھتے۔

Translate into Urdu:

1.   My house is in that direction in which you are going.

2.   He who is my friend is not your friend.

3.   The things that are pleasing to those girls are not pleasing to me.

4.   The receipts for these bags are right there where you are looking.

5.   In this country you cannot get the kind of carpets that you want.

6.   I will meet you there where no one comes or goes!

7.   Ever since Lata has come to America, she has become vegetarian.

8.   Until her beloved comes back home, she will cry for him day and night!

Combine the following sentences using appropriate relatives and correlatives:

Example:‒ لڑکی میری بہن ہے۔ لڑکی وہاں پڑھ رہی ہے becomes in combination:

جو لڑکی وہاں پڑھ رہی ہے، وہ میری بہن ہے۔

١۔   طالبِ علم ہارورڈ بزنیس اسکول میں پڑھتا ہے۔ کیا، وہ کروڑ پتی بنیگا؟

٢۔   تم مُحبّت کھو سکتی ہو۔ تم مُحبّت پا بھی سکتی ہو۔

٣۔   بہادُر لڑکا خطرناک چور سے دور بھاگا۔ بہادُر لڑکے سے ملئے۔

٤۔   کھڑکی سے دھوپ آ رہی ہے۔ کھڑکی صاف نہیں۔

٥۔   لتا منگیشکر گیت گا رہی تھی۔ پچھلے سال گیت بہت مشہور تھا۔

٦۔   رِشی ٹکٹ لینے کے لئے گیا۔ قطار لمبی تھی۔

٧۔   وہاں اونچے پہاڑ ہوتے ہیں۔ وہاں بارش زیادہ ہوتی ہے۔

٨۔   وہ ہر وقت یہ کہانی سُناتی ہے۔ میں اس کہانی سے بیزار ہوں۔

٩۔   ماں اپنی چھوٹی لڑکی کو دیکھے گی۔ ماں روئے گی۔

12.6 The Particles بھی and ہی

We have already encountered the emphatic particle بھی which means "also" or "too."

میں بھی جا رہا ہوں۔

I too am going.

When بھی is used in a negative sentence, it corresponds to the English "even."

میں بھی نہیں جاؤنگا۔

Even I will not go.

بھی must immediately follow the word it is meant to emphasize.

The enclitic particle ہی is used to emphasize any element that precedes it. Used in this manner, it may often not be easily translatable in English:

اِس سال ہی میں پاکستان جاؤنگا۔

This *year* (emphatic) I will go to Pakistan.

اِس سال میں ہی پاکستان جاؤنگا۔

This year *I* (emphatic/myself/alone) will go to Pakistan.

اِس سال میں پاکستان ہی جاؤنگا۔

This year I will go to *Pakistan* only (emphatic).

اِس سال میں پاکستان جاؤنگا ہی۔

This year I will definitely *go* (emphatic) to Pakistan.

Note that ہی can sometimes correspond to the English "only."

اِس گھر میں تم ہی کام کرتے ہو۔

In this house, only you work.

ہی can also come between the noun/pronoun and the postposition that follows:

یہ آپ ہی کی کتاب ہے۔

This is *your* (emphatic) book.

or

یہ آپ کی ہی کتاب ہے۔

This is *your* (emphatic) book.

When ہی is combined with certain pronouns, it has a special form.

مجھی	=	ہی	+	مجھ
تجھی	=	ہی	+	تجھ
ہمیں	=	ہی	+	ہم
تمہیں	=	ہی	+	تم
یہی	=	ہی	+	یہ
وہی	=	ہی	+	وہ
اِسی	=	ہی	+	اِس
اُسی	=	ہی	+	اُس
اِنہیں	=	ہی	+	اِن
اُنہیں	=	ہی	+	اُن

As far as adverbs are concerned, when ہی is combined with them in a special form, they have a meaning different from the one they have when ہی is written as a separate word:

right here	یہیں	only here	یہاں ہی
right there	وہیں	only there	وہاں ہی
right now	ابھی	only now	اب ہی
right then	تبھی	only then	تب ہی

271

۱۔ کل میں ہی کام کر رہا تھا۔

پرسوں وہی گا رہی تھی۔

یہ تمہیں کو معلوم تھا۔

یہ آپ ہی کو معلوم تھا۔

۲۔ مجھ کو یہی چیز پسند ہے۔

تم کو وہی چیز پسند تھی۔

ہم کو اِسی چیز کا نام معلوم نہیں تھا۔

اُن کو اُسی چیز کا نام معلوم نہیں تھا۔

۳۔ جان کینیڈی یہیں رہتے تھے۔

جیکی کینیڈی وہیں پڑھ رہی تھیں۔

وہ ابھی آنے والی ہے۔

یہ لڑکیاں تبھی پڑھ رہی تھیں۔

Translate into Urdu using ہی for emphasizing the italicized element in the sentence:

1.   *Those* people have no free time.

2.   *You* (informal) alone are my God.

3.   In the big house, there was a *small* child.

4.   *I* only was anxious/worried about the exam.

5.   Give your heart only to *us*.

6.   Sir, the carpet shop is right *there*.

7.   Only *here* can you buy such beautiful flowers.

12.7 The Interrogative کونسا

The interrogative کونسا acts as a marked adjective meaning "which one" and can precede both nominative and oblique nouns. The basic difference between کون (including the oblique forms کس and کن) and کونسا is that کونسا is used to inquire about a particular thing amidst many things:

آپ کو کونسا پھل پسند ہے؟

Which (out of all these) fruit do you like?

آپ کو کونسی چیز چاہیے؟

Which thing do you need?

12.7 Reading and Translation Drill

١۔ وہ کونسا گھر ہے جس میں امیتابھ بچّپن رہتا ہے؟

آپ کو یہ خوبصورت کپڑے کونسی دوکان میں ملتے ہیں؟

تمہارے بیٹے کو کونسی مٹھائی پسند ہے؟

اُن کے دوستوں کو کونسے جوتے چاہییں؟

٢۔ اس کتاب کے علاوہ اور کونسی کتابیں پڑھنے کے قابل ہیں۔

اِس ہوائی اڈّے پر کونسے ہوائی جہاز ٹھہرے؟

وہ فنکار کونسے فن کے لئے مشہور تھا؟

امیتابھ بچّپن کی فلموں کے علاوہ آپ اور کونسی فلمیں دیکھیں گے؟

12.8 Repetition of Adjectives

When non-interrogative adjectives are repeated, the repeated adjectives take on an intensified form:

وہ بُلبُل میٹھے میٹھے گیت گاتی تھی۔

That nightingale used to sing very sweet songs.

273

This sentence could also be expressed as:

وہ بُلبُل بہت میٹھے گیت گاتی تھی۔

Similarly:

اُن کے گھر میں اچّھی اچّھی چیزیں ہیں۔

In their house, there are very good things.

could be expressed as:

ان کے گھر میں بہت اچّھی چیزیں ہیں۔

The repetition of interrogative adjectives conveys a sense of variety:

آپ پاکستان میں کہاں کہاں جائینگے؟

Where "all" will you go in Pakistan?

اُن کے گھر میں کون کون رہتے ہیں؟

Who "all" lives in their house?

In order to repeat کونسا, the forms کون کونسی/کون کونسے/کون کونسا are used instead of کونسا.

تمہیں کون کونسی لڑکیاں پسند ہیں؟

Which are (all the) girls you like?

12.8 Reading and Translation Drill

۱۔ اُس دوکان میں بہت اچّھے اچّھے پھل ملتے ہیں۔
وہاں سستی سستی قالینیں ملتی ہیں۔
ہندوستان میں بڑی بڑی عمارتیں ہیں۔
اُن باغوں میں چھوٹے چھوٹے بچّے کھیلتے ہیں۔

۲۔ وہ لوگ لندن میں کہاں کہاں جائینگے؟

هم کو یہ خوبصورت چیزیں کہاں کہاں مل سکتی ہیں؟

ہارورڈ میں کون کونسے مشہور لوگ پڑھتے ہیں؟

آپ اُس بازار میں کون کونسی چیزیں خریدنی چاہتے ہیں؟

Translate into Urdu using repeated adjectives or interrogatives:

1. What "all" will you buy for me in the market?

2. He has very beautiful houses.

3. That woman has two very small children.

4. What need is there to buy very expensive clothes?

5. Whom "all" will you meet with in Delhi?

6. Where "all" will you go when you tour Pakistan?

اِن سوالوں کے جواب دیجئے:

۱۔   جب آپ اپنے گھر جاتے ہیں تب کیا کرتے ہیں؟

۲۔   جہاں آپ رہتے ہیں، وہاں اور کون رہتا ہے؟

۳۔   کیا، آپ کے پاس اُتنا پیسہ ہے جتنا بِل گیٹس کے پاس ہے؟

۴۔   پچھلے سال گرمیوں کی چھٹیوں میں آپ کہاں تھے؟

۵۔   آپ اپنے بچپن میں کیا کیا کرتے تھے؟

۶۔   کیا، آپ اور آپ کے دوست بچپن میں شرارتیں کرتے تھے؟

۷۔   آپ کو یونیورسٹی میں کونسی چیزیں پسند ہیں؟

۸۔   آپ اور آپ کے دوست کھانے کے لئے کہاں کہاں جاتے ہیں؟

۹۔   دس سال پہلے آپ کا خاندان کہاں رہتا تھا؟

۸۱ اِکیاسی

۸۲ بیاسی

۸۳ تِراسی

۸۴ چوراسی

۸۵ پچاسی

۸۶ چھِیاسی

۸۷ ستّاسی

۸۸ اٹّھاسی

۸۹ نواسی

۹۰ نوّے

۱۲.۱۰ گفتگو (Conversation)

(نرگس، راج، ریشما، روی اور رشی۔۔۔ لکھنؤ کے ہوائی اڈّے پر)

راج: دیکھو نرگس، یہ کتنی لمبی قطار ہے۔ آج کئی ہوائی جہاز ایک ساتھ جا رہے ہیں۔ ہم کو اُس قطار میں ٹھہرنا چاہئے ۔ وہ اِس سے چھوٹی ہے۔

نرگس: ہاں راج۔ آج گرمی بھی بہت ہے۔ کیا، تمہارے پاس ہمارے ٹکٹ ہیں؟

راج: ہاں، ہاں۔ میرے پاس ہم سب کے ٹکٹ ہیں۔

ٹکٹ کلرک: کیا، آپ لوگوں کے ساتھ کچھ سامان ہے؟

نرگس: جی ہاں یہ پانچ بیکس ہیں۔

کلرک: یہ تو بہت بھاری ہیں۔ ایکسیس بیگیج دینا ہے!

نرگس: کیوں؟ ہم پانچ لوگ ہیں۔ اِتنا سامان تو ضرور لا سکتے ہیں۔

کلرک:	نہیں میڈم! آج ہوائی جہاز پر بہت لوگ ہیں۔ اِتنا وزن آپ نہیں لا سکتے۔
راج:	ہم ایک مہینے کے لئے جا رہے ہیں۔ دیکھیئے گرمی بہت ہے اور میری بہن پریشان ہو رہی ہے۔ یہ چار دِن سے بیمار تھی۔
ریشما:	ہاں۔ میں کل ہی ہسپتال سے آئی!
کلرک:	اچّھا۔ آپ کے ٹکٹ بھی ریکنفرمڈ نہیں ہیں۔
نرگس:	کیا! میں خود پرسوں شہر میں ایرلائن کے دفتر پر گئی۔ یہ لیجیئے ریکنفرمیشن کی رسید ہے۔
کلرک:	ٹھیک ہے، ٹھیک ہے۔ آپ لوگ جا سکتے ہیں۔
	(دِلّی میں ایک ٹیکسی میں)
نرگس:	(ٹیکسی والے سے) ہمیں پہاڑ گنج جانا ہے۔
ٹیکسی والا:	بس، اِتنا ہی سامان ہے؟
راج:	ہاں، ہاں۔ کیا۔ تم کو پلونیا ہوٹل کا پتا معلوم ہے؟
ٹیکسی والا:	ہاں صاحب، معلوم ہے۔
نرگس:	راج، آج کتنی پُرانی یادیں واپس آ رہی ہیں۔ میں بچپن میں اپنے بھائی بہنوں کے ساتھ، ہر سال دِلّی آتی تھی۔
راج:	اچّھا!
نرگس:	ہم لوگ بہت مزے کرتے تھے۔ ہمارے نانا یہاں کام کرتے تھے اور وہ ہم کو لے کر تاریخی مقامات دکھانے کے لئے جاتے تھے۔ ہماری پسندیدہ جگہ لال قلعہ تھی۔
روی:	لال قلعہ کیا ہے؟
نرگس:	یہ مغلوں کے زمانے کا قلعہ ہے۔ یہ بہت خوبصورت ہے۔ یہاں ہر سال پندرہ اگست کو بہت بڑا جشن ہوتا ہے کیونکہ یہ ہندوستان کی آزادی کا دن

ہے۔

رشی: لال قلعہ کے علاوہ دلّی میں اور کیا کیا دیکھنے کے قابل ہے؟

نرگس: ہُمایوں* کا مقبرہ، جامع مسجد، اِنڈیا گیٹ، برلا مندر، لودھی باغ، پرانا قلعہ، اور قُطب مینار*۔ یہ سب وہ تاریخی مقامات ہیں، جہاں ہمیں جانا چاہیئے۔ یہ اچّھے مقامات ہیں۔

ٹیکسی والا: کیا، آپ کنّاٹ پلیس نہیں جائیںگے؟ وہاں وِمپیز ہے۔ وِمپیز میں بہت اچّھے برگرز ملتے ہیں۔ جب سے وِمپیز دلّی میں آئی ہے تب سے امیر لوگ وہیں جاتے ہیں۔

راج: نہیں، ہم وِمپیز نہیں جائیںگے۔ ہم وہاں جانا چاہتے ہیں جہاں مزیدار بریانی ملتی ہے!

ٹیکسی والا: بریانی تو آپ کو نِظام الدّین کے قریب ملیگی، صاحب۔

نرگس: ہاں، ہاں۔ ہمیں نِظام الدّین تو جانا ہے۔ راج، تم کو قوّالی بہت پسند ہے، نا؟

راج: ہاں، بہت! نُصرت فتح علی خان* تو مجھے بہت پسند ہیں۔ کیا، وہاں قوّالی ہوتی ہے؟

نرگس: ہاں، ہر جمعرات کی شام کو وہاں قوّالی ہوتی ہے۔ وہاں نِظام الدّین اولیاء* کا مزار ہے۔

راج: کیا یہ وہی نِظام الدّین ہیں جو ہندوستان کے بہت بڑے صوفی بُزُرگ تھے؟

نرگس: ہاں، ہاں، یہ وہی تو ہیں۔ اور اُن کے مزار کے قریب ہندوستان کے دو مشہور شاعروں، امیر نُصرو* اور مِرزا غالِب* کی قبریں بھی ہیں۔

رشی: کل جُمعرات ہے۔ ہمیں تو وہاں ضرور جانا چاہیئے!

ٹیکسی والا: صاحب، یہ آپ کا ہوٹل ہے۔

راج: تمہارا بہت بہت شکریہ۔ کتنے پیسے دینے ہیں؟

ٹیکسی والا: چار سو روپے صاحب۔

راج: یہ تو بہت زیادہ ہے۔ ہم تو ہر وقت تین سو روپے دیتے ہیں۔

ٹیکسی والا: ارے نہیں صاحب۔ یہ تو بہت کم ہیں۔ آج کل پیٹرول بھی بہت مہنگا ہے۔ میرے چار بچّے ہیں۔ مجھے اُن کو بھی پالنا ہے۔

نرگس: ٹھیک ہے۔ کیا، تم ہر روز ہمارے ساتھ چل سکتے ہو؟ کیا تم کو سب تاریخی مقامات کے پتے معلوم ہیں؟

ٹیکسی والا: جی ہاں۔ مجھے سب مقامات کے پتے معلوم ہیں۔ میں کل صبح آؤنگا۔

نرگس: اچّھا، شکریہ، کل ملینگے۔

Notes

ہُمایوں : Humayun, Mughal Emperor, died 1556.

قُطُب مینار : Qutub Minar; victory tower in Delhi built in the 13th century by the ruler Qutub ad-Din Aibak

نُصرت فتح علی خان : Nusrat Fateh Ali Khan, renowned qawwali perfomer; died 1997.

نِظام الدّین اولیاء : Nizam ad-Din Auliya, famous Muslim mystic of Delhi; died 1325.

امیر خُسرو : Amir Khusraw, a Persian poet who lived in Delhi, popularly considered to be a pioneer poet in Hindi; disciple of Nizam ad-Din Auliya; died 1326.

مرزا غالِب : Mirza Ghalib, a prominent Persian and Urdu poet; died in Delhi in 1869.

12.11 Conversation Practice

Anil: This is such a beautiful restaurant. Who is the beautiful woman who is singing?

Sonia: The woman who is singing is Anuradha. She is very famous. She and I used to study together in college.

Renu: Really? To which college did you both go?

Sonia: We went to Amherst College. As long as I was in college, I used to listen to her every

week.

Renu: Did your parents live in the United States at that time?

Anil: No, both our families used to live in India at that time. Only both of us were in this

country.

Renu: My family used to live in India five years ago, but now they also live here.

Waiter: What would you people like to eat?

Renu: The food here is very good. (use emphatic ہی)

Anil: What "all" do you like here?

Renu: Their dosas are delicious. I also like their tanduri chicken.

Sonia: I don't eat meat. I would like a dosa and a mango lassi.

Anil: I would like a plate of tanduri chicken.

Renu: I will get a dosa too.

Sonia: After we eat, we ought to go to a movie. Yesterday I was about to go to the new

Madhuri movie but I did not have a car. My brother was going to New York.

Anil: Yes, I like Madhuri very much. Is the theater very far from here?

Renu: No, no. The theater is very near. But there is always a long line in front of the theater.

For this reason we ought to go before 9 o'clock.

12.12 Songs

ا) اے میری زہرہ جبیں، تجھے معلوم نہیں

تو ابھی تک ہے حسیں اور میں جواں

تجھ پہ قربان میری جان میری جاں

یہ شوخیاں، یہ بانکپن، جو تجھ میں ہے کہیں نہیں

دلوں کو جیتنے کا فن، جو تجھ میں ہے کہیں نہیں

میں تیری آنکھوں میں پا گیا دو جہاں۔

۲) میرے سپنوں کی رانی کب آئیگی تو؟

آئی رُت مستانی کب آئیگی تو؟

بیتی جائے زندگانی کب آئیگی تو؟

چلی آ تو چلی آ!

پیار کی گلیاں، باغوں کی کلیاں

سب رنگ رلیاں پوچھ رہی ہیں

گیت پنگھٹ پہ کس دن گائیگی تو؟

۳) عشق بِنا کیا مرنا یارا

عشق بِنا کیا جینا

گُڑ سے میٹھا عشق عشق

اِملی سے کھٹّا عشق

وعدہ پکّا عشق عشق

دھاگا کچّا عشق

Glossary for Songs

زہرہ جبین = forehead radiant as Venus		گلی = alley (f)	
حسین = beautiful		کلی = flower bud (f)	
قُربان = sacrifice, offering		رنگ رلیاں = rejoicings, merriment (f)	

شوخیاں = coquetry, playfulness, flirting (f)

بانکپن = elegance, smartness; curvature (m)

جیتنا = to win, to conquer

فن = art, skill (m)

جہان = world (m)

رانی = queen (f)

رُت = season (f)

مستانی = intoxicating

زندگانی = life (f)

بیتنا = to pass, elapse

پنگھٹ = well, tank; place for drawing water (m)

بِنا (کے بِنا) = without

گُڑ = raw sugar, molasses (m)

اِملی = tamarind (f)

کھٹّا = sour, tart; harsh

وعدہ = promise (m)

پکّا = ripe; perfect; strong, firm; pure

دھاگا = thread (m)

کچّا = unripe, raw; rough; unstable; weak; brittle

12.13 Vocabulary

action/deed; mischief; movement; (f)	حرکت
airport (m)	ہوائی اڈّا
animal (m)	جانور
answer (m)	جواب
artist (m)	فنکار
ashamed, bashful, modest	شرمِندہ
to be ashamed, bashful, etc.	شرمِندہ ہونا
baggage, luggage, goods (m)	سامان
besides, moreover, in addition to	کے علاوہ
brave, courageous	بہادُر

capable, able, skillful;	قابِل
worthy of (with oblique infinitive)	کے قابِل
to cause or make listen, to tell;	سُنانا
to narrate	
celebration (m)	جشن
to climb	چڑھنا
cold (weather) (m or f)	سردی (f) / جاڑا (m)
to enjoy	مزہ کرنا
fed up	بیزار
to flee, to run away from	بھاگنا
fort (m)	قِلعہ
grave, tomb (f)	قبر
grave/tomb shrine of Sufi	مزار
holy man (m)	
heavy	بھاری
Hindu devotional hymn;	بھجن
worship (m)	
historical	تاریخی
homeland (m)	وطن
independence, freedom (f)	آزادی
invitation; feast, party (f)	دعوَت
mausoleum (m)	مقبرہ

millionaire (m)	کروڑپتی
minaret (m)	مینار
Mirabai -- a 16th century (?) poetess famous for her devotional songs to the Hindu deity Krishna	میرابائی
mischievous	شریر
mosque (f)	مسجد
mountain, hill (m)	پہاڑ
Mughal -- dynasty that ruled India from the 16th to the 19th century	مغل
nightingale (m/f)	بلبل
ninety	نوّے
place (m) (plural)	مقام (مقامات)
Premchand -- prominent author of Urdu-Hindi narrative prose; died 1936	پریم چند
prince (m)	شاہزادہ
qawwali -- spiritual-mystical song recited by Muslim mystics (f)	قوّالی
queen, empress (f)	مہارانی
queue/line (f)	قطار
rain (f)	بارش
to rain	بارش ہونا

to raise/nourish; maintain	پالنا
to protect	
receipt (f)	رسید
to return/come back	واپس آنا
revered person/ respected elder	بُزُرگ
several; some; a few	کئی
skill, art, craft (m)	فن
to smile	مُسکرانا
Sufi -- a Muslim mystic (m)	صوفی
tree, plant (m)	پیڑ
to wait; to stay	ٹھہرنا
weight (m)	وزن
to work out, to exercise	ورزِش کرنا

Chapter 13

13.1 The Simple Past Tense of Transitive Verbs

Subjects of transitive verbs in the simple past tense are marked with the particle نے. This particle puts the subject and any modifying adjective into the oblique case.

نے *with Pronouns as Subjects*

Although نے puts noun subjects into the oblique, in the case of pronouns *only the third person pronouns go into the oblique*. The third person plural pronoun "they" has a special oblique form with نے - اُنہوں or اِنہوں instead of the usual اُن or اِن.

I saw	میں نے دیکھا
You (least formal) saw	تو نے دیکھا
You (informal) saw	تم نے دیکھا
You (formal) saw	آپ نے دیکھا
He/she/it saw	اس نے دیکھا
We saw	ہم نے دیکھا
You (informal) saw	تم نے دیکھا
You (formal) saw	آپ نے دیکھا
They saw	انہوں نے دیکھا

Note: the oblique forms of the interrogative کون "who" before نے are کس (singular) and کنہوں (plural).

Verb Agreement for Transitive Verbs

The particle نے, used to mark the subject of a transitive verb in the past tense, cuts off

agreement between the subject and verb. Instead the verb agrees in number and gender with the

object, if it is explicitly mentioned. For example:

میں نے کتاب دیکھی۔

I saw the book.

In the above sentence the past participle of the verb is in the feminine singular form because its

object, "book," is feminine singular. In this tense the gender of the subject is irrelevant for

agreement for transitive verbs. Similarly, in the sentence below, the verb participle is in the

masculine plural form in agreement with the object "shoes."

میں نے آپ کے جوتے دیکھے۔

I saw your shoes.

In case the object is not explicitly mentioned or is indeterminate, the participle uses the

masculine singular form as its default form.

میں نے دیکھا۔

I saw.

In case the object is marked by کو (as, for example, is mandatory for direct animate or specific

inanimate objects), then the verb participle also remains in the masculine singular as the particle

کو cuts off agreement between object and verb.

میں نے لڑکوں کو دیکھا۔

I saw the boys.

میں نے کتاب کو دیکھا۔

I saw the book.

In both sentences above, the verb agrees with neither the subject nor the object because of the particles نے and کو which mark each of them respectively. As a consequence, the verb adopts the default form - masculine singular.

13.2 The Case of کرنا، دینا، لینا

Three of the most commonly used transitive verbs have irregular past participles: کرنا،دینا، لینا

Masculine Singular	کیا، دیا، لیا
Masculine Plural	کیئے، دیئے، لیئے اکئے، دے، لئے
Feminine Singular	کی، دی، لی
Feminine Plural	کیں، دیں، لیں

Examples:

میں نے کام کیا۔

I worked.

(The verb agrees with object کام, masculine singular.)

اُس نے چیزیں لیں۔

He took the things.

(The verb agrees with object چیزیں, feminine plural.)

میرے والد نے مجھے کپڑے دے(دیئے)۔

My father gave me clothes.

(The verb agrees with object کپڑے, masculine plural.)

13.3 Negating the Simple Past Tense

In order to negate the simple past tense, نہیں is placed right before the verb.

ہم وہاں نہیں گئے۔

We did not go there.

میں نے اُن لڑکیوں کو نہیں دیکھا۔

I did not see those girls.

Placing نہیں after the past participle results in an emphatic negation:

اس نے کھانا کھایا نہیں۔

He did not eat the food at all.

13.1-13.3 Reading and Translation Drill

۱۔ راج نے ایک سیب کھایا۔

سیما نے پچاس سیب کھائے۔

اُنہوں نے اور اُن کے بیٹوں نے وہ اچّھی مٹھائی کھائی۔

کیا، آپ نے کھانا کھایا؟

۲۔ میں نے اپنی گاڑی بیچی۔

اُس نے اپنا گھر بیچا۔

اُن لڑکیوں نے پچاس چیزیں خریدیں۔

تو نے یہ پھل کب خریدے؟

۳۔ کیا، اُن طالبِ علموں نے اپنے کپڑے دھوئے؟

کیا، طالبِ علموں نے اُن کپڑوں کو دھویا؟

ہم نے اپنے کپڑوں کو دھویا مگر ہم نے اُن کو نہیں سُکھایا۔

آپ نے مجھ کو پھل دیئے مگر میں نے اُن کو نہیں کھایا۔

۴۔ کیا، اُن ہوشیار لڑکیوں نے وہ چیز دیکھی؟

289

کیا، اُن ہوشیار لڑکیوں نے اُس چیز کو دیکھا؟

حسن نے راج کو سب چیزیں دیں مگر راج نے اُن چیزوں کو دیکھا نہیں۔

امان نے اُس چیز کو راج کو دیا مگر راج نے وہ چیز نہیں دیکھی۔

۵۔ ایک امیر آدمی نے اس کو دو ہزار ڈالر دیئے۔

پچھلے سال آپ نے اپنے گھر کا کتنا کرایہ دیا؟

اُس عورت نے ڈر کر چور کو الماری میں سے سب مہنگی چیزیں دیں۔

آپ نے میرا کام کیا یا نہیں؟

۶۔ پرسوں میں نے آپ کا بہت اِنتظار کیا۔

انہوں نے ایک بجے تک ہوائی جہاز کا انتظار کیا۔

تم یہاں میرا انتظار کرو! میں ابھی آتا ہوں۔

کسی آدمی نے بہت دیر تک اُس حسین عورت کا انتظار کیا۔

۷۔ کیا! تو نے مجھے پہچانا نہیں؟

اُس چور نے اپنے وکیل کو نہیں پہچانا۔

مُنیر نے تھیٹر میں شاہزادے چارلس کو پہچانا۔

اردو کے اس ہوشیار طالبِ علم نے ہزاروں شعروں میں سے مرزا غالب کے شعر کو پہچانا۔

Translate the following sentences into Urdu. Pay special attention to transitive and intransitive verbs.

1. Yesterday, my friend and I came from school at 4:00 pm.

2. Did you dance with your friend last Saturday?

3. Having seen the ghost, all the boys were frightened.

4. He went home with his brother.

5.   When did you wake up this morning?

6.   In my opinion, you did not do a lot of work.

7.   Did that little boy smile? Poor fellow, he was very sick yesterday. He had a high fever.

8.   At what time did they reach Islamabad?

9.   I don't know about them but I reached Islamabad at 3:30 pm.

10.   Did you (least formal) understand?

11.   With whom did she dance? I don't know; there was a big crowd at the party.

12.   I washed the clothes but I did not dry them.

13.   Did you (informal) drink tea? No, I don't like tea.

14.   They asked me a question but I did not reply (i.e., give an answer).

15.   What "all" did you write in the letter?

16.   London is very expensive. I bought only two things.

17.   Where did the President of America give his speech last night? On T.V.?

18.   His friend gave him a lot of things for his birthday.

19.   Did they fix (ٹھیک کرنا) your telephone?

20.   We cleaned our house because my brother is coming home tonight.

Change the tenses in the following sentences into the simple past tense, inserting نے when necessary, and then translate them into English. For example: ہم کل سنیما جائینگے "We will go to the movies tomorrow" will become ہم کل سنیما گئے "We went to the movies yesterday."

۱۔   گاؤں والے کپڑے دھو رہے ہیں۔

۲۔   کیا، وہ چھوٹا لڑکا پیڑ پر چڑھ رہا ہے؟

۳۔   ہم اپنے خاندان کے ساتھ آئینگے

۴۔   شیلا اُس چیز کو دیکھ رہی ہے۔

۵۔   آپ جرمنی سے ہمارے لئے کیا کیا لائینگے؟

۶۔   تم اپنے گاؤں کب جاؤگے؟

۷۔   کیا، آپ کی لڑکی روتی ہے؟

۸۔   میں چاول اور سالن کھاؤنگا۔

۹۔   روی اور نیل شراب نہیں پیتے ہیں۔

۱۰۔   کیا، راج نرگس سے لڑتا ہے؟

۱۱۔   اس کام کو کرنے میں تم کیوں دیر کر رہی ہو؟

۱۲۔   میرے خیال میں وہ لڑکی بھوت نہیں دیکھ سکتی۔

13.4 The Present Perfect Tense

The simple past tense is used to denote past actions that are completed. If these completed

actions are connected to or have bearing upon the present, then the present perfect tense is used.

Simple Past Tense:

وہ ہندوستان سے آیا۔

He came from India.

(Action completed in the past)

Present Perfect Tense:

وہ ہندوستان سے آیا ہے۔

He has come from India.

(Action completed but still relevant to the present)

In order to form the present perfect tense, the past participle of the verb is followed by the

appropriate present tense of the verb ہونا that agrees with the subject of the verb (in case of intransitive verbs) or the object of the verb (in case of transitive verbs).

	Masculine	Feminine
I have come	میں آیا ہوں	میں آئی ہوں
You (least formal) have come	تو آیا ہے	تو آئی ہے
You (informal) have come	تم آئے ہو	تم آئی ہو
You (formal) have come	آپ آئے ہیں	آپ آئی ہیں
He/She/It has come	وہ آیا ہے	وہ آئی ہے
We have come	ہم آئے ہیں	ہم آئی ہیں /ہم آئے ہیں
You (informal) have come	تم آئے ہو	تم آئی ہو
You (formal) have come	آپ آئے ہیں	آپ آئی ہیں
They have come	وہ آئے ہیں	وہ آئی ہیں

Note: for the feminine plural, the feminine past participle is not nasalized, e.g., عورتیں آئی ہیں

Examples:

Intransitive Present Perfect Tense (verb agreeing with the subject)

علی باہر گیا ہے۔

Ali has gone out.

شیلا اور ریشما باہر گئی ہیں۔

Sheila and Reshma have gone out.

Transitive Present Perfect Tense (verb agreeing with the object)

راج نے دکان سے کتابیں خریدی ہیں۔

Raj has bought books from the shop.

(verb agreeing with feminine object کتاب)

نرگس نے ریشما کو پینے کے لئے دودھ دیا ہے۔

Nargis has given Reshma milk to drink.

(verb agreeing with masculine object دودھ)

13.4 Reading and Translation Drill

۱۔ سلیم وہاں گیا ہے۔

شہلا آج ہی دِلّی سے واپس آئی ہے۔

میں ابھی نہیں جاگی ہوں۔

ہم بالکل عجیب ملک میں آئے ہیں۔

۲۔ یہ ڈاک کب آئی ہے؟

وہ ڈاک ابھی گاؤں سے آئی ہے۔

میرے خیال میں یہ ڈاک اُس چھوٹے ڈاکخانے سے آئی ہے۔

کیا، آپ نے اپنی آج کی ڈاک پڑھی ہے؟

۳۔ ہمارے دوست نے دِلّی کی عدالت نہیں دیکھی ہے۔

کیا، تو نے لاہور کا ہوائی اڈّا دیکھا ہے؟

میں نے ہوائی جہاز میں سفر نہیں کیا ہے۔

وہ وکیل ابھی ہوائی اڈّے سے عدالت گیا ہے۔

۴۔ اُس مُجرم نے لاہور کے قیدخانے میں کیا کھایا ہے؟

اُن مُجرموں نے قیدخانے میں گرم گرم روٹیاں کھائی ہیں۔

علی نے اب تک چائے بھی نہیں پی ہے۔

راجہ نے شاد کے اِنتظار میں چائے نہیں پی ہے۔

میں نے اپنے دوست کے اِنتظار میں کھانا نہیں کھایا ہے۔

تم نے اُس عجیب شہر میں کیا کیا خریدا ہے؟

۵۔ میں نے سُنا ہے کہ کل رات کو امیک نے اپنی الماری میں ایک بھوت دیکھا۔

میں نے سُنا ہے کہ اس کروڑپتی نے اپنے شاندار گھر کو بڑھایا ہے۔

میں نے سُنا ہے کہ حکومت نے آزادی کے دِن ایک شاندار دعوت کی۔

میں نے سُنا ہے کہ ہندوستان کے وزیرِ اعظم نے لال قلعہ سے ایک تقریر کی ہے۔

13.5 The Past Perfect Tense

As in English, the past perfect tense emphasizes actions completed at a given point in time in the past.

علی بھی آیا تھا۔

Ali too had come.

راج نے مٹھائی کھائی تھی۔

Raj had eaten the sweets.

As in the present perfect tense, the past perfect tense is formed with the past participle of the verb. However, instead of using the present tense of the verb ہونا as an auxiliary, this construction uses the past tense auxiliary form of ہونا namely, تھا, and its variants. Again, the participle and its auxiliary have to agree with the subject of the intransitive verb or the object of the transitive verb:

ہیر اور رانجھا اِس گاؤں میں رہے تھے۔

Hir and Ranjha had lived in this village.

ہیر اور رانجھا نے ایک آم کھایا تھا۔

Hir and Ranjha had eaten a mango.

۱۔ شاہ جہاں نے تاج محل بنوایا تھا۔

اورنگزیب نے بادشاہی مسجد بنوائی تھی۔

کیا، جارج واشنگٹن نے وائیٹ ہاؤس بنوایا تھا؟

نہیں، میرے خیال میں جان ایڈمز نے وہ عمارت بنوائی تھی۔

۲۔ آپ کی بہن نے کل رات کی دعوت کے لئے کیا بنایا تھا؟

میری بہن نے کل سموسے اور پکوڑے بنائے تھے۔

کیا، اُس آدمی نے مزیدار مٹھائی بنائی تھی؟

جی نہیں۔ اُس نے کچھ خاص مٹھائی نہیں بنائی تھی۔

۳۔ ہم ہندوستان اُس وقت نہیں گئے تھے۔

کیا، اُس مشہور اداکارہ نے وہاں کی خاص چائے پی تھی؟

جی نہیں، اُس مشہور اداکارہ نے آم کا خاص جوس (مینگو ملک شیک) پیا تھا۔

مجھے لسّی نہیں پسند۔ میں نے وہاں پھل کا رس پیا تھا۔

۴۔ پولیس نے چالاک چور کو پکڑا تھا۔

عدالت میں جج صاحب نے خطرناک مُجرم سے بہت سوال پوچھے تھے۔

چالاک وکیل نے مُجرم سے قیدخانے کی حالت کے بارے میں بات کی تھی۔

جن چوروں نے اس بینک کی چوری کی تھی، وہ بہت چالاک تھے۔

۵۔ جب اس کو اِن باتوں کی معلومات ہوئی تھیں تب وہ بہت شرمندہ ہوا تھا۔

کل مُنیر نے دعوت میں آنے والے بچّوں کے ساتھ مذاق کیا تھا۔

بچپن میں وہ بہادر آدمی ہمالیہ پر چڑھا تھا۔

میرے پروفیسر نے اپنی زندگی کی کہانی دُہرائی تھی۔

۹۱۔ اِکیانوے

۹۲۔ بانوے

۹۳۔ ترانوے

۹۴۔ چورانوے

۹۵۔ پچانوے

۹۶۔ چھیانوے

۹۷۔ ستانوے

۹۸۔ اٹھانوے

۹۹۔ نِنانوے

۱۰۰ ۔ سو

13.7 گفتگو (Conversation)

(نرگس، راج، روی، رشی اور ریشما دلّی کی ہوٹل میں)

دروازے پر دستک۔۔۔

نرگس: کون ہے؟

روم سروس والا:نمستے میم صاحب۔ ہم آپ کی چائے لائے ہیں۔

راج: اِتنی صبح! کیا، اِن لوگوں کا دماغ خراب ہے؟ (روم سروس والے سے)۔ ہم

ابھی سو رہے ہیں۔ بعد میں آؤ۔

نرگس: راج! دس بج رہے ہیں۔ ہم کو جلدی اُٹھنا چاہیئے ۔ ورنہ گرمی

بہت بڑھیگی۔

راج: تم کب جاگیں؟

نرگس: میں رات میں سوئی نہیں۔ میرے سر میں بہت درد تھا۔

راج: تم نے کچھ دوائی کھائی ہے؟ میرے سوٹکیس میں ایسپرن ہے۔

نرگس: نہیں۔ اب تو میں ٹھیک ہوں۔ تم جلدی اُٹھو، نہاؤ اور پھر ہم لال قلعہ جا سکتے ہیں۔ ریشما، رشی اور روی، تم لوگ بھی اُٹھو۔ بہت دیر ہو رہی ہے۔

ریشما: او دیدی! میں اور سونا چاہتی ہوں۔ آپ اور راج بھیّا جا سکتے ہیں۔ مجھے تاریخی جگہوں سے بالکل دلچسپی نہیں۔ دیکھیئے روی بھیّا اور رشی بھیّا کو کتنی تھکن ہے۔ وہ دونوں تو آنکھیں بھی نہیں کھول سکتے!

رشی: او ہو! صبُح صبُح اتنا شور! ہمیں اور سونا ہے!

روی: رشی بالکل ٹھیک کہتا ہے۔ تم لوگ جاؤ! ہم بعد میں سیر کریںگے۔

نرگس: کیا، تم دلّی سونے کے لئے آئے ہو؟ اچھا، ٹھیک ہے۔ ہم دونوں جائیںگے۔

روم سروس والا: میڈم! کیا آپ کو چائے چاہیئے؟

نرگس: ہاں، ہم بیس منٹ میں نیچے آئیںگے۔

(نرگس اور راج ٹیکسی میں)

نرگس: ہم کو لال قلعہ جانا ہے۔

ٹیکسی والا: اچّھا! آج اُدھر بہت بھیڑ ہے۔ میں اُدھر تھوڑی دیر پہلے ہی گیا تھا۔

راج: کیا، کوئی خاص بات ہے؟

ٹیکسی والا: ہاں صاحب۔ آج جُمعہ ہے۔ لال قِلعہ کے پاس جامعہ مسجد ہے اور وہاں سب مُسلمان آج دو پہر کو نماز پڑھتے ہیں۔ کیا، لال قِلعہ جانا ضروری ہے؟

نرگس: کیا؟! ہاں بالکل ضروری ہے۔ اُس کے بعد ہم جامعہ مسجد بھی جائیںگے۔ وہ بھی دیکھنے کے قابل ہے۔

ٹیکسی والا: ہاں۔ یہ مغلوں کے زمانے کی عمارتیں ہیں۔ یہ عمارتیں مغل بادشاہ شاہ جہاں نے بنوائی ہیں۔ کیا، آپ کو یہ معلوم تھا؟

نرگس:	ہاں۔ میں نے ہندوستان کی تاریخ پڑھی ہے۔ مجھے تاریخی مقامات بہت پسند ہیں۔
راج:	کیا، دِلّی میں چڑیاگھر نہیں ہے؟
نرگس:	کیا؟ تم چڑیاگھر جاؤگے؟
راج:	کیوں نہیں؟
نرگس:	ہاں، ہاں، مجھے معلوم ہے۔ تمہارا خاندان وہیں تو رہتا ہے۔ اُن سے ملنا بہت ضروری ہے۔
راج:	کیا؟!
نرگس:	ارے، بُرا مت مانو۔ میں تو مذاق کر رہی ہوں۔ تم بھی تو ہر وقت مذاق کرتے ہو!
ٹیکسی والا:	لو صاحب۔ یہ ہے لال قِلعہ۔ کتنا شاندار ہے!
راج:	واہ! کیا چیز ہے!
نرگس:	دیکھو راج۔ ۱۹۴۷ء میں، ہندوستان آزاد ہوا۔ ہندوستان کے پہلے وزیرِ اعظم، جواہر لال نہرو نے آزادی کے دِن یہیں سے تقریر کی تھی۔ ایک زمانے میں یہاں مغل بادشاہ رہتے تھے۔ اُس کے بعد انگریزوں نے یہاں سے حکومت کی۔
ٹیکسی والا:	آپ کی بہت معلومات ہیں۔ آپ لوگ یہاں کب تک رہینگے؟
راج:	ہم یہاں دو بجے تک رہینگے۔ اُس کے بعد ہم جامع مسجد جائینگے۔
ٹیکسی والا:	اچھا۔ میں دو بجے یہاں آپ کا انتظار کرونگا۔ صاحب آج تو دھوپ بہت تیز ہے۔ کیا، آپ اپنی ٹوپی نہیں لائے ہیں؟
راج:	ہاں۔ میں ٹوپی لایا ہوں اور ساتھ میں چھتری بھی لایا ہوں۔ وہ نرگس کے پاس ہے۔

چلو راج۔ بہت دیر ہو رہی ہے۔ لال قلعہ بہت بڑا ہے۔ ہم کو ہوٹل جلدی واپس جانا ہے۔ کیا تمہیں یاد نہیں کہ ریشما، رشی اور روی ہوٹل میں ہمارا انتظار کر رہے ہیں؟

13.8 Conversation Practice

Mother: Anil! You are watching a lot of TV. Did you do your work?

Anil: Yes, mummy. I did my work, washed the clothes, and organized my room.

Mother: Did you eat the delicious samosas that I made?

Anil: Mummy! I am not hungry. I want to watch TV. This is my favorite show.

Mother: No. First eat these samosas and then drink this milk. It has bournvita

(chocolate) in it.

Anil: I don't like milk. You know that. I ate two oranges and an apple.

Mother: Milk is good for your health. Look - your brother drinks five glasses of milk

every morning and all the girls like him. Sunita Auntie told me yesterday that

your brother is the most handsome guy in school.

Anil: Really! I did not know that. I will now drink six glasses.

Mother: Just drink one glass right now otherwise the cow will not be very happy.

13.9 Songs

۱)   میرے گھر آئی ایک ننھی پری، ایک ننھی پری

چاندنی کے حسین رتھ پہ سوار

اُسکے آنے سے میرے آنگن میں

کھل اُٹھے پھول، گنگنائی بہار

دیکھ کر اُسکو جی نہیں بھرتا

چاہے دیکھوں اُسے ہزاروں بار

میں نے پوچھا اُسے کہ کون ہے تو؟

ہنس کے بولی کہ میں ہوں تیرا پیار

میں تیرے دل میں تھی ہمیشہ سے

گھر میں آئی ہوں آج پہلی بار

٢) پیار ہوا اِقرار ہوا ہے

پیار سے پھر کیوں ڈرتا ہے دل؟

کہتا ہے دل رستہ مشکل

معلوم نہیں ہے کہاں منزل

کہو کہ اپنی پریت کا گیت نہ بدلیگا کبھی

تم بھی کہو اس راہ کا میت نہ بدلیگا کبھی

پیار جو ٹوٹا ساتھ جو چھوٹا، چاند نہ چمکیگا کبھی

راتیں دسوں دِشاؤں سے کہینگی اپنی کہانیاں

گیت ہمارے پیار کے دہرائینگی جوانیاں

میں نہ رہونگی، تم نہ رہوگے، پھر بھی رہینگی نِشانیاں

Glossary for Songs

ننّھا = little, tiny, young

پری = fairy (f)

رتھ = chariot (m)

پر سوار x = riding on

آنگن = courtyard of a house (m)

اِقرار = promise; agreement; acceptance (m)

رستہ = road, path (m)

منزل = goal, destination (f)

پریت = love; happiness, joy (f)

راہ = path, road (f)

کِھل اُٹھنا = to blossom, to flower

گُنگُنانا = to hum, to sing softly

جی بھرنا = to be content, to be satisfied

مِیت = friend, lover (m)

چمکنا = to shine, glow, glimmer

دِشا = direction (f)

13.10 Vocabulary

bad, evil, wicked	بُرا
to be affronted, to feel insulted	بُرا ماننا
beautiful	حسِین
brain, mind, intellect (m)	دِماغ
to cause to be built, constructed	بنوانا
to have X built	X کو بنوانا
to cause to laugh	ہنسانا
clever, cunning, sly	چالاک
court (f)	عدالت
criminal (m)	مُجرِم
crowd (f)	بھِیڑ
cupboard, cabinet (f)	الماری
to dry	سکھانا
facts, information (f)	معلومات
to fight x	x سے لڑنا
to forget	بھولنا
ghost (m)	بھوت
government (f)	حُکومت

to govern	حُکومت کرنا
to increase, to enlarge, to extend (intransitive)	بڑھنا
to cause to increase, enlarge (transitive; causative)	بڑھانا
interest (interesting) (f)	دِلچسپی
joke, wit; taste (m)	مذاق
journey (m)	سفر
to make a journey, to travel	سفر کرنا
juice, nectar (m)	رس
late, a long while; a long period of time, interval; lateness (f)	دیر
to delay, to be a long time	دیر کرنا
to come late	دیر سے آنا
lawyer, agent (m/f)	وکیل
to live; to be alive	جینا
to lose (a battle, contest, game)	ہارنا
mail (f)	ڈاک
moon (m)	چاند
moonlight (f)	چاندنی
Muslim ritual prayers (f)	نماز
to recite namaz	نماز پڑھنا

oath (f)	قسم
to swear by x	x کی قسم کھانا
to open	کھولنا
otherwise	ورنہ
poetry; a couplet, a verse (m)	شعر
to play the role of x	x بننا
prison, jail (m)	قید خانہ
to recognize; to know; to perceive; to discern	پہچاننا
to repeat, to double, to fold	دُہرانا
sign, memento, souvenir (m/f)	نِشان(m)/ نِشانی (f)
special	خاص
speech, recital, statement (f)	تقریر
to give a speech	تقریر کرنا
splendid, stately, grand	شاندار
theft (f)	چوری
umbrella; canopy (f)	چھتری
village (m)	گاؤں
waiting, expectation (m)	اِنتظار
to wait for x	x کا اِنتظار کرنا
wonderful; surprising; strange	عجیب
zoo (m)	چڑیا گھر

Chapter 14

14.1 لگنا Constructions

لگنا is an intransitive verb which has a wide variety of meanings, depending on the context in which it is being used. The range of its root meanings include "to be connected to," "to be attached to," "to be fastened with or hung to," "to stick or adhere to."

اُس کی تصویر اِس دیوار پر لگی ہے۔

His picture is hanging (has been hung) on the wall.

ہندوستان کے خط پر کتنے ٹکٹ لگتے ہیں۔

How many stamps for (literally, are attached to) a letter for India?

In addition to the above examples, there are many idiomatic expressions and constructions with لگنا, some of which are introduced below.

(A) لگنا in Constructions with کو

لگنا can be used to convey feelings, sensations (hunger, thirst, fear), and perceptions (to seem, to appear). It is also employed in constructions involving objects that strike or hit the body (bullets, arrows, wounds). In these constructions, the logical subject in English is marked by کو and the verb agrees gramatically with the feelings, sensations, or objects.

آج صبح پانچ بجے مجھے بھوک لگی۔

I felt hungry at five o'clock this morning.

کیا تم کو علی اچّھا لگا؟

Did Ali seem nice to you?

305

راج کو لگتا ہے کہ نرگس کسی وجہ سے ناراض ہے۔

It seems to Raj that Nargis is displeased for some reason.

گرم چائے پینے کے بعد مجھے ٹھیک لگیگا۔

After drinking tea I will feel better.

مجرم کو گولی لگی۔

The criminal was struck by the bullet.

لگنا can also mean "to require," "to take (time)," "to cost" in constructions where the logical subject (in English) is marked by کو and the verb agrees in number and gender with the object:

میں گھر دیرے سے آیا کیونکہ مجھے امیگریشن کے دفتر میں دو گھنٹے لگے۔

I came home late because it took me two hours in the Immigration office.

اُس ہوٹل میں کھانا کھانے میں بہت پیسے لگینگے۔

It will cost a lot of money to eat in that restaurant.

یہاں سے اسلام آباد پہنچنے میں کتنے گھنٹے لگینگے؟

How many hours will it take to reach Islamabad from here?

(B) Oblique Infinitive + لگنا

When لگنا follows an oblique infinitive, it conveys the sense of the commencement or beginning of the action associated with the verbal infinitive. In this construction, the verb of action always remains as the oblique infinitive and the verb لگنا agrees in number and gender with the subject. Although the "oblique infinitive + لگنا construction" occurs in all tenses, except for the present and past continuous ones, it is common to find it used in the past tense.

راج اسی ہسپتال میں کام کرنے لگا۔

Raj began to work in the same hospital.

ڈر کی وجہ سے، بچّے رونے لگے۔

The children began to cry from (on account of) fear.

ہم کل وہاں کام کرنے لگینگے۔

We will begin to work there tomorrow.

ہر روز وہ عورت دفتر سے گھر آ کر کھانا پکانے لگتی ہے۔

Every day that woman begins to cook after coming home from the office.

14.1 Reading and Translation Drill

١۔ گاندھی جی کی تصویر اُس دیوار پر لگی ہے۔

آپ کے مُنہ پر کچھ لگا ہے۔

کل صبح ہمیں بہت بھوک لگی تھی۔

کیا، آپ کو پیاس نہیں لگی؟

٢۔ مجھے وہ لڑکی بہت خوبصورت لگی۔

کیا، تمہیں وہ فِلم اچّھی لگی؟

نہیں، مجھے انگریزی فلمیں اچّھی نہیں لگتیں۔

ہمیں صرف انگریزی شاعری اچّھی لگتی ہے۔

٣۔ اِس کتاب کو ختم کرنے کے لئے بہت دِن لگے۔

آپ کے دوست کے جانے کے بعد، آپ لوگ کیا کرنے لگے؟

میں کپڑے دھونے لگا اور شیلا گھر صاف کرنے لگی۔

میرے خیال میں اب تم کام کرنے لگو۔

٤۔ شرارت کرنے والے لڑکے اپنے ماسٹر کو دیکھ کر رونے لگے۔

جُولِئیٹ رومیو کے بارے میں سوچنے لگی۔

چور اپنی ماں کی قسم کھانے لگا۔

307

ساڑھے بارہ بجے وہ پانچوں مسلمان نماز پڑھنے لگے۔

۵۔ مائیکل جیکسن کو دیکھ کر سب لڑکیاں چیخنے لگیں۔

لیجئے، یہ دوائی پیجئے۔ آپ کو ابھی کچھ منٹوں میں ٹھیک لگنے لگے گا۔

نرگس کو لگا کہ راج رادھا سے پیار کرنے لگا۔

مجھے تو لگتا ہے کہ وہ ایک بہت خطرناک چور ہے۔

Translate into idiomatic Urdu:

1.   We are (feeling) very hungry. We have to eat now.

2.   What all seemed beautiful to you in Agra?

3.   All my friends began to go home.

4.   How long (lit. how much time) does it take to go by car from Boston to New York?

5.   The girl began to laugh a lot after she heard the joke.

6.   The rich lady asked the washerman (دھوبی) how many days it would take to wash all

the clothes.

7.   Excuse me, sir, can you tell me how much a ticket to Benares would cost?

8.   The boy was wounded in the head. (wound (f) = چوٹ; to be wounded = چوٹ لگنا).

9.   It seems to me that in India mangoes are cheaper than apples.

10.   I am not feeling well. I want to go home and sleep.

14.2 Verb Stem+ چُکنا Construction

چُکنا "to finish" is an intransitive verb which is never used by itself. Like the verb سکنا "to be able

to, can," it must always be preceded by the stem of another verb. In such constructions, چُکنا

indicates the completion of the action denoted by the verbal stem which precedes it (i.e., finish

doing something). Like the "oblique infinitive+ لگنا" construction, چُکنا is found in all tenses,

308

except the present continuous and past continuous. Since it is primarily a completive auxiliary, it

occurs most frequently in past tense constructions. Translations of "verb stem + چُکنا" construction

often incorporate the word "already" to indicate the sense of completion.

راج یہ کتاب پڑھ چکا تھا۔

Raj had already read (finished reading) this book.

وہ لڑکا اپنا دودھ پی چکا ہے۔

That boy has already drunk (finished drinking) his milk.

ہمارا نوکر گھر کا کام تین بجے تک کر چُکیگا۔

Our servant will finish the house work by three o'clock.

14.2 Reading and Translation Drill

١۔   وہ لڑکے یہ کتابیں پڑھ چکے ہیں۔

ہمارے مہمان جا چکے ہیں۔

وہ لڑکیاں پھل کھا چکی ہیں۔

میں کپڑے بدل چکی ہوں۔

٢۔   کیا، آپ اِس سے پہلے بھی پاکستان دیکھ چکے ہیں؟

مجھے لگتا ہے کہ آپ دُنیا کی سیر کر چکے ہیں۔

لڑکی اپنی والدہ کو خط بھیج چکی ہے۔

ہم اپنے صنم کو دِل دے چکے ہیں۔

٣۔   جب عورتوں نے دیکھا کہ ہم کھانا کھا چکے ہیں تو وہ خود کھانے لگیں۔

جب زمیندار وہاں پہنچا تب تک وہ محنتی کِسان سب پتّھر توڑ چکے تھے۔

جب ہم ہوائی اڈّے پر پہنچے تو ہوائی جہاز نکل چکا تھا۔

جب امول گھر پہنچ چکا تھا تو اسے میرے پیسے یاد آئے۔

309

Translate into Urdu:

1.   I had already finished eating when he came to my house.

2.   The mother asked her son, "Have you already read this book?"

3.   The student had already written his essay and given it to his professor.

4.   Have you already seen a movie in which Shahrukh Khan is an actor?

5.   When he had already left, then I remembered his name!

6.   When the teacher reached the school, the students had already gone home.

7.   When Shahrukh Khan had already left my shop, I recognized him.

8.   The naughty boy had already climbed up the tree.

9.   When Nargis and Raj arrived at the zoo, it was already closed (to be closed= بند ہونا).

10.   When the doctor examined me, the fever had already come down (use اُترنا or
کم ہونا).

14.3 The Oblique Infinitive + دینا Construction

The oblique infinitive of a verb in combination with the verb دینا is used to express the idea of allowing or permitting someone to do something as well as giving permission. The infinitive always appears in its inflected form while the verb دینا agrees in number and gender with the subject.

بیمار بچّے کو سونے دیجیے۔

Let the sick child sleep!

میرے والد صاحب مجھے ایک گاڑی خریدنے دینگے۔

My father will allow me to buy a car.

The oblique infinitive + دینا construction is considered to be transitive. Therefore, in the simple

310

past tense, the subject of this construction is marked with نے with the verb دینا agreeing with the object.

انہوں نے لڑکی کو کتاب نہیں پڑھنے دی۔

They did not let the girl read the book.

(verb agreeing with object "book")

14.3 Reading and Translation Drill

۱۔ میری والدہ مجھے ٹی۔ وی۔ دیکھنے دیتی ہیں۔

کیا، آپ کے والد آپ کو فٹبال دیکھنے دیتے ہیں؟

نہیں۔ ہمارے والد ہم کو صرف خبریں دیکھنے دیتے ہیں۔

شیلا کی بہن اُس کو مٹھائی نہیں کھانے دیتی۔

۲۔ تم مجھے کام کرنے دو گے یا نہیں؟

شفیق کو بخار ہے۔ اُسے سونے دو۔

بس! اب تو مجھے رونے دیجیئے۔

راج اب تو رات کے بارہ بج رہے ہیں! نرگس کو گھر جانے دو۔

ریشما! چپ رہو! ہمیں دُنیا کے سب سے عظیم فنکار کو سننے دو!

۳۔ میرے گھر والے نے مجھے بات بھی نہیں کرنے دی۔

اُس کم بخت(wretched) مُلک کی سردی نے ہمیں باہر بھی نہ جانے دیا۔

سمیر کے باپ نے اُسے جولی سے شادی نہیں کرنے دی۔

سردار صاحب نے اپنے لڑکے کو شراب نہیں پینے دی مگر پانی پینے دیا۔

۴۔ آپ کو اپنے چھوٹے چھوٹے بچّوں کو سگریٹ نہیں پینے دینا چاہیئے۔

آپ کی یاد نے مجھے سونے نہیں دیا۔

اُس بہادُر لڑکی نے چور کو پیسیوں کی الماری (safe) کھولنے نہیں دی۔

311

میں ڈارلنگ راج کے پتاجی کو زیادہ مٹھائی کھانے نہیں دیتی ہیں۔

Translate into Urdu:

1.   We will not allow our children to play outside in this cold. They can play inside the house with their toys.

2.   When I go to Dubai, my friend lets me stay in his house. It is a splendid house with a pretty garden.

3.   I have heard that India is a beautiful country. Let your daughter go to India.

4.   His father does not allow him to stay outside after 11pm.

5.   Did you let the traveller see those photographs?

14.4 Compound Verbs

(A) Verb Stem + Aspect Indicators: لینا، دینا، جانا، پڑنا، بیٹھنا، ڈالنا

A compound verb combines the stem or root of a principal verb with the conjugated form of an auxiliary verb. Frequently, the auxiliary verb loses its original lexical meaning, serving instead as an aspect indicator that connotes a nuance or aspect of the action of the main verb. For instance, an aspect indicator verb may indicate the intensity with which an act was performed, its suddeness or that it was done foolishly. There are only a handful of verbs that can serve as aspect indicators; some common aspect indicator verbs and the nuances with which they are associated are listed below. It is necessary to keep in mind the following points concerning an auxiliary verb serving as an aspect indicator:

a) The aspect indicator verb, which acts in an auxiliary mode, loses its original meaning. For example, the verb لینا "to take" when used as an aspect indicator no longer means "to take." Instead, it indicates that the action of the principal verb has taken place for the subject's benefit or is in some manner directed toward the subject.

b) Only the aspect indicator verb inflects; the stem of the main verb remains unchanged. As auxiliary verbs, aspect indicators can be in any tense, except the continuous.

c) In the past tense, aspect indicator constructions are treated as transitive (i.e., subject will be marked by نے) only if both the aspect indicator verb and the main verb are transitive.

d) Since there are no equivalents of aspect indicators in English, accurate translations are often difficult without some elaboration.

Common Aspect Indicators

1.   لینا, "to take": When لینا is used as an auxiliary verb with the stem of another verb, it conveys the meaning that the action has taken place for the subject's benefit or is in some manner directed toward the subject:

اُس نے یہ کتاب پڑھ لی۔

He read this book (for his own benefit).

مریض یہ دوائی پی لیگا۔

The patient will drink the medicine (for himself).

2.   دینا, "to give": دینا as an auxiliary verb with the stem of another verb conveys the meaning that the action has been done for the benefit of someone other than the subject or directed away from the subject:

میں نے یہ کتاب پڑھ دی۔

I read this book (for someone else).

امیر لوگوں کو اپنا زیادہ پیسہ غریبوں کو دے دینا چاہئے۔

Rich people should give away their extra money to the poor.

313

3.   جانا, "to go": جانا may denote several aspects including the total completion of an action, the transition from one state to another, or an action that is taking place as a process:

وہ آدمی سو گیا۔

That man fell asleep.

کیا، تم کل تک وہاں پہنچ جاؤ گے؟

Will you reach there by tomorrow?

گاؤں والے لڑکے تیز بریانی کھا گئے۔

The boys from the village ate up the spicy biryani.

4.   پڑنا, "to fall": This denotes a sudden or violent change of affairs or a sudden downward motion.

وہ لڑکا پیڑ پر سے گِر پڑا۔

That boy fell down from the tree.

اُن کی باتیں سن کر میں ہنس پڑا۔

On hearing his talk, I burst out laughing.

5.   بیٹھنا, "to sit": This is similar to پڑنا since it also denotes sudden action. بیٹھنا further implies that the reasons for the action are foolish or senseless.

وہ اپنی کتابیں کھو بیٹھا۔

He lost his books.

چھوٹی لڑکی رو بیٹھی۔

The young girl cried (without any good reason).

6.   ڈالنا, "to pour, to throw down": Also indicates a violent action and further implies that the action has been completed.

کیا، آپ نے وہ کتاب پھینک ڈالی؟

Did you throw away that book?

(B) *Verb Stem* + پانا *Construction*

Not all auxiliary verbs in compound verbal formations function as aspect indicators. For instance, the verbs سکنا and چکنا are considered grammatically to be modals indicating, respectively, ability and completion. The verb پانا as an auxiliary verb also functions as a modal. It is used to underscore physical ability or capacity to perform a particular action to its completion. Stem + پانا constructions are best translated as "to manage to..." or "get a chance to..." They commonly occur in the negative. In the past tense, the subject of this construction is not marked by نے.

ہم یہ گیت نہیں گا پائے۔

We weren't able (could not manage) to sing this song.

عشق کی وجہ سے ، راج سو نہیں پاتا۔

On account of love, Raj cannot (manage to) sleep.

افسوس ہے کہ میں یہ سچ وقت پر نہیں بتا پائی ۔

I regret that I could not manage to tell this truth in a timely manner.

Unlike the verbs سکنا and چکنا, the verb پانا can be used in a non-modal context, that is, on its own, in which case it means "to find" or "to get." In this situation, it functions as regular transitive verb, with the subject being marked with نے in the past tense.

آپ نے اِس کام سے کیا خوشی پائی؟

What happiness did you get from this work?

۱- آپ کھانا کھا لیجیٔے، میں تو اپنے دوست کا اِنتظار کر رہا ہوں۔

اُس لڑکی نے پیڑ پر چڑھ کر پھل کھا لیٔے۔

اگرچہ وہ بوڑھی ہے مگر گھر کے سب کام وہ خود ہی کر لیتی ہے۔

کیا، تم گاڑی چلا لیتے ہو؟

۲- کیا، آپ میرے لیٔے کتابیں لا دینگے؟

میں نے آپ کے لیٔے اچّھی اچّھی چیزیں خرید دی ہیں۔

یہ نوکر ابھی آپ کا کمرہ صاف کر دیگا۔

کیا، اُس دھوبی نے ہمارے کپڑے دھو دیٔے ہیں؟

۳- کیا،اُن کے سب رشتہ دار اُس گاڑی کے ایکسیڈینٹ میں مر گیٔے؟

کیا، وہ موٹا لڑکا سارا کھانا کھا گیا؟

دیکھو! وہ بلّی پیڑ پر چڑھ گئی۔

ہم یہیں بیٹھ جایٔینگے۔

۴- میں لال قلعہ کے اُوپر سے جامعہ مسجد نہیں دیکھ پایا۔

اُن کے ہاتھوں پر مہندی لگی تھی۔ وہ کام نہیں کر پایٔیں۔

کیا، تم اپنا کمرہ صاف کر پایٔے؟

وہ لڑکی بیمار ہو گئی تھی۔ اِس وجہ سے وہ ہمارے گھر نہیں آ پائی ۔

۵- اُس غمناک کہانی کو سننے کے بعد، وہ لوگ رو پڑے۔

ہم سائینفیلڈ کو دیکھ کر ہنس پڑے۔

اَمر اندھیرے میں گِر پڑا۔

بیچارہ ہمٹی ڈمٹی دیوار سے گِر پڑیگا۔

۶- تم یہ کیا کر بیٹھے؟

شیلا سنیل سے محبت کر بیٹھی!

وہ پاگل آدمی ہوائی جہاز میں اُن سب مسافروں کو مار بیٹھا۔

میں اپنے ہوش کھو بیٹھی۔

۷۔ نرگس نے راج سے پیار کرکے سنیل کا دِل توڑ ڈالا۔

اُس چور نے سب گھر والوں کو مار ڈالا۔

ہمارے شریر لڑکے نے سب کھِلونے توڑ ڈالے۔

میری تصویر کو کس نے پھینک ڈالا؟

Translate the following into Urdu using appropriate aspect indicators:

1. We have cleaned the house (for our own benefit).

2. Have you written the letter (for someone else)?

3. We are not hungry. Please eat these sweets (for your own benefit).

4. All his friends died (abruptly).

5. He lost all his best toys (foolishly).

6. Look (for yourself). I have nothing in my hands.

7. Will you be able to take all your toys in this small box?

8. The traveller came home and fell asleep.

9. Nargis ought to have her blood tested (to get X tested = کا معائنہ کرانا X).

10. The cunning thief stole all the traveller's money.

11. I understood what he had to say (use اس کی بات) (completely).

12. Because of a bad cough, he could not (manage to) eat his food (use پانا).

13. He is so busy that he will not get a chance (use پانا) to go to the hospital to see his

mother.

14.5 Introduction to the Subjunctive

The subjunctive form of a verb is commonly used in situations expressing uncertainty, possibility, desire, or wish. In addition, it is used in a variety of other circumstances, some of which are described below. Subjunctives are formed in a manner similar to that of the future tense except the suffix گا، گے، گی of the future is dropped.

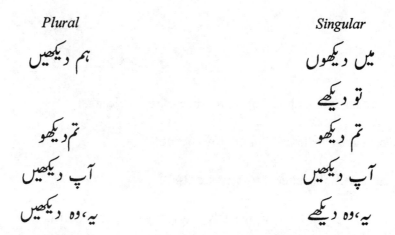

Plural	Singular
ہم دیکھیں	میں دیکھوں
	تو دیکھے
تم دیکھو	تم دیکھو
آپ دیکھیں	آپ دیکھیں
یہ، وہ دیکھیں	یہ، وہ دیکھے

Unlike other tenses, the subjunctive form of the verb distinguishes number (singular and plural) but not gender. For the negative, the subjunctive uses the particle نہ usually placed before the verb.

شاید وہ کھانا نہ پکا سکیں۔

Perhaps he is not able to cook food.

Common Uses for the Subjunctive

1. *Asking Permission (with first person)*

میں دیکھوں؟

May [should, shall] I see?

ہم جائیں؟

May [should, shall] we go?

کیا، میں سبزی کاٹوں؟

May [should, shall] I cut the vegetables?

2. *Suggestions/Indirect Commands/Reporting of Commands/Polite Imperative*

آپ ہمارے گھر تشریف لائیں۔

Please come to our house.

آپ کچھ کھانا کھائیں۔

Please eat some food.

بازار چلیں۔

Let's go to the market.

پتاجی سے کہو کہ وہ زیادہ مٹھائی نہ کھائیں۔

Tell father that he should not eat too many sweets.

3. *Desire/Wish*

تم سوا سو برس سلامت رہو۔

May you live for 125 years (A common blessing that the elderly in South Asia give).

خدا آپ کو کامیابی دے!

May God grant you (give you) success!

خوش رہو میری بیٹی!

May you remain happy, my daughter!

4. *With specific adverbs and phrases denoting desirability, contingency, suitability, doubt or possibility:*

شاید</div> - *Perhaps*

شاید وہ یہاں آئیں۔

Perhaps they may come here.

کاش - *if only/would that...*

کاش ہم روی شنکر کو سن سکیں۔

If only we are able to hear Ravi Shankar.

تاکہ - *so that....*

میں ممبئی جاؤنگا تاکہ میں سلمان خان کو دیکھ سکوں۔

I'll go to Mumbai so that I can see Salman Khan.

خدا کرے (کہ) - *May God will that....*

خدا کرے (کہ) وہ کل یہاں آئیں۔

May God will that he may come here tomorrow.

خدا نہ کرے (کہ) ہماری لڑکی روئے۔

May God not will that our daughter cry.

خدا نہ خواستہ - *God forbid (may God not will that)....*

خدا نہ خواستہ آپ کو کچھ ہو۔

May God forbid that something happen to you.

مناسب ہے کہ - *it is appropriate that....*

مناسب ہے (کہ) آپ یہاں بیٹھیں۔

It is appropriate that you sit here.

ایسا نہ ہو کہ - *let it not be that....*

دیکھو! ایسا نہ ہو کہ یہ چھوٹا لڑکا گر جائے۔

Look, let it not be that this young boy falls down.

کو چاہئے کہ x - *it is necessary for x to....*

مجھے چاہئے کہ میں آج ہی یہ کتاب پڑھوں۔

It is necessary that I read this book today.

کا اِرادہ ہے کہ x - *it is x's intention that....*

میرا اِرادہ ہے کہ میں کل تک وہ کتاب پڑھوں۔

It is my intention that I read that book by tomorrow.

ممکن ہے کہ - *it is possible that....*

ممکن ہے کہ ہم ناچیں۔

It is possible that we [may] dance.

میں چاہتا ہوں کہ - *I want that....*

میں چاہتا ہوں کہ بڑا لڑکا ایک عظیم کھلاڑی بنے۔

I want the elder boy to become a great athlete.

14.5 Reading and Translation Drill

۱۔ کیا، میں یہ تصویر دیکھوں؟

ہم یہ قالینیں دیکھیں؟

آپ وہاں دستخط کریں۔

آپ اُدھر کام کریں۔

۲۔ اُن کو چاہئے کہ دعوت کی تیاری کریں۔

مجھے چاہئے کہ میں اِمتحان کے لئے پڑھوں۔

اُس نوکر کو چاہئے کہ گھر صاف کرے۔

سیما سے کہیئے کہ کھانا پکائے۔

۳۔ تم ہزاروں برس جیوٗ۔

آپ ہزاروں سال جئیں۔

وہ سوا سو برس جئے۔

کسان کی جَے ہو۔

۴۔ شاید وہ کسان یہاں آئیں۔

کاش وہ کسان حکومت کریں۔

میں اُس گاؤں میں گیا تاکہ اُن کسانوں کو دیکھ سکوں۔

خُدا کرے کہ وہ کِسان حکومت کریں۔

۵۔ مناسب ہے کہ آپ اُس کھیت کو دیکھیں۔

ایسا نہ ہو کہ وہ آپ کا کام نہ کرے۔

اُسے چاہئے کہ وہ آپ کی مدد کرے۔

میرا اِرادہ ہے کہ میں ڈاکٹر بنوں۔

۶۔ ممکن ہے کہ آج بارش ہو۔

کاش آج بارش ہو تاکہ جانور پانی پی سکیں۔

مناسب ہے کہ آپ اس غریب آدمی کو کھانا دیں۔

ایسا نہ ہو کہ وہ بیمار مسافر مر جائے۔

۷۔ اس سے کہو کہ وہ یہاں دستخط کرے۔

دھوبی سے کہو کہ وہ کپڑے اچّھی طرح دھوئے۔

امریکہ کے صدر سے کہئے کہ وہ ہمارے گھر تشریف لائیں۔

مجھے الٹر ہے۔ آپ اپنی بیوی سے کہیں کہ وہ کھانا زیادہ تیز نہ بنائے۔

۸۔ خُدا نہ خواستہ، (کہ) وہ بیمار ہو جائے۔

خُدا کرے کہ آپ کی زندگی کامیاب ہو۔

خُدا نہ خواستہ، (کہ) ان چھوٹے بچّوں کی ماں مر جائے۔

خُدا کرے (کہ) میں جلدی ایک کروڑپتی بن جاؤں۔

Translate the following into Urdu using subjunctives wherever appropriate:

1.   May we see that?

2.   Perhaps we may see Michael Jordan. All the famous people have come here.

3.   If only we are able to study Urdu in India!

4.   I would like to go to India so that I can work in the fields with the farmers.

5.   May God will that you can come tomorrow.

6.   It is possible that we may meet that famous artist tomorrow.

7.   This seat is empty. Please sit here (تشریف رکھنا).

8.   Tell our driver that he should not wait for us.

9.   The guests are hungry. Shall we eat?

10.   It is their intention that from today they will not drink alcohol.

11.   If only all the people of this village were millionaires!

14.6 گفتگو (Conversation)

(راج، نرگس، ریشما، رشی اور روی ریل گاڑی میں)

(دلّی سے آگرہ جا رہے ہیں)

ریشما: دیدی آج بہت گرمی ہے۔ آگرہ پہنچنے میں اور کتنی دیر لگے گی؟

روی: تم ہر وقت بولتی رہتی ہو۔ نرگس دیدی سو گئی ہیں۔ اُن کو اپنے شور سے مت ستاؤ۔

راج: روی اور ریشما مت لڑو۔ وہ دیکھو کتنے ... ... اُدھر دیکھو، کسان کھیت میں ہل چلا رہے ہیں۔

روی:	ہاں، یہ کسان کتنی محنت کرتے ہیں۔ کاش ہم اِتنے محنتی بن سکیں۔ راج بھیّا، آپ نے کبھی ہل چلایا ہے؟

راج:	نہیں۔ مگر میں نے ایک بار ٹریکٹر چلایا تھا۔ مجھے بہت بہت اچّھا لگا تھا۔

روی:	میرا اِرادہ ہے کہ میں بھی ہندوستان میں اِن کھیتوں میں کام کروں۔

ریشما:	مجھے بہت بھوک لگی ہے۔ کیا میں یہ سموسہ کھاؤں۔

روی:	تم نے ابھی چار سموسے کھا لیئے ہیں۔ پیٹ خراب ہو جائیگا۔ اچّھا، کیا تم یہ کامِک بک پڑھ چکیں۔

ریشما:	نہیں، میں یہ کامِک بک نہیں پڑھ پائی۔ راج بھیّا کیا ہم آگرہ جلدی پہنچ جائینگے؟

راج:	ہاں، ہاں، بس تھوڑی دیر میں پہنچ جائینگے۔ وہ دیکھو آگرہ اِسٹیشن آ گیا۔

(راج، روی، رشی، ریشما اور نرگس تاج محل کے سامنے)

ریشما:	یہ کتنی خوبصورت عمارت ہے۔ کیا، یہاں ہندوستان کے راجہ رہتے ہیں؟

نرگس:	نہیں ریشما۔ ہندوستان کا کوئی راجہ واجہ نہیں۔ ہندوستان ایک جمہوریت ہے اور یہاں کے راجہ یہاں کے لوگ ہیں۔

روی:	جمہوریت کا مطلب کیا ہے؟

نرگس:	جمہوریت یعنی ڈیموکریسی۔ اگرچہ یہاں پر کوئی زندہ راجہ نہیں رہتا ہے، یہ ایک مقبرہ ہے۔ یہاں پر مغل بادشاہ شاہ جہاں اور اُن کی بیوی مُمتاز محل کی قبریں ہیں۔

راج:	نرگس، کیا میں اِن لوگوں کو تاج محل کی کہانی سُناؤں؟

نرگس:	ہاں، ہاں۔ کیوں نہیں؟ ضرور سُناؤ۔

راج:	اچّھا، سنو۔ شاہ جہاں پانچواں مغل بادشاہ تھا۔ وہ اپنی بیوی مُمتاز محل سے بہت پیار کرتا تھا جیسے میں نرگس سے کرتا ہوں۔ مُمتاز محل کے مر جانے کے بعد، شاہ جہاں کو بہت غم ہوا اور اس نے یہ مقبرہ بنوایا۔ یہ مقبرہ سنگِ مرمر کا ہے اور دنیا کے عجائب میں سے ایک ہے۔

324

روی: عجائب یعنی؟

راج: عجائب یعنی ونڈرز۔ تاج محل شاہ جہاں کی محبت کی نشانی ہے۔ اُردو کے ایک مشہور شاعر شکیل بدایونی* نے کہا ہے:

ایک شہنشاہ نے بنوا کے حسیں تاج محل

ساری دنیا کو محبت کی نشانی دی ہے

ریشما: میرے خیال میں یہ تو بہت مہنگی عمارت ہے۔

نرگس: ہاں، ہاں، بہت مہنگی۔ اگرچہ یہ بہت خوبصورت عمارت ہے، مگر میرے خیال میں یہ صرف امیر لوگوں کی ہی محبت کی نشانی ہو سکتی ہے۔ کیا، غریب پیار کرنے والے اپنے محبوبوں کو اِتنی مہنگی نشانیاں دے سکتے ہیں؟ شکیل کا شعر اگرچہ اچّھا ہے،مگر مجھے ساحر لدھیانوی* کا یہ شعر زیادہ پسند ہے:

ایک شہنشاہ نے بنوا کے حسیں تاج محل

ہم غریبوں کی محبت کا اُڑایا ہے مذاق

راج: نہیں نرگس۔ اگرچہ ساحر بھی بہت اچّھا شاعر تھا، مگر میرے خیال میں شاہ جہاں نے ہم غریبوں کی محبت کا مذاق نہیں اُڑایا۔ دیکھو یہاں پر امیر غریب سب لوگ آتے ہیں، اور اِس خوبصورت مقبرے کے سامنے ہم سب اپنے محبوبوں کی آنکھوں میں دیکھ کر کہہ سکتے ہیں کہ تاج محل دُنیا کی سب سے خوبصورت عمارت ہے اور تم میری زندگی کی سب سے خوبصورت چیز ہو۔

روی: او ہو! آپ لوگ صرف باتیں کر رہے ہیں۔ دیکھیئے، چاند کی روشنی میں تاج محل کتنا خوبصورت نظر آ رہا ہے۔ یہ عمارت تو خود ایک خوبصورت شعر ہے۔ کیا، بنگال کے مشہور شاعر رابندرناتھ ٹیگور* نے نہیں کہا:

تاج محل وقت کے رُخسار پر ایک آنسو ہے!

شکیل بدایونی : Shakil Badayuni, Urdu poet and lyric composer, died 1970.

ساحر لدھیانوی : Sahir Ludhianawi, Urdu poet and lyric composer, died 1980.

ربندرناتھ ٹیگور : Rabindranath Tagore, Bengali poet, winner of Nobel Prize for Literature, died 1941.

14.7 Conversation Practice

ان سوالوں کا جواب دیجیے:

۱۔ راج، روی، رشی، ریشما، اور نرگس کہاں سے کہاں جا رہے ہیں؟

۲۔ نرگس ریل میں کیا کر رہی ہے؟

۳۔ ان لوگوں کو راستے میں کیا کیا نظر آتا ہے؟

۴۔ روی ہندوستان میں کیا کرنا چاہتا ہے؟

۵۔ تاج محل کس نے بنوایا اور تاج محل میں کیا ہے؟

۶۔ دُنیا کے کتنے عجائب ہیں؟ کیا آپ کو اُن کے نام معلوم ہیں؟

۷۔ ساحر کے خیال میں شاہ جہاں نے غریب لوگوں کی محبت کو کیا کیا؟

۸۔ آپ کو شکیل کا شعر زیادہ پسند ہے یا ساحر کا شعر؟ کیوں؟

14.8 Songs

۱۔ جب کوئی بات بگڑ جائے

جب کوئی مشکل پڑ جائے

تم دینا ساتھ میرا او ہم نوا

نہ کوئی ہے نہ کوئی تھا زندگی میں تمہارے سوا

تم دینا ساتھ میرا او ہم نوا (۲)

ہو چاندنی جب تک رات

دیتا ہے ہر کوئی ساتھ

تم مگر اندھیروں میں نہ چھوڑنا میرا ہاتھ (۲)

جب کوئی ۔۔۔۔۔

۲۔ دُنیا کی سیر کر لو! (۴) اِنسان کے دوست بن کر اِنسان سے پیار کر لو!

دُنیا کی سیر کر لو! (۴) اِنسان کے دوست بن کر اِنسان سے پیار کر لو!

اَراؤنڈ دھ ورلڈ اِن ایٹ ڈالرز!

لوس اینجلیس بھڑکیلا جہاں ہولی وُوڈ ہے رنگیلا

دیکھو ڈزنی لینڈ میں آ کر پریوں کا دیش دھرتی پر

دُنیا کی سیر کر لو! (۴) اِنسان کے دوست بن کر اِنسان سے پیار کر لو!

اَراؤنڈ دھ ورلڈ اِن ایٹ ڈالرز!

ہم امن چاہنے والے ہم پیار پر مرنے والے

ایک بات کہیں گے سب سے:

"نفرت کو مٹا دو جگ سے"

اِنسان کے ہاتھ کا ٹونا مٹی کو بنایا سونا

یہ واشنگٹن البیلا نیویارک شہر کا میلا

۳۔ کیا خوب لگتی ہو، بڑی سُندر دِکھتی ہو!

پھر سے کہو، کہتے رہو، اچّھا لگتا ہے۔

جیون کا ہر سپنا اب سچّا لگتا ہے۔

کیا خوب لگتی ہو، بڑی سُندر دِکھتی ہو!

تعریف کرو گے کب تک؟ بولو کب تک؟

میرے سینے میں سانس رہیگی جب تک۔

کب تک میں رہوئگی تیرے من میں، تیرے من میں؟

سُورج ہوگا جب تک نیل گگن میں۔

پھر سے کہو، کہتے رہو، اچّھا لگتا ہے۔

جیون کا ہر سپنا اب سچّا لگتا ہے۔

کیا خوب لگتی ہو، بڑی سُندر دِکھتی ہو!

تم پیارے سے پیاری ہو، تم جان ہماری ہو!

Glossary for Songs

بِگڑنا = to go wrong, turn bad; to break down

ہم نوا = fellow-singer (m)

x کے سِوا = except for x

ساتھ دینا = to accompany; to support

بھڑکیلا = resplendent, glittering; flashy

رنگیلا = bright; showy; colorful; merry

دھرتی = the earth; earth, ground, soil (f)

امن = peace, security, safety (m)

نفرت = hatred (f)

مِٹانا = to efface, obliterate, abolish

جگ = world, universe, earth (m)

ٹونا = magic, spell; enchantment (m)

مٹّی = earth, soil, dust; dirt, filth (f)

سونا = gold (m)

البیلا = elegant, charming, smart; playful

میلا = fair, meeting, assembly (m)

خوب = beautiful, pretty; splendid

دِکھنا = to appear; to seem; to be seen

سچّا = true

تعریف کرنا = to praise

سینہ = chest, bosom, breast (m)

مَن = heart; soul; mind (m)

سُورج = sun (m)

نیل = blue

گگن = sky; heavens (m)

پیاری = precious; dear; beloved

14.9 Vocabulary

agricultural field (m)	کھیت
appropriate	مُناسِب
to break (transitive)	توڑنا
to break (intransitive)	ٹوٹنا
cheeks/countenance (m)	رُخسار
darkness (m)	اندھیرا
democracy (f)	جمہُوریت
emperor (m)	شہنشاہ
empty	خالی
to fall down	گِرنا
farmer/peasant (m)	کِسان
fat	موٹا
to finish	ختم کرنا
to fly; to cause to fly;	اُڑانا
to tease, to make fun of x	x کا مذاق اُڑانا
God willing (may God will that)	خُدا کرے (کہ)، اِنْشَاء اللہ
God forbid (may God not will	خُدا نہ کرے (کہ)،
that)	خُدا نہ خواستہ
great	عظیم
hard work (f)	محنت
hard working	محنتی

to work hard	محنت کرنا
henna (f)	حِنّا، مہندی
to hit	مارنا
if only	کاش
living	زِندہ
lover	محبوب (m) / محبوبہ (f)
marble (m)	سنگِ مرمر
once	ایک بار
perhaps	شاید
plow (m)	ہل
possible	مُمکِن
to remember	یاد آنا
for x to remember	x کو یاد آنا
signature (m)	دستخط
so that	تاکہ
sorrowful	غمناک
success (f)	کامیابی
successful	کامیاب
to tease, to annoy, to torment	ستانا
to think	سوچنا
to throw	پھینکنا
time (period of); period (m)	دوران

during this time/period	اِس دوران میں
toy (m)	کھِلونا
traveller (m/f)	مُسافِر
wall (f)	دیوار
wedding (f)	شادی
whole, entire; all; the whole	سارا
wonder (m)	عجوبہ
wonders (pl)	عجائب
museum	عجائب گھر
would that /if only	کاش
wound; injury (f)	چوٹ

Chapter 15

15.1 Condition-Result Clauses with اگر and تو

Clauses stipulating a condition are usually marked with اگر "if" and frequently precede a "result" clause that begins with تو. Example:

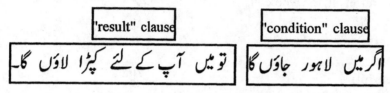

"result" clause   "condition" clause

اگر میں لاہور جاؤں گا تو میں آپ کے لئے کپڑا لاؤں گا۔

If I (will) go to Lahore, I will bring cloth for you.

Although the word اگر at the beginning of the "condition" clause may be dropped at times, the تو that marks the "result" clause is obligatory. Various verb tenses (present, future, past, or subjunctive) can occur in either "condition" or "result" clauses depending on the degree of certainty implied. The use of the subjunctive (as opposed to indicative tenses) indicates a greater degree of uncertainty or likelihood of fulfillment of a particular action. The examples below illustrate the usage of verb forms (subjunctive and indicative) in various sentences to convey degrees of certainty/uncertainty:

1. Purely hypothetical (use of subjunctive in both "condition" and "result" clauses, indicates high degree of uncertainty concerning both the condition and its fulfillment)

اگر میں ہندوستان جاؤں تو تاج محل دیکھوں۔

If I should go to India, then I may see the Taj Mahal.

2. More certainty than # 1 above ("condition" uncertain; "result" certain)

اگر میں ہندوستان جاؤں تو تاج محل دیکھونگا۔

If I should go to India, then I will see the Taj Mahal.

3. More certainty than #2 above (fulfillment of "condition" more likely or certain, "result" certain)

اگر میں ہندوستان جاؤنگا   تو تاج محل دیکھونگا۔

If I go to India, then I will see the Taj Mahal.

اگر آپ ہندوستان جا رہے ہیں تو تاج محل ضرور دیکھئیے۔

If you are going to India, do see the Taj Mahal (for sure).

At times, the "condition" clause may contain the simple past participle of a verb. In this context, the past participle often functions as a future conditional, indicating a condition that may be fulfilled in the future. Note: the past participle is not used in the "result" clause:

اگر میں ہندوستان گیا   تو تاج محل دیکھونگا۔

If I (ever) go to India (in the future) then I will see the Taj Mahal.

Improbable or contrary-to-fact conditions (*irrealis*) are expressed by using the present participle of the verb in both "condition" and "result" clauses:

اگر ہم ہندوستان جاتے تو تاج محل دیکھتے۔

Had we gone to India, we would have seen the Taj Mahal.

If the speaker wants to indicate a definite past time for conditions that are impossible to fulfill, then the past participle of a verb followed by the present participle of ہونا may also be used in both the "condition" and "result" clauses:

اگر میں ہندوستان گیا ہوتا تو تاج محل دیکھا ہوتا۔

Had I gone to India, I would have seen the Taj Mahal.

اگر ہم ایک دوسرے سے پچھلے سال ملے ہوتے تو شادی کئے ہوتے۔

333

Had we met each other last year, we would have gotten married.

اگر ہم آپس میں بات کئے ہوتے تو دوست بنے ہوتے۔

If we had talked among ourselves, we would have become friends.

*Note on usage: ایک دوسرا used to describe action involving two persons; آپس میں used to describe reciprocal action among more than two persons

15.1 Reading and Translation Drill

۱۔ اگر میں ڈاکٹر بنوں تو دُنیا کی خدمت کر سکوں۔

اگر آپ امریکہ کے صدر بنیں تو دُنیا میں امن پھیلا سکیں۔

اگر وہ کِسان بنے تو ہر روز ہل چلا سکے۔

اگر تو پھل والا بنے تو ہر وقت میٹھے میٹھے پھل کھا سکے۔

۲۔ وہ گھر آئیں تو سامان لائیں۔

تم اِسکول جاؤ تو پڑھ سکو۔

تو لندن جائے گی تو بکینگھم پیلیس دیکھے گی۔

ہم لوگ محنت کرینگے تو اِمتحان میں کامیاب ہونگے۔

۳۔ اگر ہم اِس اِمتحان میں کامیاب ہوئے تو ڈاکٹر بن جائینگے۔

اگر آپ نے یہ دوائی کھائی تو بخار کم ہو جائیگا۔

اگر وہ یہ کتاب پڑھے تو اُس کو سب چیزیں معلوم ہو جائیں۔

اگر آپ اُس پھل والے کے پاس جائیں تو میرے لئے آم ضرور لائیے۔

۴۔ اگر آج برف نہ پڑتی تو ہم باہر کھیلتے۔

اگر اِتنی دھوپ نہ پڑتی تو ہم دریا میں تیر سکتے۔

اگر اِتنا پانی نہ پڑتا تو کپڑے سوکھ جاتے۔

اگر سردی نہ ہوتی تو بچّے باہر بھاگتے۔

٥۔ اگر تم ہارورڈ میں پڑھے ہوتے تو کیا تم امریکہ کے صدر بنے ہوتے؟

اگر اُس نے اِس فلم میں کام کیا ہوتا تو اُس کو بھی آسکر ملا ہوتا۔

اگر ہینری کسنجر امریکہ میں پیدا ہوا ہوتا تو وہ اُس ملک کا صدر بنا ہوتا۔

اگر میں نے بچپن میں دودھ پیا ہوتا تو زیادہ صحت مند ہوئی ہوتی۔

٦۔ کیا وہ ایک دوسرے کو نہیں جانتے تھے؟

ہم ایک دوسرے کی طرف دیکھنے لگے۔

ہم دونوں کو چاہیئے کہ ایک دوسرے سے پیار کریں۔

آپ کے بیٹے کو چاہیئے کہ وہ گھر کا سارا کام کرے۔

۷۔ ہم نے یہ فیصلہ آپس میں کر لیا۔

اُن لوگوں کو چاہیئے کہ یہ فیصلہ آپس میں کریں۔

اُس کلاس کی لڑکیوں نے آپس میں بات کرنی شروع کی۔

آپ لوگ آپس میں کیا باتیں کر رہے ہیں؟

Translate the following sentences into Urdu:

1. If I should go to that store, then I would buy the red carpet.

2. If I go to Washington, then I will see the White House.

3. If all of you come to my house, please bring food with you.

4. Had you played with the boy, he would have liked you.

5. If you play with that boy, he will like you very much.

6. If you had been born in America, you would have become the president of this country.

7. If she would have spoken Urdu well, she would have been the prime minister of

    Pakistan.

8. If you read Ghalib, he will teach you many things.

9. If you say so, I will cook the food.

10. Had you been able to write Hindi, you could have taught this class.

15.2 Expressing Presumptions and Suppositions with the Verb ہونا

Through the future form of the verb ہونا a speaker can also express presumptions and suppositions. For example, the sentence:

$$\text{وہ عورتیں کام پر ہونگی۔}$$

Those women will be at work. (future)

can also mean:

Those women must be at work. (supposition)

Similarly, the sentence:

$$\text{وہاں بہت شور ہوگا۔}$$

There will be a lot of noise there. (future)

can also mean:

There must be a lot of noise there. (supposition)

Note the use of the English "must" in the above sentences indicates probability or likelihood rather than a sense of obligation or duty.

Presumptive and suppositional forms of various tenses can be formed by replacing the ہیں/ہے auxiliaries with the appropriate future form of ہونا. Examples:

Present continuous tense: وہ لڑکے پڑھ رہے ہیں۔ Those boys are studying.

suppositional form: وہ لڑکے پڑھ رہے ہونگے۔ Those boys must be studying.

Present tense: وہ اس لڑکے سے بات کرتے ہیں۔ They talk to this boy.

suppositional form: وہ اس لڑکے سے بات کرتے ہونگے۔ They must talk to this boy.

Present perfect tense: راج کام پر گیا ہے۔ Raj has gone to work.

suppositional form: راج کام پر گیا ہوگا۔ Raj must have gone to work.

The following table provides a review of the future tense forms of ہونا:

Feminine	Masculine	Pronoun
ہونگی (ہوؤنگی)	ہونگا (ہوؤنگا)	میں
ہوگی	ہوگا	تو
ہوگی	ہوگے	تم
ہوگی	ہوگا	وہ/یہ
ہونگی	ہونگے	ہم
ہوگی	ہوگے	تم
ہونگی	ہونگے	آپ
ہونگی	ہونگے	وہ/یہ

15.2 Reading and Translation Drill

۱۔ وہ خوبصورت لڑکیاں ضرور کشمیر سے ہونگی۔

اُن کا سارا خاندان ایران سے ہوگا۔

یہ لوگ کہاں سے ہونگے؟

نیلوفر اسلام آباد سے ہوگی۔

۲۔ جاپانی لوگ چاول کھاتے ہونگے۔

انگریز آلو کھاتے ہونگے۔

آپ کی چھوٹی لڑکی ہر روز دودھ پیتی ہوگی۔

اُس کا دوست لال لال سیب کھاتا ہوگا۔

۳۔ کل وہاں برف پڑی ہوگی۔

337

آج کل ہندوستان میں بہت گرمی ہوگی۔

اِس زمانے میں آسٹریلیا میں سردی ہوگی۔

میرے خیال میں وہاں موسم اچّھا ہوگا۔

۴۔ اُن لڑکیوں نے اُس کتاب کو پڑھا ہوگا۔

اُس نے اخبار پڑھا ہوگا۔

کیا اُن شاعر صاحب نے یہ ساری غزلیں لکھی ہونگی؟

اِس خوبصورت غزل کو کس نے لِکھا ہوگا؟

۵۔ وہ ہم کو بھول گئے ہونگے۔

میری سہیلی مجھے بھول گئی ہوگی۔

امریکہ جاکر وہ اپنے دوستوں کو بھول گیا ہوگا۔

گرمیوں کی چھٹیوں کے بعد آپ ساری اُردو بھول گئے ہونگے۔

15.2 Substitution Drill

Change the verb forms in the following sentences so that they agree with the substituted subject

or object.

۱۔ حُسین نے (کھانا) کھا (لیا ہوگا)۔

fruits

sweets

mango

yogurt

۲۔ (رام اور شیام) گھر پر (ہونگے)۔

Akbar's sister

Anita's brother

Radha's girlfriends

my cat

۳۔ (نرگس کی والدہ) شادی کی تیاری (کر رہی ہو نگی)۔

Raj's father

our family

your mother-in-law

their servants

۴۔ (وہ لڑکے) کھیلنے کے لئے (باہر گئے ہو نگے)۔

that handsome boy

those famous filmstars

our youngest daughter

his eldest son

15.3 Expressing Compulsion with the Verb پڑنا

The infinitive of a verb employed in conjunction with پڑنا is used to indicate actions that the

subject is forced, compelled, or cannot help but perform. The subject is marked by کو. This

construction is similar to the infinitive + ہے construction introduced in 9.5. There is, however,

an important difference in the nuance of the two constructions. The former construction

(infinitive + پڑنا) is used for compulsion that is external to the subject while the latter (infinitive

+ ہے) implies compulsion that stems from the subject, for example, from duty and obligation.

Compare the following examples:

حسین کو اسلام آباد جانا پڑتا ہے۔

Hussein has to go to Islamabad. (forced by external circumstances)

339

حسین کو اسلام آباد جانا ہے۔

Hussein must go to Islamabad. (from a sense of duty, obligation)

For transitive verbs, the infinitive may or may not agree with object(s) in number and gender, but forms of پڑنا must retain agreement with object(s). Examples:

مُفلسی کی وجہ سے اُن کو اپنا گھر بیچنا پڑا۔

Due to poverty, they had to sell their house.

کل شفیق کو کپڑے دھونے پڑینگے۔

Tomorrow Shafique will have to wash the clothes.

For intransitive verbs and transitive verbs with no object, both the infinitive and form of پڑنا will be masculine singular. Examples:

مجھے گھر واپس جانا پڑا۔

I had to return home.

آپ کو دینا پڑیگا۔

You will have to give.

(no object mentioned; infinitive and پڑنا in masculine singular form).

15.3 Reading and Translation Drill

۱۔   ہندوستان اور پاکستان کی حکومتوں کو کِسانوں کی مدد کرنی پڑی۔

اِس بڑی چوٹ کی وجہ سے امیت کو ہسپتال جانا پڑا۔

اگر راج نرگس سے پیار کرتا ہے تو اُس کو بھی ایک تاج محل بنوانا پڑیگا۔

ہر روز اسکول کے بعد مجھے اپنے بھائی کا انتظار کرنا پڑتا ہے۔

۲۔   کل رات کو کھانا خراب ہو گیا۔ اِس لئے ہمیں سارا کھانا پھینکنا پڑا۔

اگر آپ شادی کرینگے تو ایک ہزار لوگوں کو دعوت دینی پڑیگی۔

اِنہیں جمعرات سے ورزش شروع کرنی پڑیگی۔

طالبِ علموں کو اِمتحان کی تیاری تو کرنی پڑتی ہے۔

۳۔ ہندوستان اور پاکستان میں مُفلسی پھیل رہی ہے اور اس کے بارے میں ہمیں کچھ کرنا پڑیگا۔

پرسوں سے اُس کی طبیعت خراب ہے۔ اِس لئے کل اُس کو پیشاب، پاخانے اور خون کا مُعائنہ کرانا پڑا۔

امریکہ میں سب کو گھر میں بہت محنت کرنی پڑتی ہے۔ یہاں نوکر کہاں کہاں؟!

مُفلسی کی وجہ سے قالین والے کو اپنی دوکان بیچنی پڑی۔

۴۔ وقت کم ہے۔ اِس لئے نرگس اور راج کو شادی کی تیاری جلدی سے کرنی پڑیگی۔

زندگی میں کامیاب ہونے کے لئے سب کو محنت سے کام کرنا پڑتا ہے۔

اگلے منگل کو مُجرم کو اپنے وکیل کے ساتھ عدالت میں آنا ہی پڑیگا۔

اگرچہ ریشمہ کو تاریخی باتوں میں کوئی دلچسپی نہیں، اُس کو لاہور کی سب تاریخی جگہیں دیکھنی پڑینگی۔

۵۔ زیادہ بارش کی وجہ سے یہ راستہ بند ہے۔ سب گاڑیوں کو دوسرا راستہ اِستعمال کرنا پڑیگا۔

پتاجی کے دل کی بیماری کی وجہ سے ممی ڈارلنگ کو کھانا پکانے میں بہت کم نمک اِستعمال کرنا پڑتا ہے۔

اُس بیماری کے علاج کے لئے مریض کو مہنگی دوائی اِستعمال کرنی پڑی۔

اِس ہوٹل میں آپ ہاتھ سے کھانا نہیں کھاسکتے۔ آپ کو چُھری کانٹے کا اِستعمال کرنا پڑیگا۔

Translate into Urdu:

1. Raj had to invite Sunil to the wedding.

2. Mummy Darling will have to spend a lot of money in making the arrangements for Raj

and Nargis' wedding.

3.   My car is bad. You will have to use my father-in-law's car to take the child to the

hospital.

4.   Ravi has to consider this decision thoughtfully.

5.   He had to give her this expensive present in return for her kindness.

6.   Indian brides must wear red saris at weddings, not white ones.

7.   The rich must end poverty in the world.

8.   They were so helpless that for four months they had to eat only potatoes.

9.   Due to her helplessness, the poor girl had to agree to marry him.

10.   We will have to turn on (چلانا) the fan immediately! It is too hot in this room!

15.4 Passives

Passives in Urdu are formed by adding the inflected form of the verb جانا to the past participle of

a verb. The following examples illustrate the difference between active and passive sentences:

<u>Active sentence:</u>

میں کیلا کھاتا ہوں۔

I eat a banana.

<u>Passive sentence:</u>

کیلا کھایا جاتا ہے۔

A banana is eaten.

In the active sentence the subject (میں) is asserted and the verb agrees with it. In contrast, in the

passive sentence, the subject is not mentioned and passive verb (past participle of the verb کھانا +

the inflected form of جانا in the present tense) agree in number and gender with what was the

342

object of the active sentence -- "banana" (کیلا). Thus, the grammatical object of an active

sentence becomes in fact the subject in a passive sentence. The two sets of examples below

illustrate that the passive may be created in a variety of tenses by inflecting the verb جانا

appropriately. Study them carefully, noting the agreement of the inflected forms of جانا in various

tenses with the subject of the passive sentence.

وہ چیز دیکھی گئی۔	That thing was seen.
وہ چیزیں دیکھی گئیں۔	Those things were seen.
وہ چیز دیکھی جا رہی ہے۔	That thing is being seen.
وہ چیز دیکھی جائیگی۔	That thing will be seen.
وہ چیزیں دیکھی جاسکتی ہیں۔	Those things can be seen.
وہ چیزیں دیکھی جاتی تھیں۔	Those things used to be seen.
کیلا کھایا گیا۔	The banana was eaten.
کیلے کھائے گئے۔	The bananas were eaten.
کیلا کھایا جا رہا ہے۔	The banana is being eaten.
کیلا کھایا جائیگا۔	The banana will be eaten.
کیلا کھایا جا سکتا ہے۔	The banana can be eaten.
کیلے کھائے جاتے تھے	The bananas used to be eaten.

When passives are used in an impersonal sense, the verb is put in the third person masculine

singular form and no explicit subject is mentioned. Examples:

لکھا گیا ہے۔

It has been written.

کہا جاتا ہے۔

It is said.

<u>Re-inserting the original subject of the active sentence into a passive sentence:</u>

If the original subject of the active sentence is to be re-introduced into the passive sentence, it is

marked by the postposition سے. Reinserting the original subject into a passive sentence occurs

mostly in negative sentences, hence the construction is called the passive of incapacity.

Examples:

مجھ سے کیلا کھایا نہیں جاتا۔

I cannot eat the banana.

(literally, the banana cannot be eaten by me.)

مریض سے دوائی پی نہیں گئی۔

The patient could not drink the medicine.

(literally, the medicine could not be drunk by the patient.)

The passive of incapacity differs from the سکنا construction in the negative in that it implies that

the subject could not perform the action for physical reasons.

15.4 Reading and Translation Drill

۱۔ کل رمضان کی عید دھوم دھام سے منائی گئی۔ یہ مسلمانوں کا بہت بڑا تیوہار ہے۔

پرسوں دیوالی منائی گئی۔ یہ تیوہار ہر سال سارے ہندوستان میں دھوم دھام سے منایا جاتا

ہے۔

دسمبر میں کرسمس کا تیوہار دھوم دھام سے منایا گیا۔

۱۹۴۷ء میں ہندوستان اور پاکستان کی آزادی منائی گئی۔

۲۔ اس عمارت پر بہت کام کیا جا رہا ہے۔

کیا اُس مسجد پر کام کیا گیا تھا؟

نہیں۔ اُس مسجد پر اِس سال کام کیا جائیگا۔

کیا، کل سارے ہندوستان میں چاند دیکھا گیا؟

۳۔ روٹی پکائی گئی۔

ساڑی دھوئی گئی۔

آپ کی زندگی کے بارے میں ایک کتاب لکھی جا سکتی ہے۔

خط لکھا جائیگا۔

۴۔ اُس خوبصورت لڑکی کی تعریف کی گئی۔

دیکھو! ہمارے دوست کی تعریف کی جا رہی ہے۔

مجھے افسوس ہے مگر وہ بڑاوالا مکان خرید لیا گیاہے۔

اُن غریب بچّوں کو عید کے لئے بہت تحفے دیئے گئے۔

۵۔ کچھ بھی کام کئے بغیر دن گزارا گیا۔

جو زندگی خدا کی یاد میں گزاری جاتی ہے وہی بہترین ہوتی ہے۔

یہاں تو پنکھے کے بغیر رات نہیں گزاری جا سکتی۔

پنکھے اور ایرکنڈیشن کے بغیر ہندوستان میں گرمیاں کیسے گزاری جا سکتی ہیں؟

۶۔ ہوٹل کے کھانے پر کتنا پیسہ خرچ کیا گیا؟

اِس خوبصورت قمیض پر آپ نے کتنے ڈالر خرچ کئے؟

شادیوں پر اِتنا زیادہ پیسہ خرچ نہیں کیا جانا چاہیئے۔

پاکستان اور بھارت میں شادی پر بہت پیسہ خرچ کیا جاتا ہے۔

۷۔ مجھ سے غریبوں کی یہ حالت نہیں دیکھی جاتی۔

لیلیٰ* سے قیس کی پریشانی نہیں دیکھی گئی۔

مجھے معلوم تھا کہ اُن بیوقوف لڑکوں سے غالب کی شاعری نہیں پڑھی جائیگی۔

آشا سے اپنی بہن لتا کا گیت نہیں گایا گیا۔

* لیلیٰ = pronounced as "*Lailaa*"; the last letter is called *"alif maqsura."*

Translate the following sentences into Urdu:

1. All the food was eaten at last night's party.

2. The wedding will be celebrated with pomp and gusto at our house tomorrow.

3. Was my favorite song sung?

4. The house can be built in three months.

5. The Taj Mahal was built in Shah Jahan's time.

6. The bride and the groom are being praised.

7. The poor farmers will be helped.

8. This Urdu book will be read at all universities in America.

9. Have the preparations been made?

10. Many beautiful flowers are being bought for Raj and Nargis' wedding.

15.5 Passive Intransitive Verbs

In addition to the passive construction introduced above, Urdu has several intransitive verbs that

are often, if not always, translated into English by using the passive. In many cases, the stems of

these so-called passive intransitive verbs also have transitive counterparts. While the focus in

the intransitive form is on the action itself or the result of the action, the emphasis in the

transitive form is on the doer of the action. Examples:

Transitive form:	کھولنا	to open
Intransitive form:	کھُلنا	to be opened
Transitive form:	توڑنا	to break
Intransitive form:	ٹوٹنا	to be broken

Note the "passive" character of the English translations of the intransitive verbs in the examples below:

Transitive verb:

میں نے کھڑکی کھولی ۔

I opened the window.

Intransitive verb:

کھڑکی کھُلی۔

The window opened.

Transitive verb:

حسین نے میرا گلاس توڑا۔

Hussein broke my glass.

Intransitive verb:

میرا گلاس ٹوٹ گیا۔

My glass broke.

Complex verbs when formed with the verb ہونا may also have a passive intransitive nuance to them in contrast to those formed with کرنا which are transitive in nature. Study the pair of complex verbs listed below:

to begin, to get started	شروع ہونا	to begin	شروع کرنا
to be finished	ختم ہونا	to finish	ختم کرنا
to be prepared; to get ready	تیار ہونا	to prepare	تیار کرنا

to be born	پیدا ہونا	to produce, reproduce	پیدا کرنا
for X to be at fault	X سے غلطی ہونا	to make a mistake	غلطی کرنا

Examples:

میں یہ کام شروع کرتا ہوں۔

I begin this work (job).

یہ کام شروع ہوتا ہے۔

This work begins/gets started.

کیا آپ کھانا تیار کر رہے ہیں؟

Are you preparing food?

جی ہاں۔ کھانا تیار ہو رہا ہے۔

Yes, food is being prepared.

علی نے غلطی کی۔

Ali made a mistake.

علی سے غلطی ہوئی۔

Ali was at fault (literally, "a mistake was made by Ali").

Note: The last example, using the intransitive construction, implies that the agency for the action

was somewhat beyond the subject's control.

15.5 Reading and Translation Drill

ا۔   وہ لڑکی کام شروع کر رہی ہے۔

اُس لڑکی کا کام کب شروع ہوا؟

مائیکل جیکسن نے گانا شروع کرنے کے بعد ناچ شروع کیا۔

آپ وقت پر آئیے ورنہ فلم شروع ہو جائیگی۔

348

۲۔ آپ کا کام شام کو کب ختم ہوتا ہے؟

کیا، آپ نے اپنا کام ختم کر دیا؟

گھر میں کھانا ختم ہو گیا۔

میں پڑھائی ختم کرنے کے بعد شادی کرونگا۔

۳۔ معاف کیجیئے۔ مجھ سے غلطی ہوئی۔

تم نے بہت غلطیاں کیں۔

وہ کون ہے جس سے غلطی نہیں ہوتی۔

میں نے کونسی غلطی کی جس کی وجہ سے آپ مجھ سے ناراض ہیں؟

۴۔ آپ صبح کتنے بجے تیار ہونگے؟

کیا، رادھا نے اپنے بچوں کو تیار کیا؟

ہم سب راج اور نرگس کی شادی میں جانے کے لئے تیّار ہو رہے ہیں۔

سب چیزوں کو تیار کرکے میں وہاں گیا۔

۵۔ گاندھی جی ہندوستان میں پیدا ہوئے۔

گندگی جراثیم کو پیدا کرتی ہے۔

اگر میں امریکہ میں پیدا ہوئی ہوتی تو کیا کیا نہیں کر سکتی تھی!

آپ کونسے سال میں پیدا ہوئے؟

۶۔ یہ کھِلونا ٹوٹا ہوا ہے۔

اُس لڑکے کو مت ستاؤ اُس کا دِل ٹوٹا ہوا ہے۔

اِس سٹکھے کو میں نے نہیں توڑا۔ یہ پہلے سے ٹوٹا ہوا تھا۔

کیا آپ سنیل اور رادھا کے ٹوٹے ہوئے دلوں کو جوڑ سکلینگے؟

۷۔ تاج محل سنگِ مرمر کا بنا ہوا ہے۔

یہ دیواریں پتھر کی بنی ہوئی ہیں۔

کیا آپ کا دِل بھی پتّھر کا بنا ہوا ہے؟!

وہ جوتے کہاں کے بنے ہوئے ہیں؟

Translate into Urdu:

1.   A temple is being built at that place.

2.   The wall of the old house broke. Who broke it? I don't know.

3.   Hundreds of thousands of germs are being produced every day in this filth.

4.   A lot of money was spent on building this road.

5.   Finish him off immediately!

15.6 نا as a Rhetorical Particle

نا as a rhetorical particle has two main uses in Urdu:

1. It can be a tag at the end of a statement seeking affirmation of a fact:

تم مجھ سے پیار کرتے ہو نا؟

You love me, don't you?

2. It can be a tag at the end of a request to make it more insistent:

میری تصویر دیوار پر لگا دیجیے نا؟

Won't you please hang my picture on the wall?

15.6 Reading and Translation Drill

۱۔   آپ کو اِس بات کا پتا ہے نا؟

آپ میرے لئے پھول لائینگے نا؟

یہ گانا گا دو نا!

وہ تو بہت خطرناک جانور ہے نا؟

تم بھی میرے لئے تاج محل بنواؤ نا!

۲۔ کہو نا! پیار ہے! تم کو مجھ سے پیار ہے؟

بر کلی ٹیکساس سے زیادہ خوبصورت ہے نا؟

نرگس اور راج کی شادی دھوم دھام سے منائی گئی نا؟

دیکھو جان! میں گھر دس بجے کے بعد آؤنگا۔ تم کھانا کھا لو نا!

آپ بالکل فِکر مت کیجئے! ہم ہیں نا؟

15.7 گفتگو (Conversation)

نرگس: راج! کیا سوچ رہے ہو؟

راج: کچھ نہیں۔

نرگس: بولو نا! کیا بات ہے؟ تم صبح سے بہت خاموش ہو۔

راج: ہاں۔ کچھ بات ہی ایسی ہے۔

نرگس: کیا بات ہے؟ ہم کو ایک دوسرے سے صاف صاف بات کرنی چاہیئے۔

راج: اگر میں تم سے کچھ کہوں تو ناراض تو نہیں ہوگی؟

نرگس: نہیں۔ ناراض کیوں ہونگی؟

راج: دیکھو نرگس۔ میں تم سے بہت پیار کرتا ہوں۔ تم میری زندگی ہو۔ میں تمہارے بغیر زندگی نہیں گزار سکتا۔

نرگس: او راج۔ اور تعریف کرو نا میری!

راج: جو بھی ہو تم خدا کی قسم لا جواب ہو! میں۔۔۔میں تمہارا جیون ساتھی بننا چاہتا ہوں۔ میں تمہارے ساتھ زندگی کا ہر پل گزارنا چاہتا ہوں۔ میں تمہاری زلفوں کے سائے میں سونا چاہتا ہوں۔ تمہاری بانہوں میں جاگنا چاہتا ہوں۔

نرگس: اب۔۔۔اب کیا کہا جا سکتا ہے؟ میں۔۔۔مجھے معلوم نہیں۔ میں۔۔۔اگر ممّی ڈیڈی ہاں کہہ دیں تو۔۔۔تو میں۔۔۔میں تمہاری ہو جاؤنگی۔

351

راج:	سچ! تم۔۔تم مجھ سے شادی کروگی؟
نرگس:	ہاں۔میں تم سے شادی کرونگی۔ میرا دِل تو تمہارے پاس ہی ہے۔ اب میری
	جان بھی تمہاری ہو جائیگی۔
راج:	میں تو بن گیا ہوں
	تو میں بن گئی ہے
	میں تن بن گیا ہوں
	تو جان بن گئی ہے
	اب تو اور میں دو نہیں ایک ہیں۔۔ایک!
	اِس دُنیا میں ایک چاند ہے، ایک سورج ہے، اور ایک میری نرگس!
نرگس:	مگر تو میرا چاند ہے
	میں تیری چاندنی
	تو میرا راگ ہے
	میں تیری راگنی۔
راج:	اور یہ تاج محل۔۔۔ ہمارے پیار کا گواہ۔ وہ دیکھو شاہ جہاں اور ممتاز محل ہم کو
	مبارک باد دے رہے ہیں۔
نرگس:	اور یہ تارے کتنے خوش ہو رہے ہیں۔
راج:	یہ چاند اپنی چاندنی کا تحفہ دے رہا ہے۔
	(تھوڑی دیر بعد نرگس اپنی ممّی سے ٹیلیفون پر بات کر رہی ہے)
نرگس:	ہیلو ممّی۔ آداب۔ آپ کیسی ہیں؟
ممّی:	نرگس! میں نے تم کو آج ہی خواب میں دیکھا!
نرگس:	اچّھا!
ممّی:	ہاں۔ میں نے دیکھا کہ تم بہت خوش ہو اور ہمارے گھر میں خوشیاں منائی جا

رہی ہیں۔

نرگس: سچ ممّی! اچھا سُنئیے ۔۔راج۔۔

ممّی: کیا ہوا راج کو؟ خدا نہ کرے کہ وہ بیمار ہو!

نرگس: نہیں نہیں۔ وہ ٹھیک ہے۔ وہ۔۔۔۔وہ آپ سے۔۔۔وہ شادی کرنا چاہتا ہے!

ممّی: کیا! وہ مجھ سے شادی کرنا چاہتا ہے! کیا تم پاگل ہوگئی ہو؟!

نرگس: او ہو ممّی! آپ سے نہیں مجھ سے!

ممّی: سچ۔ یہ تو بہت خوشی کی بات ہے۔ کیا تم راضی ہو؟

نرگس: کیا آپ کو راج پسند ہے؟

ممّی: ہاں ہاں۔ اور تمہارے ڈیڈی کو بھی راج بہت پسند ہے۔ وہ ہر وقت راج کی تعریفیں کرتے ہیں۔ انہوں نے راج کو تصویروں میں دیکھا ہے۔ راج تم کو بہت خوش رکھیگا بیٹی۔

نرگس: او ممّی آج میں کتنی خوش ہوں!

ممّی: ہم کو اب شادی کی تیّاریاں شروع کرنی پڑینگی۔ دیکھو میرے خیال میں دسمبر کا مہینہ شادی کے لئے زیادہ مناسب ہوگا۔ اُس زمانے میں ہمارے سب رشتہ داروں کو چھٹیاں ہوتی ہیں۔ مجھے بہت بہت انتظام کرنا پڑیگا۔ اچھا دیکھو دوسری لائین پر فون ہے۔ ایک منٹ ٹھہرو۔۔۔۔۔ہلو! ہلو! کون؟

راج کی ماں: میں راجکماری ہوں۔۔راج کی ماں۔

نرگس کی ماں: کیسی ہو راجکماری؟

راجکماری: میں تو بس ٹھیک ہوں۔ میں تم سے کچھ مانگنا چاہتی ہوں۔

نرگس کی ماں: ہاں۔ہاں۔ کہو۔ میں تمہاری کیا خدمت کر سکتی ہوں؟

راجکماری: میں نرگس کو اپنی بیٹی بنانا چاہتی ہوں۔ اُس کے بدلے تم راج کو لے لو۔

نرگس کی ماں: او راجکماری۔ یہ تو بہت خوشی کی بات ہے۔ ہم اِس شادی کو دھوم دھام سے

353

مناٗئیںگے نا؟ اچّھا دِسمبر کا مہینہ کیسا رہیگا؟

راجکماری: یہ تو میں بھی سوچ رہی تھی ۔ اُس زمانے میں موسم بھی بہت اچّھا ہوتا ہے۔ میری نرگس کتنی حسین دُلہن بنے گی۔ وہ تو ایک چاند کا ٹکڑا ہے۔

نرگس کی ماں: ہاں اور راج بھی بہت خوبصورت دولہا بنے گا۔ لاکھوں میں ایک ہے تمہارا بیٹا۔

راجکماری: اب میرا نہیں ہے۔ تمہارا ہے۔ تمہارا۔

نرگس کی ماں: اچّھا سنو! نرگس دوسری لائین پر ہے۔ ہم دونوں ایک دوسرے سے بات کر رہے تھے اور تمہارا فون بیچ میں آ گیا۔ میں تھوڑی دیر بعد خود تم کو فون کرتی ہوں اور پھر ہم ایک دوسرے سے زیادہ تفصیل میں بات کر سکتے ہیں۔

راجکماری: ہاں۔ ہاں ضرور۔ اور تم نرگس کے ڈیڈی سے بھی کہہ دینا کہ ہم اور ہمارے گھر والے اِس رشتے سے بہت خوش ہیں۔

نرگس کی ماں: اچّھا۔ خدا حافظ۔۔ ہلو بیٹی نرگس؟

نرگس: جی مّمی!

نرگس کی ماں: تمہاری ساس تھیں دوسری لائین پر!

نرگس: او مّمی! اچّھا راج میرا انتظار کر رہا ہے۔ میں اُس کو خوش خبری دے دونگی۔ آپ ڈیڈی سے کہہ دینگی؟

مّمی: ہاں ہاں۔ جب وہ گھر آئینگے تو میں بتا دونگی۔ وہ تو بہت ہی خوش ہونگے۔ راج ہزاروں میں، نہیں، نہیں، کروڑوں میں ایک ہے۔

نرگس: مّمی آئی لو یو!

مّمی: بیٹی اردو میں بات کرو! اچّھا خدا حافظ۔

(نرگس اور راج)

نرگس: ہلو راج۔

راج: تو کیا کہا ساس جی نے؟

354

نرگس: اُنہوں نے کہا کہ مجھ کو تم سے زیادہ اچّھے لڑکے سے شادی کرنی چاہیے۔

راج: کیا؟ نہیں نہیں۔ یہ نہیں ہو سکتا۔ میں مر جاؤنگا!

نرگس: راج، میریں تمہارے دُشمن۔ ایسی بات بھی مت کرو۔ میں تو مذاق کر رہی تھی۔ ممّی نے ہاں کہہ دی ہے۔

راج: سچ۔ یہ میری زندگی کا خوبصورت ترین دِن ہے۔

نرگس: ہاں۔ راج آج میں بھی بہت خوش ہوں مگر میری زندگی کے تو سب سے اچّھے دِن اُردو کی کلاس میں گزرے! اُس کلاس کی تو بات ہی کچھ اور تھی!

15.8 Conversation Practice

(Sulochna and Shama are Nargis' friends who live in London)

Shama: Oh Sulochna, did you hear that Nargis is getting married?

Sulochna: Yes, Sunil told me. Poor guy, he had tears in his eyes when he asked me,"Sister

Sulochna how will I spend my life without Nargis?!". I was unable to bear his

distress. (مجھ سے اُس کی پریشانی نہیں دیکھی گئی!) I started to cry!! I think Nargis'

heart is made out of stone!

Shama: Her foolish heart! A book can be written about Raj, Nargis, and Sunil. Sunil

ought to stop crying. He must start studying. He is no longer 16 years old. He is

now 20. Do you know what preparations are being made for Nargis' wedding?

Sulochna: A lot of money is being spent on this wedding. I have heard that work is being

done on Nargis' house. Expensive clothes are being bought. Nargis' mother told

me to buy some clothes for her if I go to Lahore. Lahore has beautiful clothes for

brides. So when I go to Lahore next month I will bring clothes for Nargis.

Shama: You will bring clothes from Lahore? I think Karachi has better and cheaper clothes. These days, Karachi's weather must also be very good. If you go to Karachi, you must go to Rambo market. You will be able to buy some good but cheap clothes there. I think Nargis will look so beautiful in a red sari.

Sulochna: It's good that we are talking to each other about this. But I don't like Karachi very much. When I went to Karachi two years ago, I saw a dead man on the road! As soon as I saw him, I started crying. I told my mother that I will never go back to that city.

Shama: Sulochna darling, don't live in the past (departed time). Don't think of dead men! I have seen dead men on the streets of New York and Mumbai! I know the governments of India and Pakistan need to do more to help the poor but you cannot provide the medicine for all the illnesses of the world. You are not a Mother Teresa!

Sulochna: Shama, I used to think that your heart has a lot of love in it. But perhaps it is made out of stone!

Shama: Oh Sulochna, you are always crying. Your heart is made out of salt. Forgive me, don't be upset with me. If you want to help the poor, go and work with them. You will not be able to end poverty in India and Pakistan while sitting in London. Come, let's think of happy things...like Nargis' wedding. Do you want to sing a song with me? What's the latest song from Bollywood?

15.9 Songs

١) تجھے دیکھا تو یہ جانا صنم پیار ہوتا ہے دیوانہ صنم
اب یہاں سے کہاں جائیں ہم

تیری بانہوں میں مر جائیں ہم

آنکھیں میری سپنے تیرے

دِل میرا یادیں تیری

میرا ہے کیا سب کچھ تیرا

جان تیری سانسیں تیری

میری آنکھوں میں آنسو تیرے آ گئے

مُسکرانے لگے سارے غم

تجھے دیکھا تو یہ جانا صنم۔۔۔۔

(۲) دل میرا ہر بار یہ سننے کو بے قرار ہے

کہو نا پیار ہے کہو نا پیار ہے

ہاں تم سے پیار ہے کہ تم سے پیار ہے

اِن پیاری باتوں میں انجانا اقرار ہے

کہو نا پیار ہے کہو نا پیار ہے

کہا نا پیار ہے کہا نا پیار ہے

پیار جہاں میں ہوتا نہیں پھر بولو کیا ہوتا؟

دُنیا میں دل کوئی کبھی نہ دھڑکا ہوتا

دھڑکا ہے دل آ یار مل! یہ پیار کا اِظہار ہے

کہو نا پیار ہے کہو نا پیار ہے

کہا نا پیار ہے کہا نا پیار ہے

۳)   (ڈائیلاگ: یہ میری آخری اِلتجا ہے: دُنیا میں دل والے کا ساتھ

دینا دولتِ والے کا نہیں)

وفا کی راہ میں عاشق کی عید ہوتی ہے

خوشی مناؤ محبت شہید ہوتی ہے

زندہ باد، زندہ باد، اے محبت زندہ باد، اے محبت زندہ باد! (۲)

دولت کی زنجیروں سے تُو (۲) رہتی ہے آزاد

زندہ باد، زندہ باد، اے محبت زندہ باد، اے محبت زندہ باد!

مندِر میں مسجد میں تُو اور تُو ہی ہے ایمانوں میں

مُرلی کی تانوں میں تُو اور تُو ہی ہے اذانوں میں

تیرے دم سے دین و دھرم کی دُنیا ہے آباد

زندہ باد، زندہ باد، اے محبت زندہ باد، اے محبت زندہ باد!

پیار کی آندھی رُک نہ سکیگی نفرت کی دیواروں سے

خونِ محبت ہو نہ سکیگا خنجر سے تلواروں سے

مر جاتے ہیں عاشق زندہ رہ جاتی ہے یاد

زندہ باد، زندہ باد، اے محبت زندہ باد، اے محبت زندہ باد!

Glossary for Songs

مُرلی = flute (f)		صنم = beloved; idol (m/f)	
تان = tune (f)		بے قرار = restless	
اذان = Islamic call to prayer (f)		انجانا = unknown, unwitting	
دین و دھرم = religion and faith (m)		اقرار = confirmation; acknowledgment (m)	
آندھی = tempest, whirlwind; storm (f)		دھڑکنا = to beat, throb	
رُکنا = to stop, to rest; to be hindered		اِظہار = revelation; declaration; display (m)	

وفا = loyalty; faithfulness (f)	نفرت = hate; hatred (f)
شہید = martyr; one who is slain (m/f)	خون = blood; murder; slaughter (m)
دولت = riches, wealth; dominion; rule (f)	خنجر = dagger (m)
زنجیر = chain; fetters (f)	تلوار = sword (f)
ایمان = faith; belief (m)	زِندہ باد = long live

15.10 Vocabulary

to agree upon x	x پر راضی ہونا
arm, embrace (f)	بانہہ
arrangement (m)	اِنتظام
body (m)	تن
to be born	پیدا ہونا
bride (f)	دُلہن، دُلہنیا
bridegroom (m)	دُلہا
to call x on the phone	x کو فون کرنا
to celebrate, commemorate	منانا
cure (m)	عِلاج
decision (m)	فیصلہ
details, explanation; analysis (f)	تفصیل
to dial the phone	فون مِلانا
distress, misery, anxiety (f)	پریشانی
dream (m)	خواب
to dry (intransitive)	سوکھنا

359

to end, conclude (transitive)	ختم کرنا
to end, conclude (intransitive)	ختم ہونا
expenditure, expense (m)	خرچ
to spend, to expend (transitive)	خرچ کرنا
to be spent, expended (intransitive)	خرچ ہونا
fan; ventilator (m)	پنکھا
festival	تیوہار، تہوار (m)/عید (f)
filth (f)	گندگی
fork; thorn (m)	کانٹا
germs (m)	جراثیم
gift (m)	تُحفہ
healthy	صحت مند
in return for x; instead of x	x کے بدلے میں
life partner (m/f)	جیون ساتھی
melody	راگ (m)/راگنی (f)
middle	بیچ
mistake (f)	غلطی
party; invitation (f)	دعوت
to invite x	x کو دعوت دینا
to have a party for x	x کی دعوت کرنا
peace, safety (m)	امن
piece, morsel (m)	ٹکڑا

pleased; contented; agreed	راضی
to be pleased with x	x سے راضی ہونا
to agree upon x	x پر راضی ہونا
pomp and gusto (f)	دھوم دھام
potato (m)	آلو
poverty (f)	غریبی / مُفلِسی
praise (f)	تعریف
to praise x	x کی تعریف کرنا
Ramadan, Muslim month (m)	رمضان
relationship / connection (m)	رِشتہ
river (m)	دریا
road (m)	راستہ
snow (f)	برف
to spread (intransitive)	پھیلنا
to start, begin (transitive)	شُروع کرنا
to start, begin (intransitive)	شُروع ہونا
use, employment (m)	اِستعمال
to use	اِستعمال کرنا
to use x	x کا اِستعمال کرنا
without	(کے) بغیر
witness (m/f)	گواہ

Chapter 16

16.1 The *"Izafa"*

The *"izafa,"* or "addition," is a construction of Persian origin frequently used in Urdu.

Linguistically, the *"izafa"* is an enclitic, indicated by placing the subscript sign *"zer,"* i.e., ِ

(also used to represent a short *"i"* vowel) after a noun. The *"izafa"* is used to express either (i) a

possessive relationship between two nouns or (ii) an adjectival modification of a noun.

(i) <u>Possessive relationship between two nouns</u>:

In such a construction, the "possessor" noun follows the "possessed one" and the enclitic *"izafa,"*

that reflects the relationship between the two nouns, falls in the middle and can frequently be

translated as "of." Examples:

دخترِ نظام

the daughter of the Nizam.

("possessed one" daughter = دختر "possessor" Nizam = نظام)

جنگِ آزادی

the war of independence

(war = جنگ independence = آزادی)

حکومتِ امریکہ

the government of America

(government = حکومت America = امریکہ)

In highly Persianized Urdu, geographical features are frequently written with the *"izafa,"* with

362

the geographical entity preceding its proper name:

$$کوہِ طور$$

Mount Sinai

(mountain = کوہ Sinai = طور)

(ii) <u>Adjectival modification of a noun:</u>

In such a construction, the noun is followed by an attributive adjective and again, their relationship is reflected by the enclitic *"izafa"* that falls between the two. When translating such a construction into English, place the attributive adjective before the noun. Examples:

$$دلِ نادان$$

foolish heart

(heart = دل foolish = نادان)

$$اسمِ شریف$$

noble name

(name = اسم noble = شریف)

$$مغلِ اعظم$$

the Greatest Mughal

(Mughal = مغل greatest = اعظم)

$$برِّ صغیر$$

the [Indian] subcontinent

(continent = برّ small = صغیر)

16.1 Reading and Translation Drill

1. Read and translate the following couplets with the assistance of the glossary:

١۔

دِلِ ناداں تجھے ہوا کیا ہے

آخر اِس درد کی دوا کیا ہے

Glossary

ناداں = foolish

٢۔

شامِ فراق اب نہ پوچھ

آئی اور آ کے ٹل گئی

دل تھا کہ پھر بہل گیا

جاں تھی کہ پھر سنبھل گئی

Glossary

فِراق = separation (m)

ٹلنا = to pass off, to pass over

بہلنا = to be entertained

سنبھلنا = to recover

٣۔

غالبؔ چھٹی شراب پر اب بھی کبھی کبھی

پیتا ہوں روزِ ابرِ شبِ ماہتاب میں

Glossary

چھٹنا = to leave, to abandon

ابر = cloud(s) (m)

شب = night (f)

ماہتاب = moon (m)

۴۔   یہ نہ تھی ہماری قسمت کہ وِصالِ یار ہوتا

اگر اور جیتے رہتے یہی اِنتظار ہوتا

Glossary

وِصال = union, meeting (m)

یار = friend, beloved (m/f)

2. Read and translate the following passage concerning the famous Indian movie, *Mughal-e Azam (The Greatest Mughal)*

مُغلِ اعظم

مُغلِ اعظم ہندوستان کی ایک بہت مشہور فِلم ہے۔ یہ مُغل شہزادے سلیم* اور ایک کنیز انارکلی**
کی خوبصورت کہانی ہے۔ شہزادے سلیم، جو شہنشاہ بننے کے بعد جہانگیر کے نام سے مشہور
ہوئے، شہنشاہ اکبر*** کے بیٹے تھے۔ سلیم کو انارکلی سے پیار ہو گیا۔ مگر سلیم کے والد شہنشاہ
اکبر اِس بات سے بہت ناراض ہوئے۔ اُنہوں نے کہا کہ اگر سلیم انارکلی سے شادی کریں گے
تو اُن کو ہندوستان کا تخت ہمیشہ ہمیشہ کے لئے چھوڑ دینا پڑیگا۔ سلیم نے اپنے والد سے کہا کہ
انارکلی اُنہیں ہندوستان کے تخت سے زیادہ عزیز ہے۔ انارکلی کی محبت میں وہ اپنی جان بھی
دے سکتے ہیں مگر اُس سے دور نہیں رہ سکتے۔ مگر انارکلی یہ نہیں چاہتی تھی کہ شہزادہ سلیم
ہندوستان کا تخت چھوڑ دیں۔ اِس لئے اُس نے فیصلہ کیا کہ وہ سلیم کی زندگی سے نکل
جائیگی۔ مُغلِ اعظم کا ایک مشہور ڈائیلاگ:

شہنشاہ اکبر: انارکلی! ہم محبت کے دُشمن نہیں۔ اپنے اصولوں کے غُلام ہیں۔

ایک غلام کی بے بسی پر غور کرو تو شاید تم ہمیں معاف کر سکو۔

مغلِ اعظم میں ہندوستان کے بہت بڑے بڑے اداکاروں نے کام کیا۔ اکبر کا رول پرتھوی راج

کپور نے ادا کیا۔ سلیم دِلیپ کمار تھے۔ اور انار کلی۔۔۔ ہندوستان کی سب سے خوبصورت اداکارہ

مدھوبالا۔ مغلِ اعظم آج تک ساری دُنیا میں دیکھی جاتی ہے اور بہت پسند کی جاتی ہے۔ ہم کو یہ

تو معلوم نہیں کہ یہ کہانی سچ ہے یا نہیں مگر لاکھوں لوگ اس فِلم کو ایک تاریخی فِلم سمجھتے

ہیں۔ سلیم اور انار کلی ہزاروں پیار کرنے والوں کے دِلوں میں زندہ ہیں: ' زندہ باد زندہ باد

اے محبت زندہ باد!'

* Prince Salim (1569-1627); Mughal prince who on becoming emperor in 1605 adopted the

royal title Jehangir (literally "world seizer")

** Anarkali, legendary courtesan in the Mughal court, with whom Prince Salim fell in love

*** Emperor Akbar (1542-1605); considered to be the greatest emperor of the Mughal dynasty;

reigned from 1556 to 1605; father of Salim.

16.2 Some Common Uses of Present and Past Participles

Thus far we have encountered present and past participles in the context of different verbal

tenses. However, in Urdu, like in English, present and past participles can serve a variety of

other functions such as adjectives or adverbs (as in "burning fire" "while walking" and so on).

When employed in this manner, present and past participles are usually followed by the

appropriate form of the past participle of the verb "ہونا" (ہوا، ہوئے، ہوئی).

1. Present Participle as Adjective

When used in an adjectival sense, these participles and the forms of "ہونا" attached to them

decline according to the case, number, and gender of the nouns they modify. Note, however, that

in the case of feminine adjectival participles, the singular form modifies both singular and plural

366

feminine nouns. Examples:

a dancing girl	ناچتی ہوئی لڑکی
a singing boy	گاتا ہوا لڑکا
laughing actors	ہنستے ہوئے اداکار
playing girls	کھیلتی ہوئی لڑکیاں
shy bride	شرماتی ہوئی دُلہن
moving bus	چلتی ہوئی بس

In many instances, the past participle of " ہونا " may be omitted without affecting the meaning:

میں چلتی گاڑی میں کتابیں نہیں پڑھ سکتا ہوں۔

I am unable to read books in a moving car.

2. Past Participle as Adjective

Whereas the present participle of a particular verb, acting as an adjective, conveys the

progression of particular actions, the past participle as adjective connotes a state of completion

or a passive state. Thus, at times, the past participle may convey a present stative sense. For

instance: بیٹھی ہوئی عورت would mean a seated woman (that is a woman in the state of being

seated). In contrast بیٹھتی ہوئی عورت, with the present participle, would mean a woman who is

in the act or process of sitting down.

dead man	مرا ہوا آدمی
kept books	رکھی ہوئی کتابیں
written letters	لکھے ہوئے خط
fallen things	گری ہوئی چیزیں
a seated man	بیٹھا ہوا آدمی

a standing woman	کھڑی ہوئی عورت
constructed buildings	بنی ہوئی عمارتیں
a past time	گزرا ہوا زمانہ

3. Participles as Nouns

Occasionally participles, like adjectives, can be used as nouns. They may or may not be followed by the appropriate form of the past participle of the verb "ہونا" (ہوا، ہوئے، ہوئی). For example:

سوتے (ہوئے) کو اُٹھاؤ۔

Wake up /pick up the sleeping one.

پڑھتے (ہوئے) کو تنگ مت کرو!

Don't bother the person who is reading (lit. the reading one).

A famous Urdu proverb also illustrates this construction:

مرتا کیا نہ کرتا۔

What wouldn't a dying person do?

(In a desperate state, a person would not think twice about the consequences of his/her actions.)

4. Participles as Adverbs

Urdu participles used in an adverbial sense can often be translated into English with phrases beginning with "while" and often express incomplete actions. The adverbial participle phrase almost always appears in singular masculine oblique form. The usual word order in sentences that contain adverbial participles is: subject - adverbial participle - object - verb. Examples:

میں نے گھر جاتے ہوئے ایک خوبصورت لڑکی کو دیکھا۔

While going home, I saw a beautiful girl.

وہ لڑکی نہاتے ہوئے گا رہی تھی۔

While bathing, that girl was singing.

کٹی ہوئی مُرغی کو چلتے ہوئے دیکھو!

Watch the cut-up chicken walk!

(A note posted outside a trickster's stall in Lahore!)

5. Participle + ہی

In order to convey immediacy or to give the sense of "as soon as" or "immediately after," the particle ہی may be added to the masculine oblique present participle:

چھوٹا بچہ کتے کو دیکھتے ہی رونے لگا۔

The little boy started crying as soon as he saw the dog.

میں کھانا کھاتے ہی وہاں جاؤں گی۔

I will go there immediately after I finish eating.

6. Participle + وقت

Masculine oblique present participle combined with the word " وقت " connotes the simultaneity of two actions, that is, the action of the main verb taking place at the same time as the action signified by the participle + " وقت " construction. Example:

گاڑی چلاتے وقت ٹیلیفون پر بات نہیں کرنی چاہیئے۔

While driving (at the time of driving) a car, one should not speak on the telephone.

7. Repeated Participles

Present participles can often be repeated to signify that the action of the repeated participle ends or results in the action of the main verb. Repeated past participles signify a past action resulting in a continuous or repetitive state. Examples:

میں پڑھتے پڑھتے سوچنے لگا۔

I began thinking while studying.

بیچارہ مجنوں روتے روتے مر گیا۔

Poor Majnun died weeping.

جناب! آپ بیٹھے بیٹھے تھک جائینگے۔

Sir, you will tire of sitting (and sitting).

16.2 Translation Drills

Translate into idiomatic English:

۱۔ پولیس کو مرا ہوا آدمی اس روڈ پر ملا۔

۲۔ آپ لائبریری جانے سے پہلے گھر میں رکھی ہوئی کتابیں پڑھئے!

۳۔ غالب کے لکھے ہوئے خط آج بھی پڑھے جاتے ہیں۔

۴۔ اس لڑکی سے کہو کہ وہ ان گری ہوئی چیزوں کو نہ اُٹھائے۔

۵۔ وہ بیٹھا ہوا آدمی سگریٹ پی رہا تھا۔

۶۔ وہ کھڑی ہوئی عورتیں بس کا انتظار کر رہی تھیں۔

۷۔ شاہ جہاں کے زمانے کی بنی ہوئی عمارتیں مجھے بہت پسند ہیں۔

۸۔ تم گزرے ہوئے زمانے میں رہتے ہو۔ اب گزری باتوں کو یاد مت کرو۔

۹۔ اس کام کرتی ہوئی لڑکی کو دیکھئے۔

۱۰۔ کل رات جس ناچتے ہوئے لڑکے سے آپ بات کر رہے تھے، اس کا نام کیا تھا؟

۱۱۔ کتاب پڑھتے ہوئے ریشما ٹیلیفون پر بات کر رہی تھی۔

۱۲۔ وہ بچہ روتے ہوئے سو گیا۔

۱۳۔ راج نے نرگس کو سنیل کے ساتھ ٹینیس کھیلتے ہوئے دیکھا۔

۱۴۔ وہ شاعر روتے ہوئے غزل لکھ رہا تھا۔

۱۵۔ دودھ پیتی ہوئی بلّی کو مت ستاؤ۔

۱۶۔ کیا ہر ساجن کو ٹوٹے ہوئے دل اچّھے لگتے ہیں؟

۱۷۔ کام کرتے کو دیکھو!

۱۸۔ کھاتے ہوئے سے بات مت کرو۔

Translate into Urdu:

1. Give some sweets to the crying girl.

2. Do not talk to the studying boy (the boy who is studying).

3. The laughing actor burst out crying all of a sudden!

4. That man talks to dead people.

5. We cannot study while eating.

6. While studying (at the time of studying) one should not watch T.V.

7. Ask Sunil's broken heart!

8. Raj does not like shy brides.

9. As soon as he came home, Mummy darling gave Raj some food to eat.

10. This is a book written by Reshma (lit. This is Reshma's written book).

11. Please give tea to the person who is singing (lit. the singing one).

16.3 Present Participle and رہنا Construction

The present participle of a verb when combined with the verb رہنا results in the iterative form.

The iterative indicates the constant repetition of an action and is often translated as "keeps....." In this form both the present participle and the verb رہنا agree with the subject. The form cannot be employed in the negative, nor can it be used with compound verbs/aspect indicators. In addition, the present participle of رہنا cannot be used in this construction.

میں وہاں دس منٹ میں پہنچ جاؤنگا۔ آپ کام کرتے رہیئے۔

I will reach there in ten minutes. You keep working.

سُنیل نرگس کے گھر جاتا رہا مگر نرگس تو راج کے ساتھ جا چکی تھی۔

Sunil kept going to Nargis' house, but Nargis had already left with Raj.

میری گزارِش ہے کہ آپ عربی سیکھنے کے بجائے اردو سیکھنے کی کوشِش کرتے رہیئے۔

It is my request that you keep trying to learn Urdu instead of learning Arabic.

<u>Note:</u> The present participle of جانا when combined with the رہنا has two meanings: its expected

meaning "keep on going" and an idiomatic one "to disappear, to be lost."

کاش کہ ایسی بُرائیاں دُنیا سے جاتی رہیں!

If only such evils would disappear from the world!

In the past tense, the particle نے is not used even when the participle is that of a transitive verb.

16.4   Present Participle and جانا Construction

The present participle of a verb when combined with جانا can have several meanings, the most

common being: (1) persevering or deliberately continuing with an action and (2) gradual

unfolding of the action resulting in change. Since جانا the governing verb is intransitive,

constructions in the past tense do not use the particle نے.

اُس کو تیز بُخار تھا مگر وہ اپنا کام کرتا گیا۔

He had a high fever but he went on working.

تم گوشت کھاتے جاؤ اور تمہاری صحت خراب ہوتی جائیگی۔

Continue eating meat and your health will keep deteriorating.

وقت گزرتا گیا اور ہم ایک دوسرے کو بھولتے گئے۔

Time kept passing and we gradually forgot each other.

16.3-16.4 Reading and Translation Drill

۱۔ میں دیکھتا رہا اور بس نکل گئی۔

بوڑھا پھل والا محنت کرتا رہا اور اِس کا بیٹا اپنے باپ کی مدد کرنے کے بجائے کرِکٹ کھیلنے چلا گیا۔

ہم پاکستان جانے کی کوشش کرتے رہے۔

میں کام کر لوں گی۔ تمہاری طبیعت خراب ہے۔ تم سوتے رہو۔

۲۔ اگر تم اپنے والدین کا مذاق اُڑاتے گئے تو تم کو کامیابی کیسے ملیگی؟

وہ صدر تقریر کرتے گئے اور ساری دُنیا ہنستی گئی۔

آپ اپنے والدین کی دیکھ بھال کرتے جائیے اور خُدا آپ کو لمبی عُمر دیگا۔

میں کھانسی کا عِلاج کراتا گیا مگر یہ کھانسی کم ہی نہ ہوئی۔

Translate the following sentences using the present participle and رہنا construction:

1. Instead of talking to me on the phone, he kept sending me letters.

2. Thirteen years after coming to the United States, they keep on remembering Pakistan.

3. I kept trying to explain to him and he kept watching the movie.

4. On Saturday, Sarah and Salma kept dialing the telephone, but because of the rain the phone was not working.

Translate the following sentences into Urdu using the present participle and جانا construction:

1. Keep on saying your (Muslim ritual) prayers and then see how happy God is with you!

2. Shaan went on throwing the trash onto the street, but the children kept bringing it back into his house.

3. She went on narrating her (own) story and the little girl gradually fell asleep.

373

4.   Why wouldn't Rakesh be angry? Reshma kept making fun of him instead of listening to his poetry.

16.5 Present Participle in the Narration of the Past

Present participles without auxiliary verbs are frequently encountered in narrations of those past events that occurred routinely or habitually. In such cases, the narration usually begins with an initial sentence containing a present participle followed by an auxiliary, but in subsequent sentences/statements, the auxiliary is dropped and the present participle suffices on its own.

بچپن میں ساجد اپنی نانی کے گھر گرمیوں کی چھٹیوں میں جاتا تھا، آم کھاتا ، تیرتا، اور شاہ رُخ خان کی فلمیں دیکھتا۔

In his childhood Sajid would often go to his grandmother's house during the summer holidays, eat mangoes, swim, and watch Shah Rukh Khan's films.

اُپنے اِنتقال سے ایک دِن پہلے تک وہ گھر کا سارا کام کرتے تھے، خطوں کے جواب دیتے، اور غریبوں کی مدد کرنے کی کوشِش کرتے۔

Until one day before his death (literally, transfer), he did all the house work, reply to all the letters, and try to help the poor.

16.5 Reading and Translation Drill

Translate into English:

١۔   جب ہم شِکاگو میں پڑھتے تھے، ہم ہر روز مزیدار کھانا بناتے، دوستوں کے ساتھ ناچتے اور وہ ساری چیزیں کرتے جو ہمارے والدین کو پسند نہیں تھیں۔

٢۔   وہ اپنے بھائی کے اِنتقال سے پہلے اکثر دِلّی جاتی تھی۔ پُرانی دِلّی میں بریانی کھاتی اور قوّالی سُنتی۔

٣۔   جب بھی فراز پریشان ہوتا تھا یا وہ زیادہ شراب پی لیتا یا اپنے گھر والوں کو تنگ کرتا۔

٤۔ میں سمیر کو اپنے گھر آنے کی اِجازت نہیں دے سکتا۔ پچھلے سال وہ ہر روز یہاں آتا
اور میرے سارے پیسے چُرا لیتا۔

Translate into Urdu:

1. During our childhood, before our grandmother's death, we used to get up at 6 am every

    morning, swim, take a bath, drink milk, eat fresh hot rotis, and then go to school.

2. That sly boy would eat all the sweets, lie, and bother all the shopkeepers.

3. While driving her car that girl would listen to music, sing songs, and talk to her

    friends on her cell phone.

4. While walking down the streets, these mad boys would scream, throw fruits and

    vegetables, and make fun of democracy.

16.6 Past Participle and کرنا Construction

The masculine form of a past participle when combined with the verb کرنا indicates an action

performed habitually. In such constructions, only the verb کرنا inflects, agreeing in number and

gender with the subject. Since this construction is considered to be intransitive in the past tense,

the subject is not marked by the particle نے.

بیٹا، تم غریبوں کی مدد کیا کرو!

Son, go on helping [habitually] the poor.

مِّی ڈارلنگ ہمارے گھر چائے پینے کے لئے آیا کرتی تھی۔

Mummy darling habitually used to come to our house to drink tea.

آپ اپنی دوائی پی لیا کریں۔

Keep drinking your medicine [for your own benefit].

375

Note: For this construction, the verb جانا uses جایا as its past participle and not its normal form گیا.

نرگس راج کے گھر جایا کرتی ہے۔

Nargis habitually goes to Raj's house.

16.6 Reading and Translation Drill

۱۔   آپ اپنی نانی کی دیکھ بھال کیا کیجیے۔

سمیر یہ تم کو کیا ہو گیا؟ آج کل تم تو سچ بولا کرتے ہو!

جب میں کالج میں تھا تب میں صبح کے چار بجے تک جاگا کرتا تھا۔

نرگس! میرے سامنے سنیل کا نام مت لیا کرو!

وہ شریر لڑکے چھوٹی چھوٹی باتوں پر رویا کیے۔

۲۔   آپ کو یاد ہے کہ آپ میرے لئے پھل اور پھول لایا کرتے تھے۔

میری جان، ناراض مت ہو۔ میں سنیل کے ساتھ ٹینس کھیلنے کے لئے جین پارک میں نہیں جایا کرونگی۔

ہاں۔ اُن کی صحت خراب ہے۔ پھر بھی وہ بہت سگریٹ پیا کرتے ہیں۔

میں اپنے عاشق پر اپنا سارا پیسہ خرچ کیا کرونگا۔ آپ میری فکر مت کیا کریں!

ریشما ہر روز اسکول کے بعد مٹھائی کی دکان پر جایا کرتی تھی۔

Translate the following into Urdu :

1.   When we were healthy, we used to go [habitually] to that beautiful garden every evening.

2.   I never talked to his wife. I used to remain [habitually] quiet in his house.

3.   In his childhood Raj used to climb [habitually] the tree that was in front of his house.

4.   I don't know why my parents don't give me permission to go to the movies. When they

were in college they used to watch films every Friday.

16.7 The Uses of نہیں تو

نہیں تو occurs frequently in colloquial Urdu-Hindi as a substitute for ورنہ, "otherwise."

تو گرمی میں کام کرنے کا عادی ہو جا نہیں تو تجھے دوبئی میں بہت مشکل ہوگی۔

Get used to working in the heat, otherwise you will have a difficult time in Dubai.

دوائی کھا لو نہیں تو بُخار بڑھ جائیگا۔

Take (literally, eat) the medicine, otherwise the fever will increase.

آپ پولیس کو فون کیجیۓ نہیں تو میں خود کرونگا۔

You call the police, otherwise I will do so myself.

نہیں تو is also used in colloquial Urdu-Hindi, usually in the context of conversations, to respond

negatively to assertions and connotes "not really," "no way," or "no."

فراز: شاد! کیا تم لوگ آپس میں میرے بارے میں بات کر رہے ہو؟

شاد: نہیں تو! ہم آپ کے بارے میں بات کیوں کرینگے؟

Faraz: Shad! Are you talking among yourselves about me?

Shad: Not really! Why would we talk about you?

16.7 Reading and Translation Drill

۱۔   دیکھو بیٹے! محنت کرنے کے عادی ہو جاؤ نہیں تو امتحان میں کامیاب نہیں ہوگے۔
آپ لوگ آپس میں اچھّی باتیں کرنے کی کوشش کریں نہیں تو میں ناراض ہو جاؤنگی۔
تم فوراً بازار جاؤ نہیں تو دوکانیں بند ہو جائینگی۔
تم میرے گھر پر پانچ بجے کے بجائے ٹھیک چار بجے پہنچ جاؤ نہیں تو میں پارٹی میں اکیلا ہی جاؤنگا۔
میں دو دِن کے لئے کینڈا جا رہا ہوں۔ میری بلّی کی اچھّی دیکھ بھال کرو نہیں تو میں تم کو کبھی معاف نہیں کرونگا۔

377

۲۔ کیا نرگس نے سنبل کے والدین کی دیکھ بھال کی؟

نہیں تو۔ یہ کس نے کہا؟

معاف کیجئے۔ ہمارے بچے آپ کو تنگ کر رہے ہیں۔

نہیں تو۔ ہم تو اُن کے عادی ہیں!

اُن کے بھائی کا دس سال پہلے انتقال ہو گیا۔

نہیں تو! میں نے کل ہی اُن کو نیو یارک کے ہوائی اڈّے پر دیکھا۔

کیا تمہارے دفتر میں مچھر بہت ہیں؟

نہیں تو۔ ہمارا دفتر لندن میں ہے نیو یارک میں نہیں۔

16.8 Emphatic Negative Assertions

Emphatic negative assertions are created by combining نہیں with the oblique infinitive of the verb to be negated, followed by کا/کی/کے. The possessive کا agrees in gender and number with the subject.

میں سچ بولنے کا عادی ہوں۔ میں جھوٹ نہیں بولنے کا!

I am used to speaking the truth. I won't lie!

16.8 Reading and Translation Drill

۱۔ میں نے اپنے دوستوں سے کہہ دیا: اِن لوگوں نے مجھ سے جھوٹ بولا۔ میں وہاں نہیں جانے کا!

۲۔ تم اِس وقت گاڑی مت چلاؤ۔ یہ بارش نہیں ختم ہونے کی!

۳۔ اِس ملک میں بہت غریبی ہے۔ وہاں جمہوریت نہیں آنے کی!

۴۔ یہ دوائی کھا لو تو یہ کھانسی نہیں رُکنے کی!

۵۔ وہ لڑکے اِس کام کو کرنے کی کوشش نہیں کرنے کے!

Translate the following sentences into Urdu using the above construction:

1. It is appropriate that you ask her about the newspaper. I will not ask her!

378

2.   I will not call Ali!

3.   Salim can dry the clothes. I will not dry them!

4.   I will not sit in the hot sun!

5.   I have to go work now. I will not wait for the bus!

6.   I will not lie to my parents! I am used to [habituated to] telling the truth.

16.9 گفتگو (Conversation)

راج اور نرگس کی شادی ۲۵ دِسمبر کو دلّی میں بہت دھوم دھام سے ہوئی۔ دونوں کے والدین نے مہمانوں سے گزارش کی کہ تحفوں یا پھولوں پر پیسہ خرچ کرنے کی بجائے وہ اِس ہسپتال کو مدد دیں جس میں نرگس کام کرتی ہے۔ شادی کے بعد دُلہا دُلہن ہنی مون کے لئے کراچی چلے گئے۔ کراچی پاکستان کا سب سے بڑا شہر ہے۔ کراچی کی سیر کرنے کے بعد یہ سندر جوڑی اسلام آباد کے لئے روانہ ہوگئی۔ اسلام آباد دیکھنے کے بعد یہ لوگ مری جائینگے۔ مری پاکستان کا بہت ہی خوبصورت ہِل اِسٹیشن، یعنی پہاڑی مقام، ہے۔ مری اسلام آباد سے کوئی ۲۸ میل دور ہے۔ نرگس اپنے بچپن میں گرمیوں کی چھٹیوں میں مری جاتی تھی، ٹینس کھیلتی، میٹھے میٹھے پھل کھاتی اور بہت سوتی۔

کراچی سے اسلام آباد جاتے ہوئے راستے میں راج اور نرگس نے کئی دلچسپ چیزیں دیکھیں : کھیت میں کام کرتے ہوئے کسان، پاکستان کے چھوٹے چھوٹے شہروں کی زندگی، مغلوں کی بنوائی ہوئی عمارتیں، اور کرِکٹ کھیلتے ہوئے بچے۔ نرگس کے ساتھ بہت ساری کتابیں بھی تھیں جو وہ سفر میں پڑھنا چاہتی تھی مگر راج اُسے تنگ کرتا گیا۔ اب سنیئے راج اور نرگس کی گفتگو:

نرگس: کیا تمہارے پاس کوئی کتاب نہیں ہے؟

راج: نہیں جان! میں چلتی ہوئی گاڑی میں کتاب نہیں پڑھ سکتا ہوں۔ طبیعت کچھ خراب ہو جاتی ہے۔ اور پھر تم کتنی خوبصورت ہو! تم کو سامنے رکھتے ہوئے اور اِن مچھروں کے بیچ میں اور کوئی چیز کیسے کر سکتا ہوں؟!

نرگس (ہنستے ہوئے): تم کتنے رومانٹک ہو راج! میں مری پہنچتے ہی تم کو ایک اچھا سا تحفہ دوں گی۔

راج (خوش ہو کر): او ڈارلنگ، تحفہ؟ کہو نا۔ کیا تحفہ دو گی؟

نرگس (کتاب پڑھتے پڑھتے): مجھے تنگ مت کرو راج! میں تم کو مری جا کر ہی اس تحفہ کے بارے میں بتا سکتی ہوں۔

راج: مجھے جلدی بتاؤ نہیں تو میں مر جاؤں گا۔

نرگس: میں نہیں بتانے کی!

راج: پلیز! بتاؤ نا!

نرگس: اچھا سنو! تمہارا تحفہ؟ سنیل کی لکھی ہوئی غزلیں اور اچھے رومانٹک ڈائیلاگ ہیں۔ تم کو وہ ڈائیلاگ یاد کر لینے چاہئیں۔

راج (مسکراتے ہوئے): تھینک گاڈ! ہم شادی کے بعد بھی مذاق کر سکتے ہیں!!

نرگس: ہاں ہاں۔ کیوں نہیں! ہم تو مقدّر کے سکندر ہیں۔

16.10 Conversation Practice

Sunil meets Raj and Nargis after they come back from their honeymoon.

Sunil: Nargis, I kept calling you but you weren't home.

Raj: Don't you know that we had gone our honeymoon?

Sunil: I am used to talking to Nargis every evening. What more can I say?

Raj: Don't bother us Sunil. Nargis will absolutely not play tennis with you.

Nargis: Raj! Let me speak otherwise I will never forgive you. Sunil is my friend and you

need to get used to him instead of fighting with him.

Sunil: Look Nargis! I have written this ghazal for you: "I kept thinking of you all night

long, my moist eyes kept smiling all night long."

Raj: He is lying to you Nargis. This is not his own ghazal. This is a stolen ghazal!

Nargis: Sunil, is your name Makhdum? You ought to be ashamed.

Sunil: Forget about the ghazal. Have you forgotten we used to play tennis in our

         childhood, cook food, sing songs and dance? The truth is that I love you!

Raj: You ought to have your brain examined (medically). You are crazy! Nargis is my

         wife and she loves only me!

Sunil: Oh what should I do? Nargis, I will write another ghazal for you.

Nargis: Enough! Sunil, you keep on writing poetry but I won't read it (emphatic). Raj, you

         need to start writing poetry.

Raj: Listen to this song. I just wrote it: How crazy is my heart! It loves you.

Nargis: Raj, I know that you did not write this song. We learned it in Urdu class. Don't you

         you remember that you kept singing it for me every day after class? No, my dear

         Raj. It is not necessary for you to write a song for me. Your beautiful eyes have

         stolen my heart.

16.11 Songs

١)   روتے ہوئے آتے ہیں سب، ہنستا ہوا جو جائیگا

        وہ مُقدّر کا سِکندر جانِ من کہلائیگا

        وہ سکندر کیا تھا جس نے ظلم سے جیتا جہاں

        پیار سے جیتے دِلوں کو وہ جھُکا دے آسماں

        جو سِتاروں پر کہانی پیار کی لِکھ جائیگا

        وہ مُقدّر کا سکندر جانِ من کہلائیگا۔

381

٢)   چلتے چلتے (۲)

یوں ہی کوئی مل گیا تھا (۲)

سرِ راہ چلتے چلتے (۲)

وہیں تھم کے رہ گئی ہے (۲)

میری رات ڈھلتے ڈھلتے (۲)

جو کہی گئی نہ مجھ سے (۲)

وہ زمانہ کہہ رہا ہے (۲)

کہ فسانہ (۲) بن گئی ہے (۲)

میری بات چلتے چلتے (۲)

شبِ انتظار آخر کبھی ہوگی مختصر بھی

یہ چراغ بجھ رہے ہیں میرے ساتھ جلتے جلتے

٣)   غزل

مخدوم مُحی الدّین (۱۹۶۹ـ۱۹۰۸)

آپ کی یاد آتی رہی رات بھر

چشمِ نم مُسکراتی رہی رات بھر

رات بھر درد کی شمع جلتی رہی

غم کی لَو تھرتھراتی رہی رات بھر

بانسری کی سُریلی سُہانی صدا

یاد بن بن کے آتی رہی رات بھر

Glossary for songs

مُقدّر = fate (m)

سِکندر = Alexander the Great

جانِ من = my darling

ظُلم = tyranny, oppression (m)

جیتنا = to win

جُھکانا = to cause to bend

کہلانا = to be called, to be named

یوں ہی = by chance, accidentally

سرِ راہ = road side

تھمنا = to stop; to stand still

ڈھلنا = to decline, to fade, to sink

زمانہ = the world; time; age (m)

فسانہ = story, tale (m)

مُختصر = brief, short

چراغ = lamp; light (m)

بُجھنا = to be extinguished, to go out

بھر = entire, whole (suffix)

رات بھر = the entire night

چشم = eye (f)

نم = moist, wet

درد = pain (m)

شمع = candle (f)

جلنا = to burn

غم = sorrow (m)

لَو = flame (f)

بانسُری = reed flute (f)

سُریلی = musical, melodious

سُہانی = pleasing, appealing

صدا = cry, voice, call (f)

16.12 Vocabulary

to bite, to cut	کاٹنا
to bother	تنگ کرنا
consideration, deep thought (m)	غور
to consider thoughtfully	غور کرنا

383

to take x into consideration	x پر غور کرنا
dear, precious, beloved (m/f)	عزیز
death (lit. transfer) (m)	اِنتقال
to die (for x to die)	x کا اِنتقال ہونا
effort (f)	کوشِش
to try	کوشِش کرنا
enemy (m/f)	دُشمن
helpless	مجبور / بے بس
helplessness (f)	مجبوری / بے بسی
instead of	کے / کی بجائے
lie (m)	جھوٹ
to lie	جھوٹ بولنا
long live	زِندہ باد
mosquito (m)	مچھر
pair, couple (f)	جوڑی
parents (m)	والدین
to perform; to accomplish; to pay	ادا کرنا
principle (m)	اُصول
request (f)	گُزارِش
slave (m)	غُلام
slave girl (f)	کنیز
to take care of x	x کی دیکھ بھال کرنا

throne (m)	تخت
truth (m); true	سچ
to speak the truth	سچ بولنا
to be used to x, to be accustomed to x	x کا عادی ہونا

Reading Passages

Reading Passage One

برِّ صغیر کے موسم

سردی: سردی کے موسم میں ٹھنڈ ہوتی ہے اور کافی جگہوں پر برف بھی پڑتی ہے۔ اس موسم کے خُصوصی پھل سیب اور امرود ہیں۔

بہار: بہار میں نہ تو زیادہ گرمی ہوتی ہے نہ زیادہ سردی۔ ہر طرف پھول کھلتے ہیں۔ شاعر اِس موسم کو پیار کا موسم بھی کہتے ہیں۔

گرمی: اِس موسم میں تیز دھوپ پڑتی ہے۔ گرمی کے دِن لمبے ہوتے ہیں اور راتیں چھوٹی۔ آم اور تربوز گرمیوں کے خُصوصی پھل ہیں۔

برسات: گرمیوں کے بعد برسات کا موسم آتا ہے اور اِس موسم میں بارش ہوتی ہے۔ برسات کا سب سے بڑا تہوار (تیوہار) رکشا بندھن ہوتا ہے۔ رکشا بندھن کے دن بہنیں اپنے بھائیوں کی کلائیوں پر راکھی باندھتی ہیں اور بھائی یہ عہد کرتے ہیں کہ وہ تمام عُمر اپنی بہنوں کی حِفاظت (رکشا) کریں گے۔

خِزاں: خزاں کا دوسرا نام پت جھڑ ہے۔ اِس موسم میں درختوں کے پتے رنگ بدلتے ہیں اور پھر آہستہ آہستہ گِرنے لگتے ہیں۔ شُعراء اِس موسم کی کیفیت کو اپنے محبوب سے بچھڑ جانے کے غم سے تشبیہ دیتے ہیں۔

<u>Glossary</u>

برِّ صغیر	the Subcontinent	ٹھنڈ	cold (f)
سردی	winter (f)	خُصوصی	special
عام طور پر	commonly, usually	امرود	guava (m)
برف پڑنا	to snow	بہار	spring (f)

387

کافی	enough, sufficient	(پھول) کھِلنا	to blossom, bloom
گرمی	summer (f)	خزاں (f) پت جھڑ (m)	autumn; fall
تربوز	watermelon (m)	درخت	tree (m)
(تہوار (تیوہار	festival (m)	پتّا	leaf (m)
رکشا بندھن	festival in which sisters express love for their brothers (m)	راکھی	thread tied by sisters on the wrist of their brothers on the day of *Rakhsha bandan* (f)
کلائی	wrist (f)	محبوب	beloved (m)
عہد	promise, vow (m)	بچھڑنا	to be separated
تمام عُمر	entire life	تشبیہ	simile (f)
(حِفاظت (رکشا	safeguard; protection (f)	تشبیہ دینا	to compare
کیفیت	state, condition (f)	شُعراء (plural of شاعر)(m)	poets

Reading Passage Two

موسمی پیشن گوئی

آج کراچی کا مطلع جزوی طور پر ابر آلود رہے گا۔ بعض مقامات پر بوندا باندی یا تیز بارش کا بھی امکان ہے۔

زیادہ سے زیادہ درجہء حرارت : ۳۹ ڈگری (درجہ) سینٹی گریڈ

اور کم سے کم درجہء حرارت: ۲۷ ڈگری (درجہ) سینٹی گریڈ

رطوبت: ۶۴ فیصد

بارش: ۷ ملی میٹر

طلوعِ آفتاب: ساڑھے پانچ بجے

غروبِ آفتاب: سات بجے

Glossary

پیش گوئی	forecast (f)	x کا امکان ہونا	the possibility of x to
مطلع	sky, horizon (m)		happen
جزوی طور پر	partly	درجہءحرارت	temperature (m)
فیصد	percent	رطوبت	humidity (f)
ابر آلود	cloudy	طلوعِ آفتاب	sunrise (m)
بوندا باندی	drizzle (f)	غروبِ آفتاب	sunset (m)

Reading Passage Three

حیدر آباد دکّن

جنوبی ایشیا میں دو حیدر آباد ہیں: ایک پاکستان میں اور دوسرا جنوبی ہندوستان میں۔ جنوبی ہندوستان کے اس علاقے کو دکّن بھی کہتے ہیں اور حیدر آباد دکّن کا قدیم شہر ہے۔ یہ شہر ۵۰۰ سال سے برِصغیر کا تہذیبی اور تعلیمی مرکز رہا ہے۔ اس شہر کو جنوبی ایشیا کی ہندو مسلم مُشترکہ تہذیب کا گہوارہ سمجھا جاتا ہے۔ یہاں کی تاریخی عمارتوں میں سے چار مینار، گولکنڈہ قلعہ، برلا مندر، اور فلک نما پیلیس سب سے زیادہ مشہور ہیں۔ حیدر آباد کا لاڈ بازار بھی دیکھنے کے قابل ہے۔ لاڈ بازار میں ہر قسم کی چیزیں ملتی ہیں۔ جب حیدر آباد میں شادیاں ہوتی ہیں تو اکثر عورتیں یہیں سے خریداری، یعنی شاپنگ، کرتی ہیں۔ حیدر آباد کا سالار جنگ میوزیم بھی ایک نایاب عجائب گھر ہے۔ یہ عجائب گھر قیمتی چیزوں اور نادر آثارِ قدیمہ کا انمول خزانہ ہے۔ حیدر آباد کا کھانا بھی بہت ہی مزیدار ہوتا ہے۔ یہاں کی بریانی کا تو جواب نہیں! حیدر آباد کا موسم نہ تو زیادہ گرم ہوتا ہے نہ تو زیادہ سرد۔ اسی لئے اس شہر کو غیر ملکی سیاح بھی پسند کرتے ہیں۔ آج کل حیدر آباد میں لاکھوں غیر ملکی

آتے ہیں کیونکہ حیدر آباد ہائی ٹیک کا بھی مرکز بن گیا ہے۔ اس شہر کو بعض لوگ سائبر آباد بھی کہتے

ہیں۔

Glossary

عِلاقہ	area, region (m)	نایاب	rare
دکّن	the Deccan plateau (m)	عجائب گھر	museum (m)
قدیم	old, ancient	نادر	uncommon, rare
تہذیبی	cultural	آثارِ قدیمہ	archaeological objects
تعلیمی	educational	انمول	priceless
مرکز	center (m)	خزانہ	treasure (m)
مُشترکہ	shared, composite	غیر ملکی	foreign (m/f)
تہذیب	culture (f)	سیاح	tourist (m/f)
گہوارہ	cradle (m)	بعض	some, few
خریداری	shopping (f)		

Reading Passage Four

آئیے مُسکرائیں

سموسے

دعوت میں میزبان عورت نے مہمان خاتون سے کہا: اور سموسے لیجئے۔

مہمان خاتون: شکریہ۔ میں تو تین کھا چکی ہوں۔

میزبان: کھائے تو آپ نے گیارہ ہیں لیکن یہاں کون گن رہا ہے؟!

بارِش

شوہر نے اپنی بیگم سے پوچھا: کیا باہر بارش ہو رہی ہے؟

بیوی: کیا بارش کبھی اندر بھی ہوتی ہے؟!

بیچارہ مریض

ایک مریض نے گھبرا کر ڈاکٹر سے پوچھا: کیا آپ کو پورا بھروسہ ہے کہ آپ کامیابی کے ساتھ میرا آپریشن کر سکیں گے؟

ڈاکٹر: یہی تو مجھے آپ کے آپریشن کے بعد معلوم کرنا ہے۔

مریض نے اور زیادہ پریشان ہو کر کہا: آپ کے علاج سے اب تک کتنے لوگ مُلکِ عدم روانہ ہو چکے ہیں؟

ڈاکٹر: آپریشن کے بعد قبروں کو گِن کر بتا دوں گا۔ یہ سوال تو مجھ سے کئی مریض کر چکے ہیں مگر بد قسمتی سے مجھے جواب دینے کا موقع کبھی نہیں ملا!

مرزا غالِب کے دو لطیفے

۱) سردیوں کا موسم تھا۔ ایک دِن غالب کے ایک دوست، خان صاحب، ان کے گھر آئے۔ غالب نے شراب کا گلاس بھر کر ان کے سامنے رکھ دیا۔ خان صاحب غالب کا مُنہ دیکھنے لگے اور کہا: میں نے توبہ کر لی ہے۔ اب میں شراب نہیں پیتا۔ غالب مُتعجب ہو کر بولے: کیا! سردیوں میں بھی نہیں پیتے؟!

۲) ایک صاحب نے غالب سے کہا کہ شراب پینی سخت گناہ ہے۔ غالب نے ہنس کر پوچھا: اگر پئیں تو کیا ہوتا ہے؟ ان صاحب نے جواب دیا: شراب پینے والوں کی دُعا قبول نہیں ہوتی۔ غالب نے مُسکرا کر کہا: جس کے پاس شراب ہو وہ آدمی کسی اور چیز کی دُعا مانگ سکتا ہے؟!

ایک پہیلی

ایک جانور ایسا جس کی دُم پر پیسہ، سر پر بھی تاج ہے بادشاہ کے جیسا، بولو کیا ہے؟

(search glossary below for answer)

Glossary

مُسکرانا	to smile	خاتون	(respected) woman
سموسہ	samosa (m)	بیگم	wife (respected) woman
میزبان	host (m/f)	گھبرانا	to worry
مہمان	guest (m/f)	پورا	complete
بھروسہ	trust, confidence (m)	سخت	severe, hard
کامیاب	successful	گُناہ	sin (m)
کامیابی	success (f)	دُعا	prayer (f)
پریشان ہونا	to worry	قبول ہونا	to be accepted
مُلکِ عدم	land of eternity	دُعا مانگنا	to ask a favor; to pray
روانہ ہونا	to depart	پہیلی	riddle (f)
موقع ملنا	to get an opportunity	دُم	tail (f)
لطیفہ	joke (m)	پیسہ	coin (m)
بھرنا	to fill	تاج	crown (m)
توبہ	repentance (f)	مور	peacock (m)
مُتعجب ہونا	to be astonished		

Reading Passage Five

اکبر کا شاہی دسترخوان

آئیے مزیدار کھانا پکائیے! آلو گو بھی بنانے کے لئے ہمیں اِن اشیاء کی ضرورت پڑے گی: ۵ آلو، ایک پھول گو بھی، ۱ عدد پیاز، ۲ سُرخ ٹماٹر، آدھی پیالی تیل، آدھا چمچ ادرک پاؤڈر، ۱ چمچ لہسن پاؤڈر، آدھا چمچ گرم مصالحہ، آدھی چمچ ہلدی، نمک اور لال مرچ حسبِ ذائقہ، کڑھی پتّا، ہرا دھنیا۔

آلو گو بھی بنانے کی ترکیب:

آلو اور پھول گو بھی کو چھیل کر چھوٹے ٹکڑے کر لیں۔ پیاز اور ٹماٹر کو بھی باریک کاٹ لیں۔ تیل کو کڑھائی میں گرم کر لیں اور پھر اس میں پیاز کو کڑھی پتّے کے ساتھ تل لیں۔ جب پیاز کا رنگ بادامی ہو جائے تب اس میں آلو، گو بھی، ٹماٹر، ادرک، لہسن، نمک، مرچ، اور گرم مصالحہ تل لیں اور پھر ایک پیالی پانی ملا کر دھیمی آنچ پر پکنے دیں۔ جب آلو اور پھول گو بھی گل جائیں اور پانی خشک ہو جائے تب کڑھائی چولہے سے اتار لیں اور سجاوٹ کے لئے ہرا دھنیا اوپر ڈال لیں۔ آئیے گرم گرم روٹی کے ساتھ مزیدار آلو گو بھی نوش فرمائیے۔

<u>Glossary</u>

شاہی	royal	حسبِ ذائقہ	according to taste
دسترخوان	dining cloth* (m)	کڑھی پتّا	curry leaves (m)
آلو	potato (m)	ہرا دھنیا	coriander (m)
بند گو بھی	cabbage (f)	چھیلنا	to peel
پھول گو بھی	cauliflower (f)	ٹکڑا	piece (m)
ترکیب	recipe (f)	باریک	thin, fine, delicate
اشیاء	things; ingredients (f)	کاٹنا	to cut
عدد	quantity (m)	کڑھائی	skillet; frying pan (f)

393

سُرخ	red	تلنا	to fry
ٹماٹر	tomato (m)	بادام	almond (m)
پیالی	cup (f)	بادامی	brown, almond-colored
تیل	oil (m)	دھیما	slow, simmer
ادرک	ginger (m)	آنچ	fire, flame (f)
لہسن	garlic (m)	گلنا	to melt, soften
گرم مصالحہ	mixture of spices (m)	خشک	dry
ہلدی	tumeric (f)	چولہا	stove (m)
نمک	salt (m)	سجاوٹ	decoration (f)
مرچ	pepper (f)	نوش فرمانا	to eat with relish

*a sheet spread on the floor on which various dishes are placed. Traditionally, before the introduction of dining tables, family members and guests sat around this sheet as they partook of the meal.

Reading Passage Six

ریڈیو سے

السّلام علیکم۔ یہ ریڈیو پشاور ہے۔ آج ۲۷ رجب ۱۴۲۱ھ ہے اور اس وقت رات کے دس بجے ہیں۔ آج کی تازہ عالمی خبریں سماعت فرمائیے۔ امریکہ کے صدر بل کلنٹن کا دورۂ مصر آج ختم ہوا۔ صدر کلنٹن کی مصر کے دار الحکومت قاہرہ میں فلسطینی نمائندوں کے ایک وفد سے بھی ملاقات ہوئی۔ اس ملاقات کے دوران وفد کے سربراہ نے صدر کلنٹن کو بتایا کہ مغرب تیسری دنیا کے مسائل سے انجان ہے۔ انہوں نے مزید یہ بھی کہا کہ اگر مغربی مُمالک واقعی مشرقِ وسطٰی میں امن قائم کرنا چاہتے ہیں یا دہشت گردی کو روکنا چاہتے ہیں تو اُن کو چاہیئے کہ وہ فلسطینیوں کے مسائل کو

بہتر طور پر سمجھنے کی کوشش کریں۔ایک اور فلسطینی نمائندے نے صدر کلنٹن کو صاف صاف لفظوں میں یہ بھی بتایا کہ مشرقِ وسطیٰ میں انسانی حقوق، خصوصاً فلسطینی حقوق، کی پامالی ہو رہی ہے۔اس ملاقات کے بعد صدر کلنٹن نے اہرامِ مصر کی سیر کی۔آج سے امریکی صدر شام اور اُردن کا دورہ شروع کریں گے۔

Glossary

تازہ	fresh	نمائندہ	representative (m/f)
عالمی	international	وفد	delegation (m)
سماعت فرمایئے	please listen	سر براہ	head, leader (m/f)
مِصر	Egypt (m)	ملاقات	meeting (f)
دورہ	tour, trip, visit (m)	کے دوران	during
دورہ کرنا	to tour, visit	مغرب	West
دارالحکومت	capital city (m)	مسئلہ، مسائل	issue/issues (m)
قاہرہ	Cairo (m)	انجان	unaware/ignorant
فلسطین	Palestine (m)	مزید	furthermore
ملک، ممالک	country/countries (m)	حق، حقوق	right/rights (m)
مشرقِ وسطیٰ	Middle East	خصوصاً	especially
امن	peace (m)	پامالی	destruction, violation(f)
قائم کرنا	to establish	اہرامِ مصر	Pyramids of Egypt (m)
دہشت گردی	terrorism (f)	شام	Syria (m)
صاف صاف	clearly, emphatically	اُردن	Jordan (m)
لفظ، الفاظ	word/ words (m)	انسانی	human

Reading Passage Seven

اخبار سے

اقوام مُتحدہ کے نمائندے رحیم بھٹ نے کل شام کی پریس کانفرنس میں بتایا کہ ایڈز کا مرض تیزی سے جنوبی ایشیا میں پھیل رہا ہے۔ اگر اس مرض پر جلد قابو نہ پایا گیا تو لاکھوں لوگ مر سکتے ہیں۔ بھٹ نے مزید یہ بھی کہا کہ ایڈز صرف ایشیا اور افریقہ کا مسئلہ نہیں بلکہ ایک عالمی مسئلہ ہے جس کو حل کرنے کے لئے دُنیا کے سارے مُلکوں کو ایک دوسرے کے ساتھ تبادلہءِ خیال کرنا پڑیگا تاکہ ایڈز کے حِفاظتی ٹیکے کی ایجاد جلد از جلد ہو سکے۔ بھٹ کی اس رائے سے دنیا کی کئی تنظیمیں خصوصاً عالمی ادارہ صحت یعنی ورلڈ ہیلتھ آرگنائزیشن اتفاق کرتی ہیں۔

<u>Glossary</u>

اقوامِ مُتحدہ	The United Nations	جلد از جلد	as soon as possible
مرض	disease, epidemic (m)	x کی ایجاد ہونا	x to be invented
x پر قابو پانا	to bring x under control	رائے	opinion (f)
حل کرنا	to solve	تنظیم	organization (f)
تبادلہءِ خیال	exchange of ideas	ادارہ	institution (m)
حِفاظتی	preventive, protective	x سے اتفاق کرنا	to agree with x
ٹیکہ	vaccination (m)		

Note on the Calendar

In most of the Urdu-speaking world, one encounters two calendars: the Islamic lunar or *hijrii* calendar; and the Gregorian, Common Era one, called *isavii*. Dates are written from right to left, with the day first (at times followed by / sign), the month second, and the year third. The year is usually written over the ‿ sign which stand for the Arabic word for year, "*sana.*" This sign is followed either by ﮪ (the sign for Islamic *hijrii* calendar) or ؏ (the sign for the Gregorian *isavii* calendar). All months are masculine in gender.

ہجری مہینے

Rajab	رجب ۔۷	*Muharram*	۱۔ مُحرّم
Sha'abaan	شعبان ۔۸	*Safar*	۲۔ صفر
Ramzaan/Ramdhaan	رمضان ۔۹	*Rabii' ul-awwal*	۳۔ ربیع الاوّل
Shawwal	شوّال ۔۱۰	*Rabii'us-saanii*	۴۔ ربیع الثّانی
Zuu'l qadaa(Zii qaad)	ذوالقعدہ(ذیقعد) ۔۱۱	*Jamaadii ul-awwal*	۵۔ جمادی الاوّل
Zuu'l hijjaa(Ziilhijj)	ذوالحجّہ (ذی الحج) ۔۱۲	*Jamaadii us-saanii*	۶۔ جمادی الثّانی

عیسوی مہینے

July	جولائی	January	جنوری
August	اگست	February	فروری
September	ستمبر	March	مارچ
October	اکتوبر	April	اپریل
November	نومبر	May	مئی
December	دسمبر	June	جون

Sample dates:

9th Shawwal, 1388 Hijri   ھ ۱۳۸۸ شوّال ۹   10th January 1968 C.E. ؏ ۱۹۶۸ جنوری ۱۰

Urdu - English Glossary

ا

now	اب
father (m)	اَبّا
you - formal	آپ
sister (f)	آپا
your (formal)	آپ کا / آپکا
one's own	اپنا
this much	اِتنا
to pick up	اُٹھانا
to wake up, rise	اُٹھنا
today	آج
permission (f)	اِجازت
give permission to leave (got to run)	اِجازت دیجئے
these days, nowadays	آج کل
pickles (m)	اچار
good	اچّھا
newspaper (m)	اخبار
to perform; to accomplish; to pay	ادا کرنا
greetings, hello, hi	آداب عرض / آداب
actor (m)	اداکار
actress (f)	اداکارہ

human being, man, person (m)	آدمی
half	آدھا / آدھ
in this direction	اِدھر
in that direction	اُدھر
intention (m)	اِرادہ
rest (m)	آرام
to rest	آرام کرنا
to fly; to cause to fly	اُڑانا
independence, freedom (f)	آزادی
in this duration	اِس دوران میں
therefore	اِس لئے
use (m)	اِستعمال
to use	اِستعمال کرنا
to use x	x کا اِستعمال کرنا
student (m/f)	اِسٹوڈنٹ
noble name (m) (formal Urdu)	اِسمِ شریف
sky (m)	آسمان
principle (m)	اُصول
generally, often; most; many	اکثر
although	اگرچہ
although	البتّہ
cupboard, cabinet (f)	الماری

owl; fool; stupid (m/f)	اُلّو
potato (m)	آلُو
mango (m)	آم
mother (f)	امّاں
test, trial, examination (m)	اِمتحان
America (m)	امریکہ
American	امریکی / امریکن
peace, safety (m)	امن
mother (f)	امّی
rich	امِیر
to come	آنا
waiting, expectation (m)	اِنتظار
to wait for x	x کا اِنتظار کرنا
arrangement (m)	اِنتظام
death (lit. transfer) (m)	اِنتقال
to die (for x to die)	x کا اِنتقال ہونا
inside	اندر
darkness (m)	اندھیرا
human being (m)	اِنسان
tears (m)	آنسو
God willing (may God will that)	اِنشاء اللہ
his, her (formal)	اُن کا / اُنکا

their	اُن کا / اُنکا
eye (f)	آنکھ
English (adj.)	انگریزی
English (the language)	انگریزی
England (m)	انگلستان
English (adj.)	انگلستانی
finger (f)	اُنگلی
vagabond, wanderer (m/f)	آوارہ
voice, sound, noise (f)	آواز
above	اُوپر
and	اور
more, additional	اور
offspring, children (f)	اولاد
Iran (m)	اِیران
Iranian	اِیرانی
once	ایک بار

ب

father (m)	بابا
father (m)	باپ
speech, word; thing (abstract); matter; affair (f)	بات
to speak, to talk, converse	بات کرنا

sister (f)	باجی
rain (f)	بارِش
to rain	بارِش ہونا
market, bazaar (m)	بازار
garden (m)	باغ
hair (m)	بال
absolutely, completely	بالکل
arm, embrace (f)	بانہہ
cook (m)	باورچی
out, outside	باہر
to play (an instrument)	بجانا
childhood (m)	بچپن
child (m)	بچّہ
fever; wrath; steam (m)	بُخار
worse	بدتر
worst	بدترین
to change	بدلنا
Wednesday (m)	بُدھ
bad, evil, wicked	بُرا
to be offended, to feel insulted	بُرا ماننا
Britain (m)	برطانیہ
snow/ice (f)	برف

rice w/ spicy meat or vegetables (f)	بریانی
big	بڑا
grown up, elder person (m/f)	بڑا / بڑی
to cause to increase; to enlarge (transitive)	بڑھانا
to increase, to grow, to extend (intransitive)	بڑھنا
revered person, respected elder	بزُرگ
enough!	بس!
without	بغیر (کے)
to call, invite	بلانا
nightingale (f)	بلبل
cat (f)	بلّی
to make, to build, to create	بنانا
Bangladesh (m)	بنگله دیش
to be made, built, created	بننا
to play the role of x	x بننا
to cause to be built; constructed with (used with کو and سے)	بنوانا
elderly (adj.); elderly person (m)	بوڑھا
brave, courageous	بہادُر
very	بہت
better	بہتر
best	بہترین

sister (f)	بہن
helpless	بے بس
helplessness (f)	بے بسی
daughter (f)	بیٹی
to sit	بیٹھنا
middle	بیچ
poor thing/ fellow (m/f)	بیچارہ / بیچاری
to sell	بیچنا
fed up	بیزار
scores of	بیسیوں
useless, unemployed	بیکار
sick, ill (adj.); sick person (m/f)	بیمار
sickness, illness (f)	بیماری
wife (f)	بیوی

بھ

India (m)	بھارت
heavy	بھاری
to flee, to run away from	بھاگنا
brother (m)	بھائی
ghost (m)	بھوت
hunger (f)	بھوک

to forget	بُھولنا
also, too	بھی
to send	بھیجنا
crowd (f)	بھیڑ

پ

papad (crispy appetizers) (m)	پاپڑ
toilet, excrement, stool (m)	پاخانہ
Pakistan (m)	پاکستان
Pakistani	پاکستانی
crazy, mad, insane	پاگل
to raise, nourish; maintain; to protect	پالنا
to find	پانا
water (m)	پانی
father (m)	پِتا
pants, trousers (f)	پتلون
wife (f)	پتنی
address; hint, clue, trace (m)	پتا
to come to know; to find out	پتا چلنا
husband (m)	پَتی
last, past, previous; back, latter	پچھلا
on	پَر

old (thing)	پُرانا
day before yesterday; day after tomorrow	پرسوں
family (m)	پرِوار
worried	پریشان
distress, misery, anxiety (f)	پریشانی
Premchand - prominent author of Urdu-Hindi	پریم چند
narrative prose, died 1936	
studies, education (f)	پڑھائی
to study, to read	پڑھنا
pleasing (adjective); choice, preference (f)	پسند
favorite	پسندیدہ
to cook	پکانا
to catch, apprehend	پکڑنا
moment (m)	پل
bed (m)	پلنگ
fan; ventilator (m)	پنکھا
mountain, hill (m)	پہاڑ
to recognize; to know; to perceive; to discern	پہچاننا
to reach	پہنچنا
to ask	پوچھنا
quarter less than (after whole number)	پون
love (m)	پیار

to love	پیار کرنا
onion (f)	پیاز
thirst (f)	پیاس
cup (f)	پیالی
stomach (m)	پیٹ
to be born	پیدا ہونا
leg (m)	پیر
Monday (m)	پیر
money, cash, wealth; coin (m)	پیسا / پیسہ
urine (m)	پیشاب
yellow	پیلا
to drink	پینا

پھ

again	پھر
yet, still	پھر بھی
see you soon (lit. we will meet again)	پھر ملینگے
fruit (m)	پھل
fruit seller (m/f)	پھل والا / پھل والی
flower (m)	پُھول
to spread	پھیلنا
to throw	پھینکنا

ت

star (m)	تارا
date, history (f)	تاریخ
historical	تاریخی
so that	تاکہ
gift (m)	تُحفہ
throne (m)	تخت
to sit down (formal Urdu)	تشریف رکھنا
to enter (formal Urdu)	تشریف لانا
picture, photograph (f)	تصویر
praise (f)	تعریف
to praise x	x کی تعریف کرنا
details, explanation; analysis (f)	تفصیل
speech, recital; statement (f)	تقریر
to give a speech	تقریر کرنا
until	تک
you - informal	تُم
body (m)	تن
to bother	تنگ کرنا
you - least formal	تُو
to break (transitive)	توڑنا

ready	تیّار
to swim	تیرنا
swift, quick; hot (spicy), fiery, sharp	تیز
festival (m)	تیوہار

تھ

tiredness (f)	تھکن
some, few; scanty, little; less	تھوڑا

ٹ

piece, morsel (m)	ٹکڑا
hat (f)	ٹوپی
to break (intransitive)	ٹوٹنا

ٹھ

to wait; to stop; to stay	ٹھہرنا
cold (adjective)	ٹھنڈا
cold (noun, f)	ٹھنڈ
fine, good, exactly	ٹھیک
to become well	ٹھیک ہو جانا

ج

Japan (m)	جاپان
Japanese	جاپانی
cold (weather) (m)	جاڑا
to wake up, rise	جاگنا
life, soul; sweetheart; energy (f)	جان
to go	جانا
to know	جاننا
animal (m)	جانور
when	جب
germs (m)	جراثیم
celebration (m)	جشن
place, vacancy (f)	جگہ
gentleman, sir, mister (m)	جناب
Friday (m)	جُمعہ
Thursday (f)	جُمعرات
democracy (f)	جمہوریت
answer (m)	جواب
young (adj.); youth (m/f)	جوان
youthfulness, youth (f)	جوانی
shoe (m)	جُوتا

pair, couple (f)	جوڑی
lie (m)	جھوٹ
to lie	جھوٹ بولنا
no, not	جی نہیں
yes	جی ہاں
to live, to be alive	جینا
life partner (m/f)	جیون ساتھی

چ

clever, cunning, sly	چالاک
moon (m)	چاند
moonlight (f)	چاندنی
rice (pl. m.)	چاوَل
tea (f)	چائے
shut up; be quiet	چپ رہو
to steal	چُرانا
zoo (m)	چڑیا گھر
to climb	چڑھنا
to drive	چلانا
to come along, to go along, to set out, to walk	چلنا
spoon; sycophant (colloquial) (m)	چمچہ
wound; injury (f)	چوٹ

theft (f)	چوری
thief (m)	چور
to scream, yell	چِیخنا
thing (f)	چیز
China (m)	چِین
Chinese	چِینی
sugar (f)	چِینی

چھ

student (Hindi) (m/f)	چھاتر
umbrella; canopy (f)	چھتری
holiday, vacation (f)	چُھٹّی
knife (f)	چُھری
small	چھوٹا

ح

condition, state (m)	حال
condition (f)	حالت
action, deed; mischief; movement (f)	حرکت
beautiful	حسِین
truth (f)	حقِیقت
government (f)	حُکُومت

to govern	حُکُومت کرنا
henna (f)	حِنّا

خ

special	خاص
empty	خالی
quiet, silent	خاموش
family (m)	خاندان
news (f)	خبر
to finish, to end, conclude (transitive)	ختم کرنا
to finish, to end, conclude (intransitive)	ختم ہونا
goodbye (lit. God be your protector)	خُدا حافظ
God willing (may God will that)	خُدا کرے (کہ)
God forbid	خُدا نہ خواستہ
God forbid (may God not will that)	خُدا نہ کرے
service (f)	خِدمت
bad	خراب
fault, blemish (f)	خرابی
expenditure, expense (m)	خرچ
to spend, to expend (transitive)	خرچ کرنا
to be spent, expended (intransitive)	خرچ ہونا
to buy	خریدنا

letter (m)	خَط
dangerous	خَطرناک
dream (m)	خواب
beautiful	خُوبصُورت
self (reflexive); oneself	خُود
happy	خُوش
happiness (f)	خُوشی
blood (m)	خُون
thought, idea, opinion (m)	خیال

د

grandfather (paternal)	دادا
grandmother (paternal)	دادی
lentils (f)	دال
tooth (m)	دانت
pain (m)	درد
door (m)	دروازہ
river (m)	دریا
to have diarrhea	دست آنا
signature (m)	دستخط
enemy (m/f)	دُشمن
invitation; feast; party (f)	دعوَت

to invite x	x کو دعوت دینا
to have a party for x	x کی دعوت کرنا
office (m)	دفتر
shop, store (f)	دُکان / دُوکان
shopkeeper/store owner	دُکان والا / دُکاندار
heart (m)	دِل
interest (interesting) (f)	دِلچسپی
bridegroom (m)	دُلہا
bride (f)	دُلہن / دُلہنیا
brain, mind, intellect (m)	دِماغ
day (m)	دِن
world (f)	دُنیا
medicine (f)	دوا / دوائی
afternoon (f)	دوپہر
milk (m)	دُودھ
far	دُور
time (period of); period (m)	دوران
during this time/period	اِس دوران میں
friend (m/f)	دوست
friendship (f)	دوستی
second, another	دوسرا
both	دونوں

to repeat, double, fold	دُہرانا
yogurt (m)	دہی
sister (f)	دِیدی
late, a long while; a long period of time, interval; lateness (f)	دیر
late	دیر سے
to delay, to be a long time, to come late	دیر کرنا
to take care of x	x کی دیکھ بھال کرنا
to see	دیکھنا
to give	دینا
wall (f)	دیوار
mad, ecstatic	دیوانہ
sunshine, heat of sun (f)	دھُوپ
pomp and gusto (f)	دھُوم دھام
to wash	دھونا

ڈ

mail (f)	ڈاک
post office (m)	ڈاک خانہ
doctor (m/f)	ڈاکٹر
to pour, to place, to put	ڈالنا
box (m)	ڈِبّہ

fear (m)	ڈر
to fear	ڈرنا

ڈھ - ذ

Dacca (m)	ڈھاکہ
little, just; please (with تم form imperatives)	ذرا

ر

night (f)	رات
king (m)	راجہ
road (m)	راستہ
pleased; contented; agreed	راضی
to agree upon x	x پر راضی ہونا
to be pleased with x	x سے راضی ہونا
melody	راگ (m)/راگنی (f)
cheeks, countenance (m)	رُخسار
juice, nectar (m)	رَس
receipt (f)	رسید
relationship / connection (m)	رِشتہ
family, relatives (m)	رِشتہ دار
Ramadan, Muslim holy month (m)	رمضان
to depart, to set out	روانہ ہونا

rupee (Indian/ Pakistani currency) (m)	روپیہ
bread (f)	روٹی
Russia (m)	رُوس
Russian	رُوسی
to stop, to prevent	روکنا
to cry	رونا
to stay, to live	رہنا
train (f)	ریل گاڑی

ز

cold (illness) (m)	زُکام
time, age; world; fortune (m)	زمانہ
land (f)	زمین
landlord (m)	زمیندار
life (f)	زِندگی
living, alive	زِندہ
long live	زِندہ باد
a lot, very much	زِیادہ

س

beloved, sweetheart (m)	ساجَن
whole, entire, all; the whole	سارا

half (with whole numeral)	ساڑھے
mother-in-law (f)	ساس
birthday (f)	سالگرہ
curry (m)	سالن
barrage, luggage, goods (m)	سامان
breath (f)	سانس
all	سَب
vegetable (f)	سبزی
vegetarian (m/f)	سبزی خور
dream (m)	سپنا
to tease, to annoy, to torment	ستانا
true (adj.); truth (m)	سَچ
to speak the truth	سَچ بولنا
head (m)	سر
cold (noun, f)	سردی
cheap	ستا
father-in-law (m)	سسُر
journey (m)	سفر
to make a journey, travel	سفر کرنا
white	سفید
to be able to, can	سکنا
Sikh	سِکھ

to dry	سُکھانا
greetings to a Muslim (reply in parentheses)	سلام علیکم (وعلیکم سلام)
	السّلام علیکم (وعلیکم السّلام)
to explain, to cause to understand	سمجھانا
to understand	سمجھنا
to cause to listen, to tell, to narrate	سُنانا
orange (m)	سنترا
beautiful	سُندر
marble (m)	سنگِ مرمر
orange (m)	سنگترہ
to listen	سُننا
hundred	سو
one and a quarter; quarter more (after number)	سَوا
question (m)	سَوال
to think	سوچنا
to dry (intransitive)	سُوکھنا
to sleep	سونا
girlfriend (for girls) (f)	سہیلی
from	سے
before	سے پہلے
apple (m)	سیب

stroll, walk, tour, excursion (f)	سیر
to stroll, to take a walk, to tour	سیر کرنا
hundreds of	سیکڑوں / سینکڑوں
service (f)	سیوا

ش

wedding (f)	شادی
poet (m)	شاعر
vegetarian (m/f)	شاکاہاری
evening (f)	شام
splendid, stately, grand	شاندار
prince (m)	شاہزادہ
perhaps	شاید
auspicious name (m) (formal Hindi)	شُبھ نام
alcohol, wine (f)	شراب
mischief (f)	شرارت
sherbet (beverage) (m)	شربت
to be shy, reticent	شرمانا
ashamed, bashful, modest	شرمِندہ
to be ashamed, bashful, modest	شرمِندہ ہونا
mischievious	شریر
honorable, noble	شریف

to start, to begin (transitive)	شروع کرنا
to start, to begin (intransitive)	شروع ہونا
chess (f)	شطرنج
poetry; a couplet, a verse (m)	شعر
thanks (m)	شکریہ
noise, uproar, disturbance (m)	شور
hobby/ hobbies (m)	شوق
husband (m)	شوہر
town, city (m)	شہر
emperor (m)	شہنشاہ

ص

gentleman, sir, mister	صاحب
clean	صاف
morning (f)	صُبح
health (f)	صحت
healthy	صحت مند
president (m/f)	صدر
only	صِرف
Sufi - a Muslim mystic (m)	صُوفی

ض

definitely, sure	ضَرُور
necessity; need (f)	ضَرُورت
necessity, need for x	x کی ضَرُورت

ط

student (m/f)	طالبِ عِلم
temperament, health (f)	طبیعت
manner, style (f)	طرح
storm (m)	طوفان

ع

habituated; accustomed	عادی
to be habituated/used to/accustomed to x	x کا عادی ہونا
lover (m)	عاشِق
being a lover (f)	عاشِقی
wonders (pl.)	عجائِب
museum (m)	عجائِب گھر
wonder (m)	عجُوبہ
wonderful, surprising, strange	عجِیب
court (f)	عدالت

Arabic (f)	عربی
dear, precious, beloved (m/f)	عزیز
love (m)	عِشق
great	عظیم
cure (m)	عِلاج
besides, moreover, in addition to	کے عِلاوہ
building (f)	عِمارت
age (f)	عُمر
woman (f)	عورَت
festival -- Muslim (f)	عید
Christian	عیسائی

غ

poor person (m/f)	غریب
poverty (f)	غریبی
ghazal (love poem) (f)	غزل
bathroom (m)	غُسل خانہ
to bathe	غُسل کرنا
slave (m)	غُلام
mistake, error (f)	غلطی
sorrow (m)	غم
sorrowful	غمناک

consideration, deep thought (m)	غور
to consider thoughtfully	غور کرنا
to take x into consideration	x پر غور کرنا

ف

leisure, free time (f)	فُرصت
worry (f)	فِکر
skill, art, craft (m)	فَن
artist (m)	فَنکار
army (f)	فوج
to dial the phone	فون مِلانا
to call x on the phone	x کو فون کرنا
decision (m)	فیصلہ

ق

capable, able, skillful	قابِل
worthy of (with oblique infinitive)	کے قابِل
carpet (f)	قالِین
grave, tomb (f)	قبر
oath (f)	قَسم
to swear by x	x کی قسم کھانا
queue, line (f)	قطار

fort (m)	قِلعہ
pen (m/f)	قَلَم
shirt (f)	قَمِیض
qawwali - spiritual-mystical song recited by	قَوّالی
Muslim mystics (f)	
prison, jail (m)	قیدخانہ
prisoner (m/f)	قیدی
price, cost (f)	قِیمت

ک

to bite, to cut	کاٹنا
kohl, collyrium (m)	کاجل
would that	کاش
enough, sufficient, adequate	کافی
black	کالا
work, job (m)	کام
to work	کام کرنا
successful	کامیاب
success (f)	کامیابی
ear (m)	کان
fork; thorn (m)	کانٹا
when?	کب؟

since when?	کب سے؟
sometimes	کبھی
occasionally; now and then	کبھی کبھی
clothes (m)	کپڑے
book (f)	کِتاب
dog (m)	کتّا
how much, how many?	کِتنا / کِتنے / کِتنی
trash (m)	کچرا
something, anything	کُچھ
nothing	کُچھ نہیں
fare, rent (m)	کِرایہ
chair (f)	کرسی
to do	کرنا
ten millions; crore	کروڑ
millionaire (m/f)	کروڑپتی
millions of	کروڑوں
for what reason, why?	کِس لئے؟
farmer, peasant (m)	کِسان
tomorrow, yesterday (m)	کل
less	کم
to reduce	کم کرنا
to be reduced	کم ہونا

room (m)	کمرہ
comb (f)	کنگھی
to comb	کنگھی کرنا
slave girl (f)	کنیز
effort (f)	کوشش
to try	کوشش کرنا
who?	کون؟
someone; anyone (noun, m.); some, any;	کوئی
approximately (adj).	
no one; nobody	کوئی نہیں
that, which, who (rel. pronoun and conjunction)	کہ
where?	کہاں
from where?	کہاں سے
story (f)	کہانی
to say, to speak (with سے)	کہنا
to call (something a name) (with کو)	کہنا
in front of, across, facing	کے آگے
inside	کے اندر
on top of	کے اُوپر
instead of	کے/کی بجائے
in return for x; instead of x	x کے بدلے میں
regarding	کے بارے میں

out, outside	کے باہر
after	کے بعد
without	(کے) بغیر
near	کے پاس
behind	کے پیچھے
with	کے ساتھ
in front of, across, facing	کے سامنے
near	کے قریب
for the sake of, for, in order to	کے لئے
near	کے نزدیک
under	کے نیچے
kilogram	کِیلو
because of	کی وجہ سے
several; some; a few	کئی
what?	کیا؟
what sort of, what kind of, how?	کیسا / کیسی / کیسے؟
banana (m)	کیلا
why? for what reason?	کیوں؟
because	کیونکہ

کھ

to eat	کھانا
food (m)	کھانا
to cough	کھانسنا
cough (f)	کھانسی
window (f)	کھِڑکی
athlete, player (m/f)	کھِلاڑی
toy (m)	کھِلونا
to open	کھولنا
to lose (misplace something)	کھونا
agricultural field (m)	کھیت
to play	کھیلنا

گ

car (f)	گاڑی
to drive a car	گاڑی چلانا
song (m)	گانا
to sing	گانا
village (m)	گاؤں
cow (f)	گائے
hot	گرم

heat, hot weather (f)	گرمی
to fall down	گِرنا
request (f)	گُزارِش
to spend time, to pass	گُزارنا
filth (f)	گندگی
witness (m/f)	گواہ
meat (m)	گوشت
meat eater (m/f)	گوشت خور
meat curry (m)	گوشت کا سالن
round, circular; a circle	گول
song (m)	گِیت

گھ

house (m)	گھر
clock/ watch (f)	گھڑی
hour (m)	گھنٹا
horse (m)	گھوڑا

ل

answerless, speechless; unequalled, matchless	لا جواب
hundred thousand	لاکھ
hundreds of thousands of	لاکھوں

red	لال
to bring	لانا
boy (m)	لڑکا
girl (f)	لڑکی
to fight x	x سے لڑنا
yogurt drink (f)	لسّی
to write	لِکھنا
tall	لمبا
people, folk (m)	لوگ
lemon/ lime (m)	لیموں
to take	لینا

م

mother (f)	ماں
mother (f)	ماتا
to hit	مارنا
to be convinced, to listen, to obey	ماننا
sweets (f)	مِٹھائی
helpless	مجبور
helplessness (f)	مجبوری
criminal (m)	مجرم
mosquito; insect (m)	مچھر

love (f)	مُحبّت
to love	مُحبّت کرنا
lover (m)	محبُوب
hard work (f)	محنت
to do hard work	محنت کرنا
hard working	محنتی
help (f)	مدد
to help x	x کی مدد کرنا
joke, wit; taste (m)	مذاق
to tease, to make fun of x	x کا مذاق اُڑانا
pepper (f)	مرچ
chicken (f)	مُرغی
chicken curry (f)	مُرغی کا سالن
to die	مَرنا
disposition, health (m)	مزاج
how are you? (formal)	مزاج شریف
grave, tomb, shrine of a Sufi holy man (m)	مزار
to enjoy	مزہ کرنا
delicious	مزیدار
traveller (m/f)	مُسافر
intoxicating	مَست
mosque (f)	مَسجد

to smile	مُسکرانا
Muslim	مُسلِم
Muslim	مُسلمان
difficult	مُشکِل
famous	مَشہور
spices (m)	مصالحہ / مسالا
busy	مصرُوف
essay, composition (m)	مضمُون
purpose, intent; motive (m)	مطلب
forgive/ excuse me	معاف کیجِئے / کرو
examination (medical), investigation (m)	مُعائَینہ
to have something examined (medically)	مُعائَینہ کرانا
to know	معلُوم ہونا
facts, information (f)	معلُومات
Mughal - dynasty that ruled India from the 16th to the 19th century	مُغل
poverty (f)	مُفلِسی
useful/ profitable	مُفید
place (m) (plural)	مقام (مقامات)
mausoleum (m)	مقبرہ
house (m)	مکان
landlord (m)	مکان مالِک

435

but, however	مگر
country (m)	مُلک
to meet	مِلنا
possible	مُمکِن
to celebrate, commemorate	منانا
appropriate	مُناسِب
temple (m)	مندِر
Tuesday (m)	مَنگل
mouth, face (m)	مُنھ/مُنہ
patient (m)	مریض
fat	موٹا
season (m)	موسَم
Mahabharata - Indian epic	مہابھارت
Maharashtra (m)	مہاراشٹرہ
queen, empress (f)	مہارانی
thanks (f) (lit. kindness)	مہربانی
please, kindly (with آپ forms)	مہربانی سے / مہربانی کر کے
guest (m/f)	مہمان
henna (f)	مہندی
expensive	مہنگا
sweet	میٹھا
my	میرا

Mirabai - a 16th century poetess famous for her devotional songs to the Hindu deity Krishna	میرا بائی
table (f)	میز
minaret (m)	مینار
I	مَیں
in	میں

ن

to dance	ناچنا
angry; displeased; upset	ناراض
to be/ become angry; upset	ناراض ہونا
nose (f)	ناک
name (m)	نام
grandfather (maternal)	نانا
grandmother (maternal)	نانی
narcissus (f)	نرگس
near	نزدیک
flu (m)	نزلہ
sign, momento, souvenir (m/f)	نِشان / نِشانی
song (m)	نغمہ
to come out, to arise; to depart	نِکلنا
Muslim ritual prayers (f)	نماز

to recite namaz	نماز پڑھنا
lemon/ lime (m)	نمبو
salt (m)	نمک
servant (m)	نوکر
job, work (f)	نوکری
to bathe	نہانا
no, not	نہیں
blue	نیلا

و

to return, come back	واپس آنا
to go back, return	واپس جانا
father (m)	والِد
mother (f)	والِدہ
parents (m)	والدین
reason (f)	وجہ
to work out, to exercise	ورزِش کرنا
otherwise	ورنہ
weight (m)	وزن
minister (government) (m)	وزیر
prime minister (m/f)	وزیرِ اعظم
homeland (m)	وطن

time (m)	وقت
lawyer, agent (m/f)	وکیل
that, those	وہ
they	وہ / یہ
he/ she	وہ / یہ
there	وہاں

ﮦ

hand (m)	ہاتھ
to lose (a battle, contest, game, etc.)	ہارنا
every	ہر
every day	ہر دِن
every day	ہر روز
every year	ہر سال
every month	ہر مہینہ
every week	ہر ہفتہ
thousand	ہزار
thousands of	ہزاروں
hospital (m)	ہسپتال
Saturday; week (m)	ہفتہ
plow (m)	ہل
we (polite form: I)	ہم

Hindu	ہِندُو
India (m)	ہندوستان
Indian	ہندوستانی
to cause to laugh	ہنسانا
to laugh	ہنسنا
air, wind (f)	ہَوا
aerial	ہَوائی
airport (m)	ہَوائی اڈّا
air pollution (f)	ہَوائی آلودگی
airplane (m)	ہَوائی جہاز
intelligent, clever	ہوشیار

ی

or	یا
memory, remembrance (f)	یاد
to remember	یاد کرنا / یاد آنا
for x to remember	x کو یاد آنا
that is to say, i.e.	یَعنی
university (f)	یونیورسٹی
this, these	یہ
here	یَہاں
Jew	یَہُودی

440

English-Urdu Glossary

A

able	قابل
to be able to; can (always preceded by stem of another verb)	سکنا
above	اُوپر
absolutely, completely	بالکل
action (f)	حرکت
actor (m)	اداکار
actress (f)	اداکارہ
in addition to	کے علاوہ
additional (more)	اور
address (m)	پتا
aerial	ہَوائی
affair (f)	بات
to be affronted	بُرا ماننا
after	کے بعد
afternoon (f)	دوپہر
again, then	پھر
age (f)	عُمر
agent (m/f)	وکیل
to agree upon x	x پر راضی ہونا
agricultural field (m)	کھیت

air (f)	ہَوا
air pollution (f)	ہَوائی آلودگی
airplane (m)	ہَوائی جہاز
airport (m)	ہَوائی اڈّا
alive	زِندہ
all	سب
all (whole)	سارا
also, too	بھی
although	اگرچہ / البتّہ
America (m)	امریکہ
American	امریکی / امریکن
and	اور
angry	ناراض
to be/ become angry	ناراض ہونا
animal (m)	جانور
to annoy	ستانا
another	دوسرا
answer (m)	جواب
any (adj.)	کوئی
anyone/someone	کوئی
anything	کچھ
apple (m)	سیب

appropriate; suitable	مُناسِب
approximately	تقریباً/کوئی
Arabic (f)	عربی
arm, embrace (f)	بانہہ
army (f)	فوج
arrangement (m)	اِنتظام
art (m)	فن
artist	فنکار (m)/فنکارہ (f)
ashamed	شرمِندہ
to be ashamed	شرمِندہ ہونا
ask	پوچھنا
athlete/player (m/f)	کھِلاڑی

B

bad, evil	بُرا
to feel bad, to feel insulted	بُرا ماننا
bad (rotten)	خراب
baggage (m)	سامان
banana (m)	کیلا
Bangladesh (m)	بنگلہ دیش
bashful	شرمِندہ
to be bashful	شرمِندہ ہونا

444

to bathe	غُسل کرنا / نہانا
beautiful	سُندر / خُوبصورت / حسِین
because	کیونکہ
because of	کی وجہ سے
bed (m)	پلنگ
before	سے پہلے
to begin (transitive)	شُروع کرنا
to begin (intransitive)	شُروع ہونا
behind	کے پیچھے
to believe	ماننا
beloved, sweetheart (m)	ساجن
besides	کے علاوہ
best	بہترین
better	بہتر
big	بڑا
birthday (f)	سالگِرہ
to bite; to cut	کاٹنا
black	کالا
blood (m)	خُون
blue	نیلا
body (m)	تن
book (f)	کِتاب

to be born	پیدا ہونا
both	دونوں
to bother	تنگ کرنا
box (m)	ڈِبّہ
boy (m)	لڑکا
brain (m)	دِماغ
brave	بہادُر
bread (f)	روٹی
to break (intransitive)	ٹوٹنا
to break (transitive)	توڑنا
breath (m)	سانس
bride (f)	دُلہن / دُلہنیا
bridegroom (m)	دُلہا
to bring	لانا
Britain (m)	برطانیہ
brother (m)	بھائی
building (f/m)	عِمارت/مکان
to be built (intransitive)	بننا
to build (transitive)	بنانا
to cause to be built	بنوانا
to have x built	x کو بنوانا
busy	مصرُوف

but, however	لیکن/مگر
to buy	خریدنا
by, till	تک

C

cabinet (f)	الماری
capable	قابل
to call (something a name; use with کو)	کہنا
to call x on the phone	x کو فون کرنا
to call / invite	بلانا
car (f)	گاڑی
carpet (f)	قالین
cat (f)	بلّی
to catch, apprehend	پکڑنا
to celebrate, commemorate	منانا
celebration (m)	جشن
chair (f)	کرسی
to change	بدلنا
cheap	ستا
cheeks; face (m)	رُخسار
chess (f)	شطرنج
chicken (f)	مُرغی

chicken curry (m)	مُرغی کا سالن
child (m)	بچّہ
childhood (m)	بچپن
children (f)	اَولاد
China (m)	چِین
Chinese	چِینی
Christian	عِیسائی
city (m)	شہر
clean	صاف
clever	چالاک
to climb	چڑھنا
clock / watch (f)	گھڑی
clothes (m)	کپڑے
clue (m)	پتا
cold (adjective)	ٹھنڈا
cold (noun, f)	سردی/ٹھنڈ
cold (weather; winter)	سردی (f)/جاڑا (m)
cold (illness) (m)	زُکام
comb (f)	کنگھی
to comb	کنگھی کرنا
to come	آنا
to come along, to go along with, to walk	چلنا

to come back	واپس آنا
to come down, to descend	اُترنا
to come to know, to find out	پتا چلنا
to come out, to depart, to set out	نِکلنا
condition (f)	حالت
condition, state (m)	حال
consideration; careful thought (m)	غور
to consider thoughtfully	غور کرنا
to take x into consideration	x پر غور کرنا
to construct	بنانا
to cause to be constructed	بنوانا
to have x constructed	x کو بنوانا
to be convinced, to obey, to believe	ماننا
cook (m)	باورچی
to cook	پکانا
cost (f)	قیمت
cough (f)	کھانسی
to cough	کھانسنا
country (m)	مُلک
couple, pair (f)	جوڑی
a couplet (of poetry, m)	شعر
courageous	بہادُر

court (f)	عدالت
cow (f)	گائے
craft (m)	فن
crazy, mad, insane	پاگل
criminal (m)	مجرم
crowd (f)	بھیڑ
to cry	رونا
cunning	چالاک
cup (f)	پیالی
cupboard (f)	الماری
cure (m)	علاج
curry (m)	سالن
to cut; to bite	کاٹنا

D

Dacca (m)	ڈھاکہ
to dance	ناچنا
danger (m)	خطرہ
dangerous	خطرناک
darkness (m)	اندھیرا
date; history (f)	تاریخ
daughter (f)	بیٹی

day (m)	روز / دِن
day before yesterday; day after tomorrow	پرسوں
dear, precious, beloved	عزیز
death (lit. transfer) (m)	اِنتقال
to die (for x to die)	x کا اِنتقال ہونا
decision (m)	فیصلہ
deed (f)	حرکت
definitely, sure	ضرُور
to delay, to be a long time	دیر کرنا
delicious	مزیدار
democracy (f)	جمہوریت
to depart, to set out	روانہ ہونا
to descend	اُترنا
details, particulars; explanation; analysis (f)	تفصیل
to dial the phone	فون مِلانا
diarrhea (m)	دست
to have diarrhea	دست آنا
to die	مرنا
difficult	مُشکِل
to discern; to recognize	پہچاننا
disposition, health (m)	مِزاج
how are you? (formal)	مِزاج شریف

distress, misery, anxiety (f)	پریشانی
to do	کرنا
doctor (m/f)	ڈاکٹر
dog (m)	کتّا
door (m)	دروازہ
to double; to repeat	دُہرانا
dream (m)	خواب / سپنا
to drink	پینا
to drive	چلانا
to drive a car	گاڑی چلانا
to dry (transitive)	سُکھانا
to dry (intransitive)	سُوکھانا

E

ear (m)	کان
to eat	کھانا
effort (f)	کوشِش
to try	کوشِش کرنا
elderly (adj.); elderly person (m)	بوڑھا
to be embarassed	شرمِندہ ہونا
emperor (m)	شہنشاہ
empress (f)	مہارانی

empty	خالی
to end, conclude (transitive)	ختم کرنا
to end, conclude (intransitive)	ختم ہونا
enemy (m/f)	دُشمن
England (m)	اِنگلستان
English (adj.)	انگریزی / انگلستانی
English (nationality)	انگریز
English (the language)	انگریزی
to enjoy	مزہ کرنا
to enlarge, to expand, to cause to spread (transitive)	بڑھانا
to increase; to grow; to spread (intransitive)	بڑھنا
enough!	بس!
enough (sufficient); a lot	کافی
to enter (formal Urdu)	تشریف لانا
entire	سارا
essay / composition (m)	مضمُون
evening (f)	شام
every	ہر
every day (m)	ہر روز / ہر دِن
every month (m)	ہر مہینہ
every week (m); every Saturday	ہر ہفتہ

every year (m)	ہر سال
evil, bad	بُرا
exactly	ٹھیک
examination (test) (m)	اِمتحان
examination / investigation (medical, m)	مُعائنہ
to have something examined (medically)	مُعائنہ کرانا
excrement (m)	پاخانہ
to exercise	ورزِش کرنا
expenditure, expense (m)	خرچ
to expend, to spend (transitive)	خرچ کرنا
to be expended, to be spent (intransitive)	خرچ ہونا
expensive	مہنگا
to explain, to cause to understand	سمجھانا
to extend (intransitive)	بڑھنا
to extend, to expand (transitive) (causative)	بڑھانا
eye (f)	آنکھ

F

face (m)	مُنھ/مُنہ
facts (f)	معلومات
to fall down	گرنا
family (m)	پریوار / خاندان

454

famous	مشہور
fan; ventilator (m)	پنکھا
far	دُور
fare; rent (m)	کرایہ
farmer (m)	کِسان
fast, quick	تیز
fat	موٹا
father (m)	والِد / لَلّا / پِپّا / باپ / بابا
father-in-law (m)	سُسر
fault, blemish (f)	خرابی
favorite	پسندیدہ
fear (m)	ڈر
to fear	ڈرنا
feast; party (f)	دعوت
fed up	بیزار
festival	تہوار / تیوہار (m) / عید (f)
fever (m)	بُخار
few	تھوڑا
to fight	لڑنا
to fight x	x سے لڑنا
filth (f)	گندگی
to find	پانا

to find out	پتا چلنا
fine	ٹھیک
finger (f)	اُنگلی
to finish	ختم کرنا
to flee	بھاگنا
flower (m)	پُھول
flu (m)	نزلہ (فلو)
to fly	اُڑنا
to cause to fly	اُڑانا
food (m)	کھانا
fool (m)	اُلّو
for the sake of, for, in order to	کے لئے
to forget	بُھولنا
forgive / excuse me	معاف کیجئے / معاف کرو
fork; thorn (m)	کانٹا
fort (m)	قِلعہ
freedom (f)	آزادی
free time (f)	فُرصت
Friday (m)	جُمعہ
friend (m/f)	دوست
friendship (f)	دوستی
from	سے

from where	کہاں سے
fruit (m)	پھل
fruitseller (m/f)	پھل والا / پھل والی

G

garden (m)	باغ
generally	اکثر
gentleman, sir, mister (m)	جناب / صاحب
germs (m)	جراثیم
to get, to obtain	مِلنا (with کو)
ghazal (love poem) (f)	غزل
ghost (m)	بھُوت
gift (m)	تُحفہ
girl (f)	لڑکی
girlfriend (for girls) (f)	سہیلی
to give	دینا
give permission to leave (got to run)	اِجازت دیجیئے
to go	جانا
to go back	واپس جانا
God forbid (May God not will that)	خُدا نہ کرے (کہ) / خُدا نہ خواستہ
God willing (May God will that)	اِنشاء اللہ / خُدا کرے (کہ)
good	اچّھا

goodbye (lit, God be your protector)	خُدا حافظ
goods, luggage (m)	سامان
government (f)	حُکُومت
to govern	حُکُومت کرنا
grand	شاندار
grandfather (maternal)	نانا
grandfather (paternal)	دادا
grandmother (maternal)	نانی
grandmother (paternal)	دادی
grave (f)	قبر
grave, tomb, shrine of a Sufi holy man (m)	مزار
great	اعظم / عظیم
greetings, hello, hi	آداب/آداب عرض/نمستے
"Peace on you" [to a Muslim] (reply in parentheses)	سلام علیکم (وعلیکم سلام) السّلام علیکم (وعلیکم السّلام)
grown up, elder person (m/f)	بڑا / بڑی
guest (m/f)	مہمان

H

habituated; accustomed	عادی
to be habituated/used to/accustomed to x	x کا عادی ہونا
hair (m)	بال

half	آدھا / آدھ
half (with whole numeral)	ساڑھے
hand (m)	ہاتھ
happiness (f)	خوشی
happy	خوش
hard work (f)	محنت
to work hard	محنت کرنا
hard working	محنتی
hat (f)	ٹوپی
he / she	وہ / یہ
head (m)	سر
health (f)	صحت / طبیعت
healthy	صحت مند
heart (m)	دِل
heat, hot weather (f)	گرمی
heavy	بھاری
help (f)	مدد
to help	مدد کرنا
to help x	x کی مدد کرنا
helpless	بے بس / مجبور
helplessness (f)	بے بسی / مجبوری
henna (f)	حنا / مہندی

here	يہاں
here (in this direction; hither)	اِدھر
hill; mountain (m)	پہاڑ
Hindu	ہندُو
Hindu devotional hymn (m)	بھجن
hint, clue, trace; address (m)	پتا
his / her (informal)	اُس کا / اُسکا
his / her (formal)	اُن کا / اُنکا
history; date (f)	تاریخ
historical	تاریخی
to hit	مارنا
hobby / hobbies (m)	شوق
holiday, vacation (f)	چُھٹّی
homeland (m)	وطن
horse (m)	گھوڑا
hospital (m)	ہسپتال
hot	گرم
hot (spicy)	تیز
hour (m)	گھنٹا
house (m)	مکان / گھر
how much / how many?	کِتنا / کِتنی / کِتنے
human being (m)	اِنسان

human being, man, person (m)	آدمی
hundreds of	سیکڑوں / سینکڑوں
hundreds of thousands of	لاکھوں
hunger (f)	بھوک
husband (m)	شوہر / پتی

I

I	مَیں
if	اگر
if only /would that	کاش
in	میں
in front of, across, facing	کے سامنے / کے آگے
in return for x	کی/کے بجائے
to increase (intransitive)	بڑھنا
to increase (transitive)	بڑھانا
independence (f)	آزادی
India (m)	بھارت / ہندوستان
Indian	ہندوستانی
information (f)	معلومات
injury; wound (f)	چوٹ
inside	اندر
inside of	کے اندر

instead of	کی/کے بجائے
to feel insulted / hurt	بُرا ماننا
intellect (m)	دِماغ
intelligent, clever	ہوشیار
intent; meaning (m)	مطلب
intention (m)	اِرادہ
interest (f)	دِلچسپی
interesting	دِلچسپ
intoxicating	مست
investigation (m)	مُعائنہ
invitation (f) (also party)	دعوت
to invite x	x کو دعوت دینا
Iran (m)	اِیران
Iranian	اِیرانی

J

jail (m)	قیدخانہ
Japan (m)	جاپان
Japanese	جاپانی
Jew	یَہُودی
job / work (m)	کام(m)/نوکری (f)
joke (m)	مذاق

to tease; to make fun of x	x کا مذاق اُڑانا
journey (m)	سفر
to make a journey	سفر کرنا
juice (m)	رس

K

king (m)	راجہ
knife (f)	چھری
to know	جاننا
to know (facts)	پتا ہونا / معلوم ہونا
to know (skills)	(x کو) آنا
to know; to recognize	پہچاننا
to come to know; to find out	پتا چلنا
kohl, collyrium (m)	کاجل

L

land (f)	زمین
landlord (m)	زمیندار / مکان مالِک
last, past, previous, back, latter	پچھلا
late (adj); a long time; interval (f)	دیر
late (adv)	دیر سے
to be late	دیر ہونا
to come late	دیر سے آنا

lateness (f)	دیری
to laugh	ہنسنا
to cause to laugh	ہنسانا
lawyer (m/f)	وکیل
leg (m)	پَیر
leisure (f)	فُرصت
lemon, lime (m)	نِمبُو / لیمُو
lentils (f)	دال
less	کم
less	تھوڑا
letter (m)	خط
lie (f)	جھُوٹ
to lie	جھُوٹ بولنا
life	جیِون (m) / زندگی (f)
life, soul, sweetheart, energy (f)	جان
life, lifetime; age (f)	عُمر
life partner (m/f)	جیِون ساتھی
line (queue) (f)	قطار
to listen	سُننا
to cause or make listen	سُنانا
little	تھوڑا
to live, to be alive	جینا

to live, to stay	رہنا
living	زِندہ
long live	زِندہ باد
a long while, a long period of time; late (f)	دیر
to lose (misplace something)	کھونا
to lose (a battle, contest, game)	ہارنا
a lot, very much	زیادہ
love	پِیار (m)/ مُحَبّت (f)/ عِشق (m)
to love	پِیار کرنا/ مُحَبّت کرنا
lover	محبُوب (m)/ محبُوبہ (f)
lover (m)	عاشِق
being a lover (f)	عاشِقی
luggage (m)	سامان

M

mad, ecstatic	دِیوانہ
to be made, built, created	بَننا
Mahabharata- a famous Indian epic	مہابھارت
Maharashtra (m)	مہاراشٹرہ
mail (f)	ڈاک
to maintain	پالنا
to make, to build, to create	بَنانا

mango (m)	آم
manner (f)	طرح
marble (m)	سنگِ مرمر
market, bazaar (m)	بازار
matter; affair (f)	بات
mausoleum (m)	مقبرہ
meaning (m)	مطلب
meat (m)	گوشت
meat curry (m)	گوشت کا سالن
meat eater (m/f)	گوشت خور
medicine (f)	دوا / دوائی
to meet	ملنا (with سے)
melody	راگ (m)/راگنی (f)
memento, souvenir	نشان (m)/نشانی (f)
memory, remembrance (f)	یاد
to remember x	x کی یاد آنا / x کو یاد کرنا
middle	بیچ
milk (m)	دُودھ
millionaire (m/f)	کروڑپتی
millions of	کروڑوں
minaret (m)	مینار
mind (m)	دِماغ

minister (government) (m/f)	وزیر
Mirabai - a 16th century poetess famous for her devotional songs to the Hindu deity Krishna	میرا بائی
mischief (f)	حرکت
mischief (f)	شرارت
mischievious	شریر
mistake (f)	غلطی
to mock	مذاق اُڑانا
moment (m)	پل
Monday (m)	پیر
money; cash; wealth; coin (m)	پیسہ / پیسا
moon (m)	چاند
moonlight (f)	چاندنی
more	زِیادہ
more, additional	اور
moreover	کے عِلاوہ
morning (f)	صُبح
mosque (f)	مسجد
mosquito (m)	مچّھر
most	اکثر
mother	والِدہ / امّاں / امّی / ماں / ماتا
mother-in-law	ساس

467

motive (m)	مَطلَب
mountain (m)	پہاڑ
mouth (m)	مُنہ / مُنھ
movement (f)	حَرکت
Mughal - dynasty that ruled India from the 16th to the 19th century	مُغَل
museum (m)	عجائب گھر
Muslim	مُسلِم / مُسَلمان
Muslim ritual prayer (f)	نَماز
my	میرا

N

name (m)	نام
noble name (formal Urdu) (m)	اِسم شَریف
auspicious name (formal Hindi) (m)	شُبھ نام
narcissus; Nargis (f)	نَرگِس
to narrate	سُنانا
near	کے قَریب / کے نَزدیک / کے پاس
near	نَزدیک
necessity; need (f)	ضَرُورت
necessity, need for x	x کی ضَرُورت
nectar /juice (m)	رَس

news (f)	خبر
newspaper (m)	اخبار
night (f)	رات
nightingale (f)	بُلبُل
no, not	جی نہیں / نہیں
noble, honorable	شریف
nobody	کوئی نہیں
noise (f)	آواز
noise, uproar, disturbance (m)	شور
nose (f)	ناک
nothing	کچھ نہیں
now	اَب
now and then	کبھی کبھی

O

oath (f)	قسم
to obey	ماننا
occasionally	کبھی کبھی
office (m)	دفتر
offspring (f)	اَولاد
often	اکثر
old (thing)	پُرانا

on	پر
on top of	کے اُوپر
once	ایک بار
oneself	خود
onion (f)	پیاز
only	صرف
to open	کھولنا
or	یا
orange (m)	سنترہ (سنگترہ)
otherwise	ورنہ
our (also mine)	ہمارا
out, outside	باہر / کے باہر
owl (m)	اُلّو

P

pain (m)	درد
pair, couple (f)	جوڑی
Pakistan (m)	پاکستان
Pakistani	پاکستانی
pants, trousers (f)	پتلون
papad (crispy appetizers) (m)	پاپڑ
parents (m)	والدین

party (f) (also invitation)	دعوت
to have a party for x	x کی دعوت کرنا
to pass, to spend time	گزارنا
patient (m)	بیمار / مریض
to pay	ادا کرنا
peace, safety (m)	امن
peasant (m)	کِسان
pen (m/f)	قلم
people, folk (m)	لوگ
pepper (f)	مِرچ
to perceive	پہچاننا
to perform; to accomplish; to pay	ادا کرنا
perhaps	شاید
permission (f)	اِجازت
to pick up, to lift	اُٹھانا
pickles (hot) (m)	اچار
picture, photograph (f)	تصویر
piece, morsel (m)	ٹکڑا
place, station (m)	مقام
place, vacancy (f)	جگہ
to place, to put	ڈالنا
to play	کھیلنا

to play (an instrument)	بجانا
to play the role of x	x بننا
please, kindly (with آپ forms)	مہربانی سے / مہربانی کر کے
please, kindly (with تم forms)	ذرا
pleased, contented; agreed	راضی
to be pleased with x	x سے راضی ہونا
pleasing (subject marked by کو) (adjective)	پسند
choice, selection (f) (noun)	
plow (m)	ہل
poet (m)	شاعر
poetry (m)	شعر
pomp and gusto (f)	دھوم دھام
poor fellow (m)	بیچارہ
poor person (m)	غریب
possible	ممکن
post office (m)	ڈاک خانہ
potato (m)	آلو
to pour	ڈالنا
poverty (f)	غریبی / مفلسی
praise (f)	تعریف
to praise x	x کی تعریف کرنا

Premchand - prominent author of Urdu-Hindi narrative prose, died 1936	پریم چند
president (m/f)	صدر
to prevent	روکنا
price (f)	قیمت
prime minister (m/f)	وزیرِ اعظم
prince (m)	شاہزادہ
principle (m)	اُصُول
prison (m)	قید خانہ
profitable	مُفید
to protect	پالنا
purpose (m)	مطلب
to put	ڈالنا

Q

qawwali - spiritual-mystical song recited by Muslim mystics in South Asia (f)	قوّالی
queen (f)	رانی، مہارانی
question (m)	سَوال
queue (f)	قطار
quick; fast	تیز
quiet	خاموش

R

rain (f)	بارِش
to rain	بارِش ہونا
to raise, nourish	پالنا
Ramadan, Muslim holy month (m)	رمضان
to reach	پہُنچنا
ready	تیّار
reason (f)	وجہ
receipt (f)	رسِید
to recite namaz (Muslim ritiual prayer)	نماز پڑھنا
to recognize	پہچاننا
red	لال
to reduce	کم کرنا
to be reduced	کم ہونا
regarding	کے بارے میں
relationship / connection (m)	رِشتہ
relatives (family) (m)	رِشتہ دار
to remember	یاد کرنا / یاد آنا
to remember x	x کو یاد کرنا / x کی یاد آنا
to repeat	دُہرانا
request (f)	گُزارِش

respected elder	بُزُرگ
rest (m)	آرام
to rest	آرام کرنا
to return	واپس جانا
in return for x / instead of x	x کے بدلے میں
revered person	بُزُرگ
rice (m, pl.)	چاول
rice w/ meat or vegetable (f)	بریانی
rich	امیر
to rise	اُٹھنا / جاگنا
river (m)	دریا
road (m)	رستہ / راستہ
room (m)	کمرہ
round, circular, a circle (m)	گول
to run away from	بھاگنا
rupee (Indian/Pakistani currency) (m)	روپیہ
Russia (m)	رُوس
Russian	رُوسی

S

salt (m)	نمک
Saturday; week (m)	ہفتہ
to say, to speak	کہنا
scanty	تھوڑا
scores of	بیسیوں
to scream, yell	چیخنا
season (m)	موسم
second, another	دوسرا
to see	دیکھنا
see you soon (lit. we will meet again)	پھر ملینگے
self (reflexive)	خود
to sell	بیچنا
to send	بھیجنا
servant (m)	نوکر
service (f)	خدمت / سیوا
several; some; a few	کئی
sharp	تیز
sherbat (beverage) (m)	شربت
shirt (f)	قمیض
shoe (m)	جوتا

shop, store (f)	دُکان / دُوکان
shopkeeper/store owner	دُکان والا /دُکان دار
shut up, be quiet	چُپ رہو
to be shy, reticent	شرمِندہ ہونا /شرمانا
sick, ill (adj.), sick person (m/f)	بیمار
sickness, illness (f)	بیماری
sign, memento, souvenir	نِشان (m) / نِشانی (f)
signature (m)	دَسْتَخَط
Sikh	سِکھ
silent	خاموش
since when	کب سے
to sing	گانا
sister (f)	بہن
sister (f)	دِیدی / باجی / آپا
to sit	بیٹھنا
skill (m)	فَن
skillful	قابِل
sky (m)	آسمان
slave (m)	غُلام
slave girl (f)	کنیز
to sleep	سونا
sly	چالاک

small	چھوٹا
to smile	مُسکرانا
snow, ice (f)	برف
so that	تاکہ
some; little; few	تھوڑا
some; any (adj.)	کوئی
someone/somebody	کوئی
something	کچھ
sometimes	کبھی
song (m)	گیت / گانا / نغمہ
sorrow (m)	غم
sorrowful	غمناک
sound (f)	آواز
souvenir (m)	نِشان
to speak, to talk, converse	بات کرنا
special	خاص
speech	بات
speech (f)	تقریر
to give a speech	تقریر کرنا
to spend time	گزارنا
spices (m)	مصالحہ / مسالا
spicy hot	تیز

splendid	شاندار
spoon/also sycophant (m)	چمچہ
to spread	پھیلنا
star (m)	تارا
to start, to begin (transitive)	شروع کرنا
to start, to begin (intransitive)	شروع ہونا
stately	شاندار
statement; speech, recital (f)	تقریر
to stay, to live	رہنا
to stay awake	جاگنا
to steal	چرانا
stomach (m)	پیٹ
stool (excrement) (m)	پاخانہ
to stop; to prevent	روکنا
to stop, to wait; to stay	ٹھہرنا
storm (m)	طوفان
story (f)	کہانی
strange	عجیب
stroll, walk, tour, excursion (f)	سیر
to stroll, to take a walk, to tour	سیر کرنا
student (m/f)	طالبِ علم / اسٹوڈنٹ / چھاتر (ہندی)
studies, education (f)	پڑھائی

to study, read	پڑھنا
stupid (m)	اُلّو
style (f)	طرح
success (f)	کامیابی
successful	کامیاب
Sufi - a Muslim mystic (m)	صوفی
sugar (f)	چینی
suitable	مُناسِب
Sunday (m)	اِتوار
sunshine, heat of sun (f)	دھوپ
surprising, strange, wonderful	عجیب
to swear by x	x کی قسم کھانا
sweet (adjective)	میٹھا
sweets (f)	مِٹھائی
swift, quick, hot (spicy), sharp	تیز
to swim	تیرنا
sycophant (colloquial) (literally, spoon) (m)	چمچہ

T

table (f)	میز
to take	لینا
to take someone	لے جانا

to take care of x	x کی دیکھ بھال کرنا
to take out, remove	نِکالنا
tall	لمبا
tea (f)	چائے
tears (m)	آنسو
to tease	ستانا / مذاق اُڑانا
tooth (m)	دانت
to tell (to narrate)	سُنانا
to tell, say (use with سے)	کہنا
temperament (f)	طبیعت
temple (m)	مندِر
test, trial; examination (m)	اِمتحان
thanks (lit. kindness) (f)	مہربانی
thanks (m)	شکریہ
that, those	وہ
that, which, who (rel. pronoun and conjunction)	کہ
that is to say, i.e.	یعنی
theft (f)	چوری
their	اُن کا / اُنکا
there	وہاں
there (in that direction; thither)	اُدھر
therefore	اِس لئے

these days, nowadays	آج کل
they	وہ / یہ
thief (m)	چور
thing (concrete) (f)	چیز
thing, matter (abstract) (f)	بات
to think	سوچنا
thirst (f)	پیاس
this, these	یہ
this much	اِتنا
thorn; fork (m)	کانٹا
thought; idea, opinion (m)	خیال
thousands of	ہزاروں
throne (m)	تخت
to throw	پھینکنا
Thursday (f)	جُمعرات
till	تک
time (m)	وقت
time, age, world, fortune (m)	زمانہ
time (period of); period (m)	دوران
during this time/period	اِس دوران میں
tiredness (f)	تھکن
today (m)	آج

toilet (m)	پاخانہ
tomb (f)	قبر
tomorrow; yesterday (m)	کل
to torment	ستانا
to tour	سیر کرنا
town (m)	شہر
toy (m)	کھِلونا
trash (m)	کچرا
to travel	سفر کرنا
traveler (m/f)	مُسافر
true (adj.); truth (m)	سچ
to speak the truth	سچ بولنا
truth (f)	حقیقت
Tuesday (m)	منگل

U

umbrella; canopy (f)	چھتری
under	کے نیچے
to understand	سمجھنا
unemployed	بیکار
university (f)	یونیورسٹی
until	تک

upset, displeased, unhappy	ناراض
to be / become upset, displeased etc.	ناراض ہونا
urine (m)	پیشاب
use, employment (m)	اِستعمال
to use	اِستعمال کرنا
to use x	x کا اِستعمال کرنا
to be used to/ habituated/accustomed to x	x کا عادی ہونا
useful	مُفید
useless	بیکار

V

vagabond, wanderer (m/f)	آوارہ
vegetable (f)	سبزی
vegetarian (m/f)	سبزی خور
vegetarian	شاکاہاری
verse (of poetry) (m)	شعر
very	بہُت
village (m)	گاؤں
voice (f)	آواز

W

to wait, to stop; to stay	ٹھہرنا
waiting, expecting (m)	اِنتظار

to wait for x	x کا اِنتظار کرنا
to wake up	اُٹھنا / جاگنا
to walk	چلنا
wall (f)	دیوار
to wash	دھونا
water (m)	پانی
we	ہم
wedding (f)	شادی
Wednesday (m)	بدھ
weight (m)	وزن
well, fine, okay	ٹھیک
to become well	ٹھیک ہو جانا
what?	کیا؟
for what reason, why?	کس لئے؟
what sort of, what kind of, how?	کیا / کیسی / کیسے؟
when?	کب؟
when	جب
where?	کہاں؟
where (in which direction)?	کِدھر؟
where	جہاں / جدھر
which	جو
which one?	کونسا / کونسے / کونسی

485

white	سفید
who?	کون؟
whole	سارا
why?	کیوں؟
wicked	بُرا
wife (f)	پتنی / بیوی
wind (f)	ہَوا
window (f)	کھِڑکی
wine, alcohol (f)	شراب
wit, joke (m)	مذاق
to make fun of, to tease	مذاق اُڑانا
with (instrumental); from	سے
with (in the company of)	کے ساتھ
without	(کے) بغیر
witness (m/f)	گواہ
woman (f)	عورَت
wonder (m)	عجوبہ
wonderful	عجیب
wonders (pl. m)	عجائب
word (f)	بات
work (m)	کام
to work	کام کرنا

to work out (to exercise)	ورزِش کرنا
world (f)	دُنیا
worried	پریشان
worry (f)	فِکر
worse	بدتر
worst	بدترین
worthy of (use with oblique infinitive)	کے قابِل
would that/if only	کاش
wound (f)	چوٹ
to write	لِکھنا

Y

year (m)	سال
yellow	پیلا
yes	جی ہاں / ہاں
yet, still	پھر بھی
yogurt (m)	دہی
yogurt drink (lassi) (f)	لسّی
you (least formal)	تُو
you (informal)	تُم
you (formal)	آپ
young (adj.); youth (m/f)	جوان

youthfulness (f)	جوانی
your (least formal)	تیرا
your (informal)	تمہارا
your (formal)	آپ کا / آپکا

Z

zoo (m)	چڑیا گھر